AN
AMERICAN
DIALOGUE

AN AMERICAN DIALOGUE

*A Protestant
Looks at Catholicism
and a Catholic
Looks at Protestantism*

by
ROBERT McAFEE BROWN
and GUSTAVE WEIGEL, S.J.
With a Foreword by Will Herberg

DOUBLEDAY & COMPANY, INC.
Garden City, New York

Grateful acknowledgment is made to the following copyright owners for permission to reprint material in this book:

Blackfriars Community, Cambridge, England: *Divided Christendom* by Fr. M. J. Congar

The Christian Century: excerpts from the magazine. Copyright 1959 by *The Christian Century.*

Christianity and Crisis: excerpts from "A Roman Catholic View of American Protestantism" by William Clancy, and from "The Ideologists and the Missing Dialogue" by Thomas O'Dea, from the June 8, 1959, issue.

Civilta Cattolica: excerpts from the first issue of April 1948.

Robert M. McBride, Co.: "Heretics All" from *Sonnets and Verses* by Hilaire Belloc

The Month: excerpts from "Truth and Human Fellowship" by Jacques Maritain

Rutgers University Press: excerpts from *Dogmatism and Tolerance* by Etienne Gilson

Charles Scribner's Sons: excerpts from *Christians and the State* by John Bennett

The Tablet: "German Protestants and the Coming Council" by Fr. Gerard Hughes, from the September 19, 1959 issue

Contents

Contents

Foreword
by Will Herberg

The kind of religious pluralism that has come to characterize American society in the past generation both encourages and sets limits to communication between the three major religious groups in this country. The developing Protestant-Catholic dialogue, to which the two essays in this book constitute so significant a contribution, is profoundly affected by the shape of this pluralism.

From this standpoint, the basic factor in the situation is the transformation of America, in the course of the past generation, from a Protestant nation into a three-religion country.

Writing just about thirty years ago, André Siegfried described Protestantism as America's "national religion," and he was largely right, despite the ban on religious establishment in the Constitution. Normally, to be born an American meant to be a Protestant; this was the religious identification that quite naturally went along with being an American. Non-Protestants felt the force of this conviction almost as strongly as did the Protestants; Catholics and Jews, despite their vastly increasing numbers, experienced their non-Protestant religion as a problem, as a mark of their foreignness, as an evidence that they were not really and truly American. In a very significant sense, Protestantism—not any of the multiplying denominations, but Protestantism as a whole—constituted America's "established church."

This is no longer the case. Today, to be born an American is no longer taken to mean that one is necessarily a Protestant; Protestantism is no longer the obvious and "natural" religious identification of the American. Today, the evidence strongly suggests, America has become a three-religion country: the normal religious implication of being an American today is that one is either a Protestant, a Catholic, or a Jew. These three are felt to be, by and large, three different forms of being religious in the American way; they are the three "religions of democracy," the "three great faiths" of America. Today, unlike fifty years ago, not only Protestants, but increasingly Catholics and Jews as well, feel themselves to be Americans not apart from, or in spite of, their religion, but because of it. If America today possesses a "church" in the European sense—that is, a form of religious belonging which is felt to be involved in one's belonging to the national community—it is the tripartite religious system of Protestant-Catholic-Jew.

This transformation of America from a Protestant into a three-religion country has come about not as a result of any marked increase in Catholics or Jews—the Protestant-Catholic ratio has remained more or less the same for the past thirty years, and the proportion of Jews in the general population has probably been declining. It has come about, as I have argued elsewhere, as an accompaniment of the shift in the source of pluralistic diversity from ethnicity to religion. In effect, America has been transformed in little more than a single generation from a land of immigrants, where ethnic identification was normal and prevalent, into a tripartite society in which identification (aside from race understood as color) is increasingly in terms of religious belonging. Contemporary American pluralism is characteristically religious pluralism.

Within this emerging pattern of religious pluralism, the three major religious groups have had to relate themselves in two very different contexts. On one level, these religious groups are cultural sub-communities, defining three variant ways of being an American. On another level, however, they are three religious systems, with their own beliefs, traditions, and institutional loyalties. Communication between the three groups proceeds in very different ways and in altogether different forms of these two levels.

On the first level, on the level of social and cultural confrontation, the emerging pattern of American pluralism makes for close, though by no means always harmonious, relations under the rubric of "interfaith." The interfaith movement, and, even more, the interfaith "idea," articulates the new shape of American life, and therein lies its extraordinary appeal to the American mind. Indeed, as the older ethnic identifications tend to fade out, there is a growing feeling that unification along interfaith (i.e., tri-faith) lines is the most appropriate way of expressing the comprehensive unity of

the American people. Since the pluralism of American life is so
largely a religious pluralism, the symbol of all-American co-operation in every good cause naturally becomes "interfaith."

Within this large framework defined by the interfaith idea, there
are, of course, multiple tensions. The transformation of America
from a Protestant nation into a three-religion country in the course
of a single lifetime was bound to exacerbate the strains and stresses
of group life, but these strains and stresses are now essentially the
internal tensions of a multi-group society rather than the manifestations of hostility to foreigners and outsiders. Jews and Catholics
have at last become Americans, related to other Americans in the
complex pattern of American group life. It is a pattern in which
the conflicts, however sharp, are sooner or later subsumed in the
over-all unity of a common Americanness, so well expressed in the
already classic formula of interfaith: "After all, we're all Americans . . . "

But the very facility of communication on this level, without
which life in a pluralistic society would be impossible, has, paradoxically enough, served to confuse and impede communication on
the higher level of religious dialogue. In a situation in which the
underlying unity, and even the recognized forms of diversity,
among Americans has been defined in terms of a common Americanness, any effort to probe deeper so as to uncover unities and differences on a theological level, and to make these unities and
differences a matter of public discussion, must inevitably appear as
offensively divisive and productive of "un-American" controversy.
One's religious beliefs are one's own business, not something to
parade in public or argue about with other Americans. At appropriate times, Sunday mornings on TV or through arranged visits
to houses of worship, we tell our neighbors something about them,
but in a carefully "uncontroversial" manner so as to preclude all
genuine communication and understanding. As a consequence, we
have that strange paradox, frequently noted by foreign observers:
Americans live and work together with their fellow Americans of
other faiths, co-operate and quarrel with them in business, community affairs, and politics, but know virtually nothing about their
religious life, and appear unconcerned, even reluctant, to find out.
Interfaith co-operation and religious isolation seem to be the two
opposed poles of American religious pluralism.

A genuinely religious dialogue among the three major faiths is

thus seriously impeded by the prevailing interfaith ethos, which itself but reflects the essential nature of American religious pluralism.
Even when some such dialogue does emerge, it is, as a rule, stulti-
fied by the same cultural forces. For what Americans are prone to
do when making a case for their religion is to show how well and
how truly it embodies and expresses American preconceptions, the
"moral and spiritual values of democracy." The entire discussion
is kept confined within these limits, from which it is almost impossible to break out. And this is true not only of uninstructed laymen, but of theologians and church leaders as well. A distinguished
church leader and educator highly placed in one of the great
religious communities recently congratulated himself that his church
is so well "suited to the American temperament, which it has always expressed and embodied in all its actions and viewpoints,"
that it is indeed the "church of America"! Like documentation to
cover most other religious groups would not be hard to find.

Genuine religious communication thus runs counter to the way
of American religious pluralism, yet is all the more necessary if
this pluralism, so welcome on other grounds, is not to turn into a
device for stifling religious authenticity and converting the three
major faiths into three variants of the "culture-religion" of the
American Way. Without some sort of confrontation and dialogue on
a truly religious level, it is hard to see how (humanly speaking)
Protestantism, Catholicism, and Judaism in America can preserve
their authentic heritage of faith and meet their historical responsibility as they themselves understand it. It has become a religious
imperative, it seems to me, not only to take advantage of forms of
co-operation which American religious pluralism encourages, but
also to break through the limitations it imposes.

Fortunately, in recent years, multiplying evidence has appeared
that the barrier is being broken through in this country, at least
so far as Protestants and Catholics are concerned. (A resumption
of the classical Jewish-Christian dialogue still remains for the
future.) Largely as a consequence of the rapprochement between
Protestants and Catholics on the Continent for mutual support and
a common witness in the total crisis of our time, a new spirit has
come to dominate religion in America, at least on the higher levels.
The impermeability to religious communication which has so
largely characterized the American three-religion pluralism has
been ruptured at many points, and the beginnings of conversation

initiated in books, publications, and face-to-face conferences. This new departure has been facilitated—indeed, I should say made possible—by the great theological renascence of recent decades, for it is in terms of the newer religious thinking that the Protestant-Catholic dialogue has been taken up. Once again it has been demonstrated that only to the degree that a religious group returns to its own true sources of faith and life is it able to open creative communication and talk responsibly with the other religious groups of its society and culture. Not the attrition of religious self-consciousness, but its enhancement and clarification, is the requirement and result of genuine religious dialogue.

In the two essays included in this volume, this Protestant-Catholic dialogue is continued, and (it seems to me) carried to higher levels. Perhaps no two men could be found in this country better qualified for this task. Both are theologians of great distinction, and both have a sharp eye for social and cultural reality. Each is well acquainted with the community he is writing about, and each is truly capable of the sympathetic understanding of a religious way not his own that makes religious dialogue possible. The subtle interplay of historical, sociological, and theological factors that marks the thinking of both of these men endows their comments with a multidimensional reality that alone can do justice to religion.

To have in one volume, addressed to each other, an essay by Gustave Weigel on Protestantism and another by Robert McAfee Brown on Catholicism is itself a major event in American religious life, and a convincing sign that we are really beginning to emerge out of the intellectual parochialism and self-isolation that has hitherto been so characteristic of American religious pluralism.

This volume, of course, has its special interest in a Presidential year marked by a sudden flare-up of religious controversy. But this interest, though real, is surely no more than secondary. The true significance of this volume is to be measured by how well it articulates and carries forward the great "American dialogue" that both religion and democracy, each in its own way, require for the actualization of its reality and promise.

May 1, 1960   WILL HERBERG

PART

I

A PROTESTANT
LOOKS AT CATHOLICISM

by Robert McAfee Brown

1

Introductory

When I was a graduate student in theology, I once developed such a head of steam over the activities of a certain Roman Catholic prelate who shall remain nameless, that I finally exploded with a blistery and self-righteous editorial—a kind of three-page Manifesto to The West, as I recall it—denouncing the whole Catholic Church and urging The West to realize that its ultimate foe was located not in Moscow but in Rome. Wiser and cooler heads prevailed upon me not to publish it, and it went the way all such manifestos should—from filing cabinet to wastebasket to city dump.

I cite this incident for the edification of both Catholic and Protestant readers: for the former so that if they think I am occasionally too rough, they will realize that I have at least moved some distance toward temperateness and civilized conversation; and for the latter so that if they think I am occasionally too soft, they will realize that my present position involves the conscious disavowal of some of the things they might have hoped I would say. I spent four years at college and two years as an ordained minister in the Commonwealth of Massachusetts, and I have spent five years of graduate study and seven years of teaching in New York City. And I state without prejudice that as far as I was concerned, there would have been better places than Massachusetts and New York City in which to develop an appreciation of American Catholicism. In the providence of God, however, I spent two years in Minnesota, where for the first time in my life I encountered a Roman Catholicism that was creative and vigorous, and whose adherents were full of grace and charity. I became acquainted with Catholic laymen and Catholic monks, and I discovered that we were brethren even though we were separated brethren.

Since then I have been trying to understand Catholicism, rather than merely examining it for ammunition to place in both barrels of my Protestant shotgun. I have tried to discover how and why men can accept the Roman Catholic faith. I cannot myself accept it; indeed, I feel that at certain points it involves fundamental distortions of the Christian gospel, as I shall point out later. But I can now understand, I think, how and why a man other than myself could accept it, be nurtured by it, and increase thereby in wisdom and stature and in favor with God and man. This means that if I am going to express my fears and concerns about certain aspects of Catholicism I can only honestly and fairly do so in the context of expressing my admiration and gratitude for certain other aspects—and vice-versa.

I am acutely conscious of the fact that both Catholics and Protestants will be reading these pages. And I can almost anticipate the reaction of each. The Protestant will be looking for places where he can say, "You're not tough enough. Now if you only knew the priest in *our* town . . ." And the Catholic will be looking for places where he can say, "You obviously don't understand our position. If you did, you would never say that . . ."

What shall I say to these readers, caught as I am between their crossfire?

To the Protestant I can only say: "I *do* know that priest in your town. I've tangled with him myself. But I have learned as a result that it's very dubious logic and even more dubious theology to generalize from that priest to the whole Roman Catholic church. If he represents its worst, there are other Catholics who represent its best, and before you see a Torquemada hiding behind every collar and cowl, you'd better see a Francis Xavier preaching to the Japanese, and a John XXIII washing the feet of postulants, and a Baron von Hügel kneeling in adoration before the Reserved Sacrament. We must see Catholicism at its best before we are entitled to be belligerent about its worst, and neither its best nor its worst can really be understood apart from the other. I not only know the Catholic priest in your town. I know some of the Protestant ministers as well, and heaven help Protestantism if it is to be judged by the criteria with which you propose to judge Catholicism."

To the Catholic I can only say: "I have tried to place myself 'within' your faith as much as one can do without himself being a Catholic. But I am quite aware that no one can do this fully, and if I have failed to do even minimal justice to your faith in the pages that follow, *let that be my contribution to the ensuing discussion.* For my failures will at least indicate some of the places where you need to redouble your efforts to communicate the meaning of your faith to outsiders. That God can make creative use of human error is the only basis on which a Protestant could ever dare set pen to paper. But beyond that, it may be salutary for you to see how you look to an outsider. You may have been creating impressions you had no intention of creating, or you may discover that the things most transparently obvious to you are hidden from the gaze of one who stands elsewhere."

Whatever else the following pages represent, then, they are an attempt to start a conversation. As I shall point out on numerous occasions in the following pages, the first thing Protestants and Catholics must do is learn to talk to one another. This book is a *first step* in such a conversation—exactly that and no more. Father Weigel and I are trying to begin a conversation, not conclude one. And we have decided that the best place to begin is by telling each other how we look from the outside, to see ourselves as others see us. The second step in the conversation will take place when a Catholic says to me, or a Protestant says to Father Weigel, "No, no, you've got us all wrong. That isn't what we are at all. It's this way . . .", after which Father Weigel and I may want to interpose a "Yes, but . . ." from time to time. And what we shall all find is that before too long we will not only be looking at the other, but looking at ourselves again, only this time it will be with the tremendous advantage that we can now see ourselves in a fresh perspective. And this will be clear gain.

Part of the problem in the past has been that most American discussion of "Protestant-Catholic relations" has been hampered by what some Catholics might choose to call "the absolute wall of separation between church and sect." That is to say, Catholics have told Catholics what was wrong with Protestantism, in Catholic books published by Catholic publishers for Catholic consumption, while Protestants have told Protestants what was wrong with Catholicism, in Protestant books published by Protestant publishers for Protestant consumption—and never the twain did meet. Until recently.

Recently Sheed & Ward, an established Catholic publishing house, asked six non-Catholics to write whatever they felt called upon to write about American Catholicism, so that American Catholics could see what kind of an image they had projected upon American life. The result, *American Catholics: A Protestant-Jewish View*, edited by Philip Scharper, has begun a breakthrough in religious insularity. It is to be hoped that the present book will foster the further cultivation of this kind of exchange. Perhaps, who knows, an enterprising Protestant publisher will invite half a dozen non-Protestants to contribute to a symposium entitled *American Protestantism: A Catholic-Jewish View*.

* * *

The plan of my half of this book is fairly straightforward. Chapter 2 attempts to create a proper atmosphere for discussion and it is quite the most important chapter. I have become convinced that the atmosphere in which something is said is almost as important as what is said, and at this stage in the dialogue the creation of an atmosphere is probably the most important thing that can be done.

Chapter 3 attempts to be descriptive of the Catholic church in America as a non-Catholic sees it, and Chapter 4 tries to come to grips with the *immediate* source of tension between Catholics and non-Catholics, a source which I believe is located in the concerns of non-Catholics about "Catholic power." I do not feel that this is the *ultimate* source of difficulty, for when we press behind the surface irritations we come to more fundamental matters which lie in the realm of theology, and I make no apologies whatsoever for raising "theological issues" in Chapters 5 and 6. The lay reader must begin to think in these terms or he will never get beyond mere surface-scratching as he copes with the perplexing problem of why he and his neighbor are so near in some ways and so tragically far apart in others. Chapter 7 emphasizes the fact that the discussion is not finished but has only begun, and suggests some of the ways in which it could continue.

I was privileged to contribute to the Sheed & Ward symposium mentioned above, and it should be obvious that no one can write two essays about American Catholicism without repeating some of the same ideas. But the present essay is not a repetition of the former one save at a few unavoidable points in Chapters 4 and 5, and although Sheed & Ward were most willing to let me use material under their copyright, I have tried not to take excessive advantage of their charity. The portion of Chapter 2 entitled "Ground Rules for Fruitful Dialogue Today" was, in a somewhat shortened form, published simultaneously in *The Christian Century* and *The Commonweal* in February 1960, and I am grateful to both journals for the ecumenical gesture that this simultaneous publication represented.

I have included what may seem like a pretentious number of footnotes. These are included simply so that documentation on what may seem like a lot of debatable points will be available for those who desire it. My essay could serve no better end than that of pushing people to read some of the books cited.

To certain Roman Catholics, I must express particular thanks. I am grateful to Father Weigel for his willingness to collaborate in this joint venture and to lend his esteemed name to the present volume. The fact that the actual draft was written on sabbatical leave in Scotland, has made it possible for me to profit from the friendship and help of the Rev. Bernard Leeming, S.J., of Heythrop College, Chipping Norton, Oxfordshire. Father Leeming has been extraordinarily generous with his time and learning, both in conversation and correspondence; he has supplied me with much material, and graciously gave me access to the manuscript of his book, since published, on *The Churches and the Church*, (The Newman Press: New York, 1960), one of the most significant pieces of contemporary Catholic ecumenical writing. I will have indicated the measure of my gratitude to him if I state that he incarnates the "principles of Catholic ecumenism" which I have quoted from his writings on pp. 113–115 below.

A final word of gratitude. Were dedications still in order, mine would go something like this: "To Gene and Abigail and Father Godfrey, that the dialogue they helped initiate may continue."

2

Preliminaries That Are Really Conclusions

If all of us, Catholics and Protestants alike, are to "look at" one another properly today, we must first of all distinguish some of the ways in which we have looked at one another in the past. There are two good reasons for doing this: (a) we can gain some perspective on our present situation, and (b) we can rule out some ways of looking which have either spent their usefulness or were wrong from the very start.

1. How Catholics and Protestants have looked at one another in the past

1. During the Reformation period, Catholics and Protestants confronted one another in what was, in the most literal sense that words can have, *a battle to the death.* They engaged in Wars of Religion, persecutions, inquisitions, interdicts, bullyings, and torturings. Catholics burned Protestants, and Protestants drowned sectarians. A man's life was endangered by the degree to which he departed from strict orthodoxy. Orthodoxy was, among other things, geographically determined; in a Catholic territory it meant one thing, in a Protestant territory it meant something else. Poor Servetus, already condemned by the Inquisition and fleeing from Catholic persecution, foolishly went to Protestant Geneva where his orthodoxy was also found wanting, so that even there he did not escape the stake.

2. When the initial fury had spent itself, and people began to realize that the annihilation of a man's life was not only unwise but un-Christian, the struggle shifted to the annihilation of a man's ideas, which seemed not only wise but Christian, since error must be exposed with all the vigor orthodoxy could muster. Christendom entered the age of great *polemics.* As a result, much subsequent Protestant literature has been motivated not so much by a desire to show how right Protestants are as by a desire to show how wrong Catholics are, and to a surprising degree Catholic theology since Trent has been explicitly formulated in conscious repudiation of the Protestant heresies.

3. Another attitude of the past, paradoxically enough, has been *studied indifference,* the assumption being that the opposing position was so obviously wrong as to be unworthy of serious examination. American Catholics have often been educated as though Protestantism simply did not exist as a *religious* possibility for men. They have known, of course, that there is a sociological entity called "Protestantism," but their ignorance of what Protestantism really is, has been appalling. Since Luther was lecherous, Calvin cold, and Knox nasty, the whole venture was doomed from the start, and Catholics could profitably move on to learn about more consequential things. The Protestant counterpart of this attitude has been only slightly different. (It is harder for a Protestant to be studiously indifferent to the existence of Catholicism, for it is so much more externally apparent than Protestantism.) But many Protestants have been convinced that Catholicism is so wrong and out-of-date and irrelevant, that they have not believed that any intelligent person could any longer be "taken in" by it. They have assumed that Catholicism will still be around for awhile, but since it is clearly so contrary to the beliefs of modern man, they have believed that it is no more than a medieval anachronism out of place in a stainless steel culture.

4. In other quarters, there has been what both sides would now call a *false irenicism,* i.e. an attempt to dwell solely on points of agreement between Catholicism and Protestantism, to agree to disagree about the rest without any further clamor, and from then on to work together on social service projects where matters of "faith" presumably did not intrude themselves. There was an era of surface good feeling in the United States around the turn of the century, when it was popular for Protestants and Catholics to appear on the same platforms and give allegiance to certain common social ends,

but to say no more. This undoubtedly did some good to the health of the body politic, but it did some harm as well, for it gave the impression that the unmentioned points of difference didn't really matter, whereas they mattered and continue to matter tremendously —as later generations of Catholics and Protestants have discovered to their dismay.

5. Another stance has been the motive, either overt or covert, of *conversion*. There are special groups within Roman Catholicism devoted solely to the task of converting non-Catholics to the faith. And although Protestant converts to Catholicism seem to be much better publicized in the American press than Catholic converts to Protestantism, this route of conversion is one on which traffic seems to travel in both directions with about equal force. It is to the credit of American Catholicism that, so far as one can observe, it does not rush people into conversion, but makes sure that their motives are right, and that they are well instructed before they make their first communion. A similar circumspection would benefit American Protestantism, which is more ready to receive new members casually from whatever source they come. But the phenomenon of conversion is not an unmixed blessing. Many converts, travelling the Catholic-Protestant road in either direction, discover that the lane is not nearly as inviting on the other side of the dividing strip as they had anticipated that it would be, and there is a sorry spectacle of those who can find no permanent spiritual home but seem to vacillate between altar and communion table.[1]

6. The posture in Catholic-Protestant relationships which seems to have become the norm in the United States is *political jockeying*. Protestantism has had the power in the past and is naturally reluctant to relinquish that power; Catholicism has been the minority in the past and is naturally eager to transcend that status. The steady increase of Roman Catholics in national political life is hailed by one group as proof that Catholics are beginning to be responsible public citizens, and by the other group as a menacing portent of how the tentacles of the Vatican are gradually crushing the nation's capital in a death grip. Let either group gain some supposed "privilege" and the other group is crying for equal time or equal recognition. Mayors, governors, presidents, and all who make political appointments, are deathly afraid of offending one group by appointing too many from the other group. Each group keeps an eye on *Time* magazine to make sure that the other does not receive more than its proportionate number of column inches.

All of these ways of "looking at" one another seem to me to be either wrong or *passé*, in terms of the current situation in America. I have no desire to burn Catholics, and I do not really think (some of my Protestant friends to the contrary notwithstanding) that they desire to burn me. Sheer polemics will not do, since we share many convictions as well as disputing some. Studied indifference is no longer even a formal possibility in America, and even if it were it is no more than an ostrich-like attitude which will leave all who adopt it right where the ostrich is—buried in the sands of time. A sentimental irenicism is no real antidote to harsh polemics, for deepseated differences must be acknowledged along with the deepseated similarities. And while one obviously cannot be "against conversion," there is no reason to expect that this will ever be more than a small-scale operation in the total problem of Catholic-Protestant relationships. The posture of political jockeying, being the most widespread at the present time, is also the most complex, and we shall have to deal with it further in Chapter 3. That Catholics and Protestants are both, among other things, "power blocs," must, I suppose, be acknowledged. But only if we can see one another as basically *other* than "power blocs," can we keep the situation from deteriorating even more than it already has.

2. Ground rules for fruitful dialogue today

If the above approaches are inadequate ones for today, what is the alternative? The alternative is described by an important word which is in danger of becoming trivialized by overuse, but which remains an essential word nevertheless. That word is *dialogue*. A dialogue is not a speech in which one person talks and the other listens, or in which one participant has certain advantages which are denied to the other. A dialogue implies that two people, or two groups, are both speaking and listening (though not, one hopes, simultaneously), each saying what he has to say, and each listening to what the other has to say.

So much is a commonplace in every treatment of Catholicism and Protestantism these days. Everybody agrees that there should be dialogue. But what is not so clear is how the dialogue should be conducted. And I should like to try to go beyond the genial generality that Dialogue Is A Good Thing, to propose some of the conditions that ought to prevail if the dialogue is to prove fruitful. We have arrived at that rather awkward moment when we realize that we must talk to one another, and we do not quite know how to begin. Here, then, are six possible ground rules:

1. *Each partner must believe that the other is speaking in good faith.* This is the indispensable minimum of any kind of dialogue. As long as the Catholic feels that the Protestant is simply trying to get the inside story on hierarchical politics, so that he can exploit it afar, the Catholic is going to be understandably reticent about speaking openly and frankly. And as long as the Protestant feels that Catholic talk about "democracy" or "tolerance" is expediency, designed to cover up the "real" Catholic position, he will preclude the possibility of any good emerging from the discussion. *Any* dialogue must assume a common devotion to truth.

But in the Catholic-Protestant dialogue, we must count on something much more significant than a common devotion to truth. We must count on a common devotion to the One who said, "I am the . . . truth." The reason why, in this particular dialogue, we must believe that the other partner speaks in good faith is not merely because he is a civilized man, but because we are both servants of Jesus Christ. Catholic-Protestant discussion possesses this tremendous advantage which is not present in other "inter-faith" discussions: both partners share a common faith in Jesus Christ.[2]

Sharing this faith makes us "brethren." Some of my Protestant friends feel that there is an attitude of condescension in the Catholic description of Protestants as "separated brethren." I do not share this feeling. I think the phrase an excellent one, for it describes exactly what we are. No matter *who* has done the "separating,"[3] separated we are, nonetheless. But we are also and most basically "brethren." The adjective may modify the noun but it does not displace it. We are "brethren" because we share a faith in the Lord Jesus Christ, and a baptism in the Triune name recognized by each as valid. And I am heartened by the feeling that in the current dialogue, Catholics are tending to speak less and less of "*separated* brethren," and more and more of "separated *brethren*." The nuance is of incalculable importance. We shall return to it in Chapters 5 and 6.

Here is a place where the attitude which one brings to the dialogue is crucial. I have recently read a substantial Catholic treatment of the doctrine "outside the church there is no salvation." The author is particularly worried by Roman Catholic attempts to relax the most rigorous possible interpretation of this ancient formula. His greatest concern, it seems, is to limit salvation to the fewest possible recipients. His book abounds in documentation, scholarship, learning, and dialectic. It abounds in everything, in fact, save love.

2. *Each partner must have a clear understanding of his own faith.* This implies an eagerness to articulate his position, and a willingness to have it scrutinized. I see no problem here for the Catholic. At the present time any Catholic participant in the dialogue must be carefully chosen and approved, and will be instructed that the fullness of the Catholic faith must be presented without compromise or "watering down" to make it initially more palatable.[4] Something of a problem exists here for the Protestant, both because Protestant faith by its very nature cannot be articulated with quite the precision of Catholic thought, and also because of a long standing and baleful American tendency to equate the Protestant faith with "what-I-find-appealing." Part of the ensuing Protestant task, therefore, will be not only to articulate its position *vis-à-vis* Catholicism, but to engage in some strenuous intramural debate, so that it may discover more accurately what things are and are not essential to its proclamation. (The existence of the World Council of Churches has considerably hastened this process.) A better informed Protestantism is an indispensable minimum to the ongoing of the dialogue; we can count on an informed Catholicism.

3. *Each partner must strive for a clear understanding of the faith of the other.* This is both a precondition of dialogue and a result of it. It is a *precondition* in the sense that neither partner has a right to waste the other's time by starting the dialogue in total ignorance of the other's position. Both groups are required to do some serious homework in advance. There are plenty of misunderstandings that can be dispelled by a little honest reading.

However, not even honest reading will ever provide a full understanding of the faith of the other. This can only come as a *result* of dialogue. For it will only be in some kind of give-and-take, face-to-face encounter, that the most deep-seated misunderstandings will be cleared up. It was not until I had had a long discussion with a Catholic friend that I could see anything more than a bit of scholastic logic-chopping in the distinction between the "worship" of God and the "veneration" of Mary. And I hope that on his part he now realizes that Protestantism is not just "an aggregate of different religious forms of free thought," as Gabriel Monod has so wrongly asserted.

Now there are two important corollaries to this mutual striving for a clear understanding of the faith of the other:

a. The first of these is *a willingness to interpret the faith of the other in its best light rather than its worst*. This sounds very obvious in principle but it is far from obvious in practice. Too many Protestants, when they do trouble to read a papal encyclical, read it simply to discover further examples of what they politely call papal dominance and less politely call thought-control; they study Catholic literature simply to add fuel to their anti-Catholic fires. (Ironically enough, the fact that there is increasing self-criticism in modern Catholic circles helps to make the blaze burn more brightly, but the irony of this fact escapes the fire-watchers.) So, too, there are Catholics who would be constitutionally incapable of taking seriously the notion that anything good came out of the Reformation, or that Martin Luther was anything but an arrogant monk who couldn't submit to the discipline of obedience. There are plenty of sins on both sides to be exploited. Those who want to exploit them can have a field day. They can have everything, in fact, except fruitful dialogue.

This does not mean glossing over problems or pretending that grievous sins were never committed—a matter to which we shall presently come. It does mean that the best becomes our norm rather than the worst. If Protestants want to be appraised in terms of Reinhold Niebuhr rather than Carl McIntyre, they must be willing to evaluate the papacy in terms of John XXIII rather than John XXII.

b. A second corollary follows from the attempt to get a clear understanding of the faith of the other. Each partner must maintain *a continual willingness to revise his understanding of the faith of the other*. Dialogue can be a very dangerous pastime, for it may force us to give up some of our most cherished caricatures—and these die hard. It is really rather comfortable for a Protestant to believe that the Roman version of the formula "outside the church there is no salvation" is the equivalent of saying, "All non-Catholics go to hell," for then he can use words like "intolerance," "bigot," and "spiritual pride." But if he thinks that that is the actual teaching of the church, the process of dialogue will let him in for some real surprises, and he will have to change his tune. The Catholic may also have some rude shocks in store for him. I have found that most

Roman Catholics look on Protestantism as sheer private individualism, each person believing whatever he pleases, subject to no higher authority than the whim of the moment. It will be truly disconcerting to Roman Catholics to discover Protestants who live under the corporate discipline of the Word of God, who believe expressly that they must live in utter subjection to that Word, and who believe in the real presence of Jesus Christ in the sacrament, to say nothing of affirming that "outside the church there is no salvation."

Let the work of dialogue proceed, then, if only that both partners may engage in the noble work of caricature-assassination.

4. *Each partner must accept responsibility in humility and penitence for what his group has done, and is doing, to foster and perpetuate division.* Canon Southcott, an Anglican parish priest, reports a discussion with a Roman Catholic priest, during the course of which the latter said, "You know, it was our fault at the Reformation." To which, Canon Southcott comments, there are only two possible replies: either, "Of course it was," or, "It was our fault too." The latter response is beginning to carry weight in Protestant-Catholic discussions and is being voiced on both sides. No reputable Catholic historian any longer denies that things were in a sorry state in sixteenth century Christendom.[5] And Pope Adrian VI's statement about the church deserving judgment for its iniquities is coming back into circulation. Conversely, few Protestants any longer try to make the sixteenth century into the Golden Age of Protestantism. If we do not subscribe to the notion that the Reformation threw the baby out with the bath, at least in the somewhat calmer ecclesiastical atmosphere of the twentieth century we are re-examining the possible use of some of the things that were thrown out.

Many Roman Catholics are saying today that the perpetuation of the divisions of Christendom is not simply due to Protestant wrongheadedness, but also to the wrong kind of Catholic intransigence. Protestants can acknowledge that for centuries the Protestant tendency was to divide Christendom ever and ever more disastrously, and that if the ecumenical movement is reversing this trend it is still building on the wreckage of three centuries.

Such admissions are not simply a matter of being polite. They are a matter of recognizing that we all contribute to the perpetuation of division in a Christendom which Christ clearly wills to be one. Each side, in other words, bears responsibility for the fact that Christendom is and remains divided. Fortunately, one of the prayers which Catholics and Protestants are permitted to pray together contains the phrase, "Forgive us our trespasses."

5. *Each partner must forthrightly face the issues which cause separation, as well as those which create unity.* If certain disputants simply want to stress the difference between Catholicism and Protestantism, there are others who in the name of a false kind of Christian charity are unwilling to face the differences lest the atmosphere be soiled. Either avenue leads to the destruction of dialogue, the first because cynicism deepens separation, and the second because sentimentality issues in disillusionment. Far better that each partner recognize at the start that no amount of emphasis upon points held in common will dissipate the differences which still remain. There is no half-way house, for example, between believing (a) that the pope is infallible, and (b) that the pope is not infallible. Not even the combined genius of Catholic and Protestant theology could produce a satisfactory middle term; there is no such thing as being "a little bit infallible." The differences ought to be recognized directly and forthrightly and openly, so long as they are not the only factors that are recognized. If they are stressed first, they may provide psychological deterrents to the initiation of dialogue. If they are stressed fifth (as they are here) they may keep the dialogue on a realistic track.

There is always the possibility, of course, that *some* of the differences may turn out to be less divisive than was originally thought. Catholic theologians in Germany are now discussing what the Council of Trent really meant by "justification," and some are arguing that the best restatement of Trent has been given by the Protestant theologian Karl Barth![6] If this should be so, it will represent real gain for both sides; there will be one less area for nasty polemics, and one more area for joyful sharing of belief.

But let no one forget that the airing of differences may also make clear that the cleavages are much deeper than the partners to the dialogue had previously thought. The Protestant who naively hopes that Catholics will "give up" certain beliefs for the sake of unity (such as the infallibility of the pope) is in for a depressing experience. The Catholic who hopes that Protestants can be brought back into Catholicism by the concession of some "fringe benefits" (such as a married clergy or permission to sing Charles Wesley's hymns during the mass) is going to discover that Protestant convictions run a little deeper than that.

All of which may sound very depressing. If the recognition of differences is liable to accentuate them, what is the point of talking at all? The atmosphere would indeed be depressing if there were not a final ingredient necessary for the dialogue, the most important of them all.

6. The final ingredient is this: *Each partner must recognize that all that can be done with the dialogue is to offer it up to God.* What "happens" as a result of the dialogue must be left strictly in His hands. If something is to issue from it, He will see to it that something does. If we attempt to manipulate the dialogue, or "use" it, we may be sure that we will thwart whatever potential good lies within it. If, in typical American fashion, we are immediately impatient for "results," we will simply have to learn something about the patience of God—or we will try his patience yet further. While there is always a possibility that conversion may result from conversation, it will be a betrayal if we feel that the dialogue has been a failure because conversion has not taken place.

We must not, in other words, participate in the dialogue with preconceived notions *of ours* as to precisely where it should lead. We would agree that it should lead ultimately to the unity of all Christians, to the fulfilling of the prayer of Christ "that all may be one." But we must not attempt, at this juncture anyhow, to be too sure just how that ought to come. If we talk together, and offer our talking to God, we can be sure that he will show us the next steps. Humanly speaking, the gulf between us seems an unbridgeable one, since the terms of reunion which Catholics and Protestants now set are mutually exclusive. Reunion does not seem to be humanly possible.

And if we believed only in what is humanly possible, we would despair. But no Christian is entitled to believe only in what is humanly possible. We have to affirm—and really mean it—that "With men it is impossible, but with God all things are possible." This is a theme to which we shall have to return. And it tells us why the dialogue is so important: not because we know what will come of it, but precisely because we do *not* know what may come of it. We have no way of predicting what use the Holy Spirit may make of our conversations. This is why we must not presume to manipulate the course of the dialogue with too heavy a hand. All we can really do is to say in penitence and yet in hope that we disagree and that we agree that it is wrong to disagree. All we can really do is to proceed in faith and hope and love, believing that God can use our imperfect words, and that out of them His Word for us will emerge with greater clarity.

This means, of course, that the atmosphere of dialogue is above all and before all and beneath all the atmosphere of prayer. If we are really willing to leave the outcome in God's hands (with all the attendant possibilities and risks which that involves), this means simply that we are offering our dialogue up to Him in prayer, asking Him to do with it as He wills, rather than as we will, and recognizing that whatever repairing is to take place in the broken walls of Christendom will be accomplished by Him and not by us. For the moment our task is to come to know one another, both in our similarities and our differences, in our respective glories and our respective sins, and to offer this common endeavor to God, for whatever use He may deign to make of it.

So much, then, for six conditions of fruitful dialogue:

1. Each partner must believe that the other is speaking in good faith.

2. Each partner must have a clear understanding of his own faith.

3. Each partner must strive for a clearer understanding of the faith of the other. This implies:

   a. his willingness to interpret the faith of the other in its best light rather than its worst; and

   b. a continual willingness to revise his understanding of the faith of the other.

4. Each partner must accept responsibility in humility and penitence for what his group has done, and is doing, to foster and perpetuate division.

5. Each partner must forthrightly face the issues which cause separation, as well as those which create solidarity.

6. Each partner must recognize that all that can be done with the dialogue is to offer it up to God.

There may be other conditions which should be added to these. If there are, it will be one of the gifts of the dialogue to make them apparent.

3

American Catholicism and How It Got That Way

The textbook picture of American history is the picture of a great land providing a haven for the persecuted and oppressed, who could come to its sheltering shores and worship God in freedom, without fear of reprisal for their religious convictions. It is an inspiring picture, and a picture which communicates the truth. But it does not communicate the whole truth. For it is a picture painted from a Protestant (or at least a non-Catholic) orientation, and it does not show what Protestants did to Catholics in the new world. Some glimpse at a Catholic canvas is therefore necessary.[1]

1. "What every Protestant should know" about the history of Catholicism in America

There are at least four facts from American Catholicism's past that we need to see with new eyes, if we are to look at American Catholicism's present with understanding eyes, and look to our joint future with creative eyes.

The *first* thing Protestants need to remember about the history of American Catholicism is that from the very beginning Catholics were an alien minority. They were never part of the colonial "in-group"; they were, on the contrary, the curious outsiders, who not only were not "like" the rest, but were at first so few in number that the majority groups made no attempt to integrate them into colonial life. This alien status was even more pronounced, though

in a different way, in the nineteenth century, when the great waves
of immigration brought hundreds of thousands of Catholics to
America, very few of whom were Anglo-Saxons. Many if not most
of them were non-English-speaking. Those who were English-speaking were Irish, and British-descended Americans found the Irish
even more alien to their ways than the Italians. The lack of esteem
was mutual, being fed by the bitter hostility which had existed
for generations between the English and the Irish on the other
side of the water.

This suggests a *second* fact which is even more important in
understanding the contemporary Catholic mentality: American
Catholics found themselves not only in an alien but in an actively
hostile environment, and were subjected to discrimination and active persecution. I do not think many American Protestants are
aware of the extent to which this was true, and we must dwell on
the point a little longer. Will Herberg reports, "Catholics had by no
means an easy time of it in colonial America. Their church was proscribed in most of the colonies and actively persecuted in some."[2]
Father Ellis puts the point in even stronger terms, and speaks, on
the basis of considerable documentation, of the fact that "a universal
anti-Catholic bias was brought to Jamestown in 1607 and vigilantly
cultivated in all thirteen colonies from Massachusetts to Georgia."[3]

The facts are certainly clear concerning discriminatory legislation against Catholics in American colonial history. The facts are
likewise unhappily clear concerning what happened when American Protestants decided to take direct action against the Catholic
"intruders." In 1834, a Protestant mob burned down the convent
of the Ursuline Sisters at Charlestown, Massachusetts. A decade
later there was a terrible outburst against Catholics in Philadelphia;
for three days the City of Brotherly Love was in total chaos. Thirteen persons were killed and many injured, as Protestants burned
two Catholic churches, a Catholic seminary, and many blocks of
Catholic homes. A year later, in 1855, nearly one hundred Catholics
were slain and scores of Catholic homes burned to the ground in
Louisville, Kentucky, on what came to be known as "Bloody Mon-
day."

Protestants who are so vocal about what American Catholics will
"do" if they get to be 51% of the population, might more frequently
remember such incidents as these, engaged in by Protestants who
were considerably more than 51%; and Protestants who are always
urging Catholics to "repudiate the Inquisition" might expend some

of their energy organizing a few days of Protestant penitence for these and other deeds of violence against Catholics which stain the Protestant past.

It cannot be countered that such events as have been cited were merely sporadic outbursts of mob violence. For there was also reflective and carefully cultivated nativist opposition to Catholicism, epitomized in the Know-Nothing Party, and later on (from 1887 until about the turn of the century) in the American Protective Association, which was distinctly anti-Catholic in its aim and program.

Third, it was this fact of persecution which, more than any other one thing, perhaps, led to the development of what Catholics themselves have frankly called a "ghetto mentality." Since Catholics were not accepted in the predominantly Protestant society, they were forced by the very nature of the case to live by themselves. If American Protestants dislike this trait, they must realize that Protestant suspicion and superiority are in large part responsible for making the development of distinctively Catholic structures a necessity of Catholic survival. This is the background of the astonishing proliferation of specifically Catholic organizations, which so many Protestants bewail: Catholic trade unions, Catholic Boy Scouts, Catholic War Veterans, Catholic educators' groups, Catholic policeman's guilds, Catholic charities, Catholic hospitals, Catholic orphanages, Catholic social clubs, Catholic lobbies in Washington, etc.

Through the latter part of the nineteenth century, a *fourth* factor was shaping American Catholicism. During this period the church was going through some significant inner struggles, as well as going through the outer struggle of trying to relate itself to the rest of American culture. The various waves of Catholic immigrants came from many different parts of Europe, and they did not all take kindly to the dominance which the Irish had achieved over the control of American Catholic life. These nationalistic loyalties at work within the life of the church immensely complicated its adjustment to American life. To this must be coupled the fact that most of the immigrants came from poor and even unlettered backgrounds, so that little intellectual leadership was emerging from the ranks during this period. (In 1948, as many Catholic writers have pointed out, not a single Catholic archbishop was the son of parents who had had a college education.)

This very mixed heritage has had its obvious effect upon the character of contemporary American Catholicism. It has meant that until quite recently Catholic energy has had to go largely into "bricks and mortar," e.g. the sheer task of providing churches and schools for a variety of constituencies. It has meant that since many groups within Catholicism were not "indigenous Americans," Catholicism has remained on the defensive, fearful of renewed outbreaks against persons with the triple disadvantage of a different religion, a different language, and a different cultural background, from the dominant Protestant majority.

These four facts, (a) that Catholicism has been an alien minority from the very start, (b) that it has been the victim of discrimination and active persecution, (c) that it has been forced into a ghetto mentality, and (d) that it has had to make tremendous internal adjustments due to the varieties of races and cultures within its midst, are important facts to bear in mind in any intelligent appraisal of American Catholicism today.

2. A new fact, and what it means

As we turn from a discussion of Catholicism in the past to Catholicism in the present, we have to take account of a new fact on the American scene. It is a fact that can be stated in a number of ways. The gentlest way to state it is to say that America has become a pluralistic culture. It has become (in an image Will Herberg has popularized) a "triple melting-pot," in which one identifies himself not as a Scot, an Italian, or a German, but as a Protestant, a Catholic, or a Jew.[4]

But there is a stronger way of stating the new fact, which goes like this: America is no longer a "Protestant nation." Until fairly recent times it could be claimed that America *was* a Protestant nation. But this is no longer true. It is now a nation in which the presence of Jew and Catholic makes it impossible for the Protestant to claim the special privileges he had in the past. America is no longer a Protestant nation, nor is it a Catholic nation, nor yet a Jewish nation. It is an amalgam of all three.

Now adjustment to this fact is not going to be easy for Protestants. Many of them have not yet faced up to this new reality. Many of them still hope for the time when Catholicism will recede and "Protestant values" (whatever they are) can again become the dominant values of American life—and many of them are going to surrender every inch of Protestant ground at the cost of as much bloodshed as possible. But such people are going to have to adjust to the new fact, which can now be put in yet another way: Catholicism is here to stay. The wise thing for Protestants to do will be to learn how to live with their Catholic neighbors, rather than trying to keep them under heel. As Thomas O'Dea, a Catholic sociologist has said, "Protestants must now move over a bit. That men do not move over graciously is one of the few undeniable generalizations from history."[5]

None of this means, it must be emphasized, that America, no longer a "Protestant nation," is becoming a "Catholic nation." We must explore this further. Statistics are notoriously unreliable in this kind of situation (and the 1960 census will soon give us lots of new figures with which to play), but as nearly as can be determined at the time of writing, the facts appear to be these. In the United States, roughly 115,000,000 persons over 14 years of age have indicated a religious preference. Of this number, about 79,000,000 are Protestants, about 31,000,000 are Catholics, and the rest are Jews or affiliates of other faiths. This means that roughly one out of three Americans with a formal religious affiliation is a Roman Catholic. In terms of the *total* population, the number is about one out of five, or 20%.

The statistics do not bear out the "fear" expressed in many Protestant circles that Catholics are gaining much more rapidly in terms of over-all population than Protestants, and that they will shortly become 51% of the population, at which time all sorts of dire events will take place. "Neither Protestantism nor Catholicism has been gaining appreciably at the expense of the other in the past quarter of a century," Herberg reports. "Both have been growing, because of the general growth of church membership in this period, but not in such a way as to indicate serious inroads on either side."[6] He cites the following figures:

Year	Percentage of total population	
	Protestants	Catholics
1926	27.0	16.0
1940	28.7	16.1
1950	33.8	18.9
1955	35.5	20.3
1958	35.5	22.8

The two groups, in other words, seem to have come to more or less of a statistical balance.

But to see the picture fully, something more must be said, for it lies close to the center of the Protestant "fears" we shall have to examine in our next chapter. Roman Catholicism may stay in the neighborhood of 33-35% of the religiously affiliated, and 20-30% of the total population, which means that it will remain a numerical minority. But in actual fact it will occupy—and almost occupies now —a kind of quasi-majority status by virtue of the fact that it is far and away the largest single religious body in America, and possesses a degree of organizational discipline that no other religious group can begin to approach. This means that the concerted action of American Catholicism on any given issue in American life is far more potent than the diffused efforts of Protestants, or even the combined efforts of large groups of Protestant denominations banded together.

In summary, then, America has become a pluralistic culture. It is no longer a "Protestant nation," nor will it become one again. Catholicism is here to stay, but it is not likely that it is going to achieve overwhelming numerical superiority. On the other hand, numerical superiority is not necessarily a significant index of political strength.

3. A Protestant impression of American Catholicism today

I turn now to the rather presumptuous undertaking of trying to describe Catholicism in America today, as it appears to an outsider. Needless to say, this is only part of a description, and I shall discuss only those impressions which have a direct bearing on the subject matter of this book.[7] Six of these seem worthy of attention.

1. Despite the fact that Catholicism is the largest single religious body in the United States, and appears to have a quasi-majority status, American Catholics still seem to feel themselves an oppressed minority group. This comes out repeatedly in Catholic literature and in discussions with individual Catholics. It will sound like nonsense to Protestants who live in large cities where the political machinery is almost totally in Catholic hands, and where Catholicism seems anything but obsessed with its minority status. But it is nevertheless a fact that many American Catholics live with memories of the not-too-distant past when their Catholicism was a definite handicap

socially, politically, and economically. We have examined some of the historical factors which make this attitude quite understandable.

But I think there is also one way in which Catholics in their turn keep the minority-status feeling at an unfortunate fever pitch. This is by a device which I shall call the "bigot-reflex." Any public attitude which is contrary to Catholic belief or Catholic practice is interpreted by certain Catholics as though it were a direct attack upon the Catholic church. The "bigot-reflex" is partly a conditioned reflex, cultivated by occasional over-zealous priests, and fosters an impression of anti-Catholic animus where I am sure it often does not exist. A person who advocates birth control, let us say, is a "bigot" because he is attacking what Catholics believe to be an inviolable part of the moral law, and is therefore trying to destroy the Catholic faith. Any number of neat syllogisms can be constructed from this stance:

> Jones is for birth control.
> The Catholic church is against birth control.
> Therefore Jones is against the Catholic church.

> The Catholic church advocates parochial school education.
> Smith advocates public school education.
> Therefore Smith is anti-Catholic.

Unfortunately, those who employ this kind of reasoning have never heard of the Fallacy of the Undistributed Middle, nor are they likely to be too impressed if it is drawn to their attention. They are too deep in their own Undisturbed Muddle.

Thus, although there are many sound historical reasons why Catholics still feel themselves to be a persecuted minority in America, some of the fears, at any rate, are either self-imposed or self-induced.

2. These comments will have already suggested another fact: there is tremendous variety within American Catholicism. There is a Protestant stereotype of Catholicism which sees it as a vast monolithic structure, in which all people think alike, speak alike, and act alike——since the priest tells them exactly what to think, speak, and do. The basis of this stereotype is, of course, the fact that in matters of faith and morals Catholics do indeed "think alike," and the church will brook no questions or denials in the area of defined dogma. But what non-Catholics do not sufficiently grasp is that there remain many areas in the life of the Catholic that do not involve defined dogma, so that Catholics can and do have violent

disagreements among themselves. Politicians do not automatically count on a "Catholic vote." Catholics who move to the suburbs tend to switch their political allegiance from Democratic to Republican just as easily as their Protestant neighbors. A reader who gazed synoptically at issues of *The Brooklyn Tablet* and *The Commonweal* would wonder what the two possibly had in common. (What they have in common is that both are edited and written by Roman Catholics.)

These differences extend to Catholic participation in political life as well. The whole case for the variety within American Catholicism could be symbolized by the difference in political hue of two Roman Catholic senators of the same name. Senator Joe McCarthy of Wisconsin was a demagogue, a blusterer, a right-wing Republican, and a subverter of American democratic procedures. Senator Eugene McCarthy of Minnesota is a thoughtful, educated, and cultured contributor to American democratic procedures, a liberal Democrat who has earned the admiration even of that most hardened group of observers of the political scene, the Washington press corps.

3. The state of scholarship in American Catholicism has been the subject of considerable Catholic self-criticism.[8] With the exception of a few contributions in the direction of a new approach to the church-state issue, which we shall note in the next chapter, American Catholicism has not yet taken the place in the world of scholarship that could have been expected of it.

D. W. Brogan, for example, one of the most acute non-American observers of the American scene, has commented that ". . . in no western society is the intellectual prestige of Catholicism lower than in the country where, in such respects as wealth, numbers and strength of organization, it is so powerful."[9] If this judgment seems harsh, we need only take account of Father Ellis' comment on it: "No well-informed American Catholic will attempt to challenge that statement."[10]

If this is the fact, why is it the fact? The following are some of the reasons suggested by Father Ellis, Father Weigel, and others: (a) anti-Catholic prejudice (which we have previously noted) has excluded many Catholics from full participation in the intellectual life of the country, (b) many American Catholics have come from poorly educated and non-English-speaking immigrant backgrounds, (c) American Catholics like most other Americans have found themselves more interested in the acquisition of the Almighty Dollar through commerce, than in the service of the Almighty God through scholarship, and (d) Catholics in posts of leadership in the church have not taken seriously enough the vocation of the intellectual, with the result that too little attention has been paid to the development of Catholic schools and colleges of high calibre. Father Ellis comments:

> The chief blame, I firmly believe, lies with Catholics themselves. It lies in their frequently self-imposed ghetto mentality which prevents them from mingling as they should with their non-Catholic colleagues, and in their lack of industry and the habits of work . . .[11]

We must take account of a further charge that Protestants sometimes bring against Roman Catholicism and scholarship. Many of them would claim that the nature of Catholicism is such that it cannot encourage independent scholarship, since no scholar is permitted to come to conclusions at variance with those of the church. That this has often been the case in Biblical studies, for example, would seem, at least to the outsider, to have some real truth; for whatever else the "Modernist movement" may have shown, it showed very clearly that Catholic Biblical scholars could not venture into speculation which threatened the established conclusions of the church.[12] But even in this area, there has been a considerable change in the Catholic attitude toward Biblical studies since 1907, and the 1943 encyclical, *Divino afflante spiritu*, shows a remarkable adaptation to new currents in the study of scripture, as we shall have occasion to note in Chapter 5 below.

However, the notion that the Catholic church inhibits independent scholarship cannot really be given much weight in areas apart from the direct examination of faith and morals, which are of course, held to have been divinely revealed and therefore beyond human questioning. To be sure, the church is extremely cautious about accepting new data in the field of the sciences and philosophy, and the 1950 encyclical *Humani Generis* certainly did not encourage Catholics to greater degrees of intellectual venturesomeness, but it is significant that even that encyclical stressed the need for Catholic scholars to acquaint themselves with modern speculation, not simply so that error could be refuted, but in order to discover that "there is some truth underlying even these wrongheaded ideas."

Furthermore, the Protestant must try to realize that from the Catholic perspective there could be no such thing as a "truth" discovered in the realm of, say, natural science, that was at variance with the

Catholic faith. The remarkable breadth and comprehensiveness of
Thomist philosophy insures that ultimately a place will be found
for new "truths of reason" which never contradict the "truths of faith."
Protestants may have some basic questions about Thomism as a philosophy, but they are not our concern at the moment; our concern is
to make quite clear that the Catholic does not feel himself caught
in an intellectual straightjacket when he pursues truth. That significant and creative scholarship can emerge from Catholic circles is
too patent a fact to need demonstration. Actually, the reason for
lack of more creative Catholic scholarship on the American scene
is probably that thus far the church has had to do too many other
things, assimilating its immigrant structure, building churches, con-
solidating its constituency, etc. The period of creative and responsible Catholic scholarship lies just over the threshhold, and it is a
major frontier that American Catholicism is already beginning to
face. Journals like *Thought*, produced at Fordham University,
Theological Studies, produced at Woodstock College, *Cross-Currents*,
a Catholic-sponsored journal dedicated to fostering (among other
things) the Protestant-Catholic dialogue, and *The Commonweal*,
the most well-informed and thoughtful religious journal in the land,
are at least straws in the wind, and give reason to hope that the
image non-Catholics have of American Catholicism will gradually
cease being triggered by the word "bingo" and begin to be nurtured
by some word more fitting to the life of the mind.

4. One area, however, where neither American Catholic scholarship nor the Catholic lay mind have sufficiently exerted themselves,
has been in the area of knowledge of Protestantism. American Catholics, as a whole, are singularly ill-informed about American Protestantism, and hardly prepared for the Protestant-Catholic dialogue
which is so urgently needed in this country, and which the present
volume hopes to further.[13]

I base this estimate not simply on my own limited experience
with Catholics, but on the almost unanimous testimony of Catholics
who have made their own appraisals of the American scene. In an
issue of *Christianity and Crisis* (June 8, 1959) devoted to the
Protestant-Catholic dialogue, three Catholic writers, writing inde-
pendently of one another, each made the same point. The experience of one of them is probably typical of most Catholics:

> I do not believe that Catholics generally have anything that ap-
> proaches an adequate understanding of what Protestantism actually

is. Most of them know only what it is *not.* And this is a major failure in Catholic education . . .

In primary and secondary [Catholic] schools I learned the standard things, all negative: Protestants reject the authority of the Pope; they do not honor the Virgin Mary; they deny the efficacy of good works; they acknowledge only two sacraments, etc. In the college I attended I learned nothing more. (But the history department offered a two-semester course under the interesting title, "The Protestant Revolt and the Catholic Reformation.") Through eighteen years of Catholic education I heard nothing positive about Protestantism.[14]

Nor is this ignorance confined to laymen. As we shall see in Chapter 5, a great deal of Roman Catholic literature about Protestantism is being produced, but almost none of this originates in the United States. It is the product of European Catholics. (My colleague in the present volume is one of the few notable exceptions to American Catholic indifference to things Protestant, and he cannot forever be expected to symbolize American Catholic concern for Protestantism.)

I think this is a deplorable situation. I know that there are many reasons for it, both historical and cultural, and at this juncture all I would say to my Catholic readers is that they need not live in this religiously insulated atmosphere. In the light of the tremendous creativity of European Catholicism in dealing with Protestant ecumenism, I shall want to suggest later that it is not a sign of being a "bad" Catholic to be informed about Protestantism, but that on the contrary it is a very necessary part of being a responsible Catholic in the world of today.

We must not wax too lyrical at this point, however. Professor O'Dea, in the issue of *Christianity and Crisis* referred to above, has doubts that we can even begin to duplicate in America what goes on in Europe. "The best we can do is to work for a growing openness as we build some basis in mutual trust and friendship."[15] But this is surely a significant way to start, and if volumes like the present one have any value, it will be not because they say the definitive word about Protestant-Catholic relationships, but simply because they *open up the issue,* and demonstrate that Protestants and Catholics can discuss with one another within the covers of the same book. If this is shown to be possible, Catholics and Protestants may shortly begin to discuss with one another in the same room and around the same table. And until the eschatological moment when we can break bread together around the Lord's Table, we must foster a spirit that will at least make it possible for us to break bread together around a dining room table.

5. A notable Protestant contribution to this new situation would be an attempt by Protestants to realize that most American Catholics feel *no conflict whatsoever* between being Roman Catholics and being American citizens. If there is a dilemma here it is a dilemma which Protestant polemics has created for them. One can sympathize with a Catholic layman when he says,

> What does bother me a good deal is the challenge, still given us, to "prove" our Americanism, and we hear this challenge even at "advanced" inter-faith gatherings. I, for one, am very tired of explaining that, no, I *really* feel no conflict between my Americanism and my Catholicism. The day is rapidly coming—I think it has come for me—when American Catholics will refuse to answer such challenges, no matter how well they are meant——and will return them for the insults they are.[16]

One can sympathize, I say, with the statement, but I am afraid that for better or for worse, the "challenge" will continue to be uttered. *To Protestants* I say that there are plenty of reasons for taking absolutely at his word the Catholic who affirms the integrity of his American citizenship, and we shall examine some of these reasons in the next chapter. And *to Catholics* I say that I hope very much that they can be fortified with supernatural grace to such a degree that they can continue with patience to try to answer the question. For what lies behind the question is not a desire to insult, but a desire simply to be reassured. A lot of history lies behind the question, as we shall presently see. It may be a very distorted reading of history, and it may need a great deal of correction, but it is history nonetheless, and if the Protestant is going to re-learn the meaning of that history, he is going to need all the help the Catholic can give him.

But there is yet a further word, and this word must be addressed *to both Catholics and Protestants,* who may someday have to make common cause together in this area. For the issue of "conflicting loyalties" is by no means confined to the Catholic. In fact, one can say that the issue could only properly be raised by someone with an exclusively nationalistic mentality, one for whom there can be no higher loyalty than loyalty to one's country. And against this presupposition Catholics and Protestants must indeed make common cause. As a Protestant I must state that my highest loyalty is *not* to the United States of America; my highest loyalty is to God and to the God specifically made known in Jesus Christ. God, at last report, was *not* an American (some prominent Protestant clergymen in Washington, D.C., to the contrary notwithstanding), and Jesus Christ is not an Anglo-Saxon nor even a European, but one who lived his entire life in that very suspect part of the world known as the Middle East. In most things I am sure that I can serve God through the fact of my American citizenship, but if it should come to a point where the two loyalties are *in clear conflict*, I am quite sure where my ultimate loyalty belongs, and only hope that I would have the moral courage not to falter in that choice: "We must obey God rather than men." (Acts 5:29). I would expect any Roman Catholic to come to the same conclusion, and would defend him in that choice, even though I might be quite prepared to argue with him about the specific place where he had drawn his line of demarcation between loyalty to God and loyalty to country.

6. The problem raised by this line of demarcation can be posed by considering a final fact, which is this: *American* Catholicism, whatever American stresses and configurations it may have, is first, last and always *Roman* Catholicism. No Catholic is ashamed of this fact, and no Catholic tries to disguise it. American Catholicism is simply Roman Catholicism as it happens to be practiced in the United States. No Catholic would have it otherwise. Indeed, if he wanted to, he would soon discover that by the very wish he had severed himself from the Roman Catholic faith. It is sheer nonsense, then, for non-Catholics to assume that American Catholics will "repudiate the pope," or reject other items of the Catholic faith in order to make themselves more agreeable to non-Catholics on the American scene. No matter how pleadingly certain writers may ask American Catholics to institute "democratic procedures" in their church rather than "hierarchical" ones, this will not happen. For at the very basis of the Catholic conception of the church is the belief that it contains two orders within it, the sheep and the shepherds, that this is the way God willed it to be, and that therefore this is the way it shall remain. There can be changes in the life of Catholicism where revealed dogma is not involved, and American Catholics will have an increasing role to play in the evolution of such changes, but there will be no basic shift in Catholic faith and conviction. American Protestants might as well accustom themselves to this fact, and think about the nature of Protestant-Catholic relations in the light of it. In any other light, Protestants would be

making an impossible demand on Catholics, saying in effect, "You must first of all cease to be true Catholics, if we are to continue to live together."

Now curiously enough, and tragically enough, it is this very fact, that American Catholicism to have inner integrity must be Roman Catholicism, that is at the basis of so many Protestant "fears." This, many Protestants will say, is precisely why Catholicism constitutes a "problem" in America. We shall have to examine the reasons for this contention in the next chapter. But the recognition that American Catholicism is also Roman Catholicism is here cited not simply to define a "problem," but also to define for us the context in which the rest of our discussion must be framed. For we cannot take a real "look" at American Catholicism just by confining our glances to the American scene. Our chief concern, indeed, will remain the American scene, but for the rest of our discussion we shall have to view Catholicism as a world-wide phenomenon, and not merely as an American phenomenon, if we are even to begin to do justice to what we see within our own shores.

4

Beer, Ballots, Birth Control, Bingo—and All That

A look at the immediate issues

We stated at the end of the last chapter that American Catholicism can only be understood as Roman Catholicism. On one level, this is an unimaginative type of simple descriptive statement, no more, indeed, than a tautology. But on another level it conjures up, in a certain kind of Protestant mind, the most horrendous images possible, and far from being a simple statement of fact is a statement fraught with sinister implications.

The purpose of the present chapter is to examine some of the reasons why American Protestants have so many "fears" about American Catholicism, and to do so, if possible, in reasoned fashion. Sometimes the fears are stated in such hysterical fashion that they merit indeed the swift response of "bigot." But it should be possible to state them in civilized fashion so that they do not merit even the reflective response of "bigot."

It is of utmost importance to the health of the dialogue that the fears be stated, rather than suppressed. Then, if the fears are misplaced, if they flow from a faulty understanding of Catholic faith or from a biased interpretation of Catholic activity, it will be the Catholic contribution to the dialogue to tell Protestants just that, and to indicate a proper interpretation of the matter. If, on the other hand, the fears are well-founded, Catholics should realize that Protestants will feel bound to continue re-stating them, and will desire continual clarification from their Catholic partners in the dialogue.

Now even with the best will in the world, I am sure that the next few pages are going to irritate a lot of Catholic readers. They will object that the things being described are peripheral to the genius of Catholicism, atypical of the Catholicism they know, and that it is unfair to highlight them and then generalize therefrom about the whole of Catholicism. I agree that the issues are not the central issues; I agree that they are atypical of Catholicism at its best; I agree that is unfair to indict the whole of Catholicism in these terms. But I would be quite naive if I were to attempt to report Protestant feelings about Catholicism without calling attention to them. To by-pass these issues would be to cry "Peace, peace, when there is no peace."

1. The Bogey of "Catholic power"

What, then, are these issues? What is the source of these fears? The problem can be summed up bluntly in the words "Catholic power," and the bogey of Catholic power is the immediate source of friction between Protestants and Catholics.

Now a "bogey" is a bugbear, which in its turn is defined by Webster as "a kind of imaginary goblin or specter, used to excite needless fears, as in children; now, any object of dread." Thus the term is not quite adequate, for it would be improper to define Catholic power as an *"imaginary . . . specter, used to excite needless fear."* But I retain the term because I want to imply that at least some of the fears are both needless and imaginary.

Some, but not all. Therefore, we must have recourse to the latter part of our definition, which goes, "an object of dread." And this quite accurately defines what most Protestants feel about Catholic power; it is to them indeed an object of dread, and in the course of this chapter we must try to make clear why.

The immediate sources of Protestant irritation
The issues over which Protestant-Catholic tension will be stretched in the next decade will not be the ultimate issues of the theological validity or invalidity of the dogma of the Immaculate Conception, or the religious adequacy or inadequacy of the dogma of Papal Infallibility. Nor will the average Protestant be noticeably upset by the content of papal encyclicals during that period, or by Catholic pronouncements concerning the heretical character of Protestant ordination. Rather, what will upset the average American Protestant

will be some local incident, perhaps (although perhaps not) trivial in itself, which he will interpret as "one more step" in the attempt of Roman Catholicism to "seize power" in the United States, or at least, to put itself in such a vantage point that it can further its own interests at the cost of denying the interests or rights of non-Catholics. Incidents like these:

The only hospital in the neighborhood, a Catholic hospital, will dismiss a surgeon from its staff because the surgeon was heard to say that birth control information should be given to non-Catholic married women whose lives would be jeopardized by another pregnancy.

A convent will buy a large tract of land and the tax money formerly paid for the land will no longer appear in the annual town revenues.

A newspaper editor will print an article about "Catholicism in Spain" and a group of Catholic-owned department stores will withdraw their advertising.

A priest will urge, and even insist upon, his parishioners voting in favor of a bill to legalize gambling in the town, so that he can run his bingo parties legally.

A public-spirited citizen will write a letter to the local paper urging federal aid for public school education, and find himself attacked as a bigot who is out to deprive Catholic children of the right to a parochial school education.

A state legislator will introduce a bill to regularize the divorce proceedings in his state, and find himself pictured in the Catholic press as an immoral man who is urging people to flout the moral law given by God.

A movie-house owner will discover that the bishop has forbidden Catholics to attend a film (which Catholics in other parts of the country are quite free to see), and will be warned that if he continues to show the film no Catholic will be allowed to enter his theatre for a period of one year.

Some of these things may sound trivial; others are not so trivial. But they are all incidents of the sort that arouse very bitter feelings locally, and they are the kinds of incidents that are the source of very deep animosities, for they seem to have a common theme running through them. That theme goes: Catholics will employ whatever means can be employed to achieve the ends Catholics feel desirable, and will employ whatever means can be employed to see that non-Catholic ends are thwarted, defeated, and crushed.

Wherever they turn, Protestants see things that *to them* seem to be further examples of this tendency. And since they naturally do not share the aim which these actions seem designed to promote, they tend to resist, and to fight back, in order to thwart what they feel is the Catholic effort to "gain control."

A word to Protestants: inconsistencies and stereotypes in Protestant polemics

The immediate Catholic reaction is probably to feel that this is all very high-handed and unfair, and the feeling is likely to be coupled with rising resentment over this typically jaundiced Protestant view. And as a Protestant, I must state that I see considerable ground for this Catholic consternation, and must address a word of warning to my fellow Protestants. It is not only important for Protestants to "look at" Catholicism, but it is even more important for them to look at it in the right way. And part of the mind-set of contemporary Protestantism, unfortunately, is a mind-set which is convinced in advance that Rome is so wrong that anything it does must be examined until it can be seen in an unfavorable light. Any stigma, as has been said, will do to beat a dogma. Therefore, in ways which must seem quite bewildering to the Catholic, Protestants offer indictments of "Rome" which are characterized by almost every quality save consistency, and in their unhappiness about "Catholic power," Protestants will make, in almost the same breath, the most feverishly contradictory assertions and demands.

In the late '40s, for example, whenever a bishop commented adversely on a bill for, say, federal aid to education, the Protestant cry was that the hierarchy was too involved in politics. Then in the early '50s when McCarthyism became a menace stalking the land, the Protestant cry changed without any Protestant being aware of the change. Now it went, "Why doesn't somebody in the hierarchy condemn McCarthy?" Roman Catholics could thus have met all Protestant objection by the simple expedient of simultaneously (a) staying out of politics and (b) getting into politics.

The point must be driven home. How are Catholics to react when they are pilloried on such charges as these?

1. The church exerts too much control over her members (excommunicating members in Italy who vote communist); the church exerts too little control over her members (not excommunicating members in Spain who persecute Protestants).

2. The church is too committed to beliefs of the past (a doctrine of transubstantiation based on Aristotelian metaphysics); the church is too committed to novelties which have no basis in beliefs of the past (the promulgation of the dogma of Papal Infallibility).

3. The church is too closely confined to Scripture (the conservative conclusions of the Biblical Commission); the church is not closely enough confined to Scripture (the non-Scriptural dogma of the assumption of the virgin).

4. The church is too "this-worldly" (the lavish pomp of the papal court); the church is too "other-worldly" (the curious vows of the religious of poverty, chastity and obedience).

5. The church insists that everybody believe the same things (nobody can question the dogmas); the church has too many conflicting opinions (whom are we to believe about the relationship of church and state?).

6. The church is basically a political entity (American Cardinals who vote for a pope should be deprived of citizenship and forced to register as aliens); the church is not a political entity at all (therefore we should not send an ambassador to the Vatican).

7. The church urges its members to stick to themselves (Catholic War Veterans, Catholic Boy Scouts, etc.); the church urges its members to "infiltrate" the rest of society so they can take over (Catholic support of a Catholic for President).

Now I submit to my fellow Protestants that they cannot have it both ways. And as long as Protestants continue to demand that Catholics do two mutually exclusive things at the same time, Catholics will have every right to respond either in bewilderment or despair.

A word to Catholics: the concern behind the inconsistencies and stereotypes

But a word must be addressed to Catholics beyond the word of the legitimacy of bewilderment and despair. The word to Catholics must be a plea to bear with this curious jumble of criticisms long enough to do two things. The first is to eschew the temptation to conclude that since the charges are contradictory, they merely cancel one another out and can on those grounds be ignored. It may be that one of the charges is right and the other wrong, or that one is at least partly right and the other only partly wrong.

But the more important plea to Catholics is the plea that they be willing to help disentangle the *valid* concerns that may lie imbedded within the tissue of downright error or unfortunate misunderstanding in which the charges have been clothed, so that we may properly discuss real issues together and not waste our time on pseudo-issues.

Let us take as one example the typical charge of Protestant

hysteria that Catholicism is "priest-ridden." Now this is a fighting
word, for which the usual Catholic response is another fighting word,
"bigot." End of discussion.

But suppose Protestants could tone down the stridency of their
language and Catholics could be fortified with supernatural charity,
and both could examine the issue a little more temperately. The
Protestant might now say that by "priest-ridden" he means, really,
thåt the life of the church is directed by the clergy, that the people
have no real "say" in the life of the church, that it is, in short, "un-
democratic." Now these may still be fighting, or at least emotionally-
laden, words for the Protestant, but at this point the Catholic (if he
is still fortified with supernatural charity) can reply, "Of course," in
such a way that the Protestant, the wind somewhat deflected from
his sails, can proceed to ask in lucid tones, "But you mean you don't
mind?"

And from this point on there is a chance for reasoned discussion
to take place. For the fact of the matter is that the Roman Catholic
does *not* mind. His church *is* directed by the clergy, and he would
never try to assert that it is democratically run. Catholics find this
neither disturbing nor menacing (nor, to anticipate, does it make
it difficult for them to believe in democracy in the life of the state).
Their definition of the church makes a clear-cut distinction between
sheep and shepherds, as the encyclical *Vehementer Nos* makes clear:

> The church is the Mystical Body of Christ, a body ruled by pastors
> and teachers, a society of men headed by rulers having full and per-
> fect powers of governing, instructing and judging. It follows that this
> society is essentially an unequal society, that is to say, a society com-
> posed of two categories of persons; pastors and the flock: those who
> rank in the different degrees of the hierarchy and the multitude of the
> faithful; and these categories are so distinct in themselves that in the
> pastoral body alone resides the necessary right and authority to guide
> and direct all the members towards the goal of society. As for the
> multitude, it has no other right than that of allowing itself to be led,
> and, as a docile flock, to follow its shepherds.

Thus even such an epithet as "priest-ridden," harsh and disagree-
able as it is, is groping after something, and is recognizing something,
namely that there is a basic difference between Protestant and Catholic conceptions of the church. This fact ought to be recognized
in Catholic-Protestant dialogue, and even such an unpromising initial
exchange as "priest-ridden," and "bigot" can give way to civilized
discussion if there is the will and intent on both sides.

I would hope, incidentally, that this traffic could flow both ways. When I hear Protestantism described as "everyone believing what he wants," I am sure I have roughly the same emotional reaction that the Catholic has when he hears a phrase like "priest-ridden." In my angrier moments I want to say, "If you don't understand us any better than that, keep quiet!" In my less belligerent moments I want to say, "That's crazy; now listen to me and I'll set you straight." But in my more serene moments I want to say, "Protestantism *isn't* that, but let's see if we can discover together what within Protestantism could have led you to that conclusion, and then see what partial truth may be contained within so palpable an error."

A word to Protestants and Catholics: the reservoir of charity

I wish there were a way to ensure that such objectives as these could be kept in mind the next time a "local incident" flares up. I do not know what proximate resources will be available in local skirmishes—an understanding Catholic layman, perhaps, or a group of citizens who can talk sanely together about the public welfare. But I do know of an ultimate resource which is available to both Catholics and Protestants alike, if they will be humble enough to avail themselves of it. This is the reservoir of charity. I know that it is often the destiny of love and charity to be defeated, but I do not believe I am naive in assuming that a reservoir of charity, filled over a period of months and years from the springs of prayer and active goodwill, could extinguish at least some of the fires of ill-will which seem to arise by spontaneous combustion whenever Catholics and Protestants get too close to one another. I remember to my sorrow an incident where this reservoir did not exist. I was once a member of a Protestant ministers' association in a small town, and we became very much disturbed because the local Catholic priest had become very much disturbed about a course on sex education in the public high school. There were what we like to call "prophetic sermons" hurled from all the pulpits in town, and there were some sharp exchanges in the local press. But never in the course of the entire battle did it occur to one of us Protestant men of God to seek out, meet, and talk with the Catholic priest. (Most of us had never even met him.) I am not guaranteeing that controversy would have been averted or abated by our action—but it could not have gotten worse and might well have gotten better. We might at least have understood why we disagreed, and not had to impute the worst possible motives to one another.

2. A Protestant "attack" on Catholic power— an attempt to get the issues focused clearly

What, then, is the substance of the Protestant "fear" of Catholic power? I shall try to state the argument as forthrightly as I can. I think there are three main reasons why Protestants feel that Catholicism is gathering its forces to "take over." I hope Catholics will be willing to listen to these arguments, even if they become impatient at the Protestant obsession with what to them are only archaic angularities of the Catholic faith.

1. The first of these reasons is *historical*, even though to Catholics it often sounds hysterical. As Protestants look at the past history of Roman Catholicism, they see an impressive accumulation of evidence to suggest that when Roman Catholicism has had sufficient power it has persecuted those who differed from it, and has been intolerant of those holding minority opinions. The proper idea that "truth has not the same rights as error" has been transformed by the church into the improper idea that "persons in error have no rights at all." (I will later want to suggest that this conclusion is based on narrowly selective reading of Catholic history, but surely there is sufficient evidence of past Catholic persecution and intolerance so that the present day Catholic should be able to see how a Protestant could feel uncomfortable about it.) Certain Protestant memories die very hard. Protestants remember the Inquisition—as the Catholic wearily discovers every time "toleration" is discussed. I write these lines within a stone's throw of the "Martyr's Monument" at St. Andrews in Scotland. In this town four men were burned at the stake for their beliefs, one of them lingering six hours in the fire. That story has its repetition all over Europe. Perhaps Protestants remember these things a little too often or make too many easy jumps from the sixteenth century to the present day. But they know that the Catholic church once persecuted those who disagreed with it, and they find no very clear evidence that the *principle* of persecution has been disavowed; what they find are statements that it is no longer "expedient" to enlist the power of the state in destroying heretics. I know the guilt was not all on one side. I know that my Calvinistic forefathers burned Servetus. But a later generation of those forefathers erected a "monument of expiation" on the spot

where Servetus was burned, disavowing the act as inconsistent with the principles of Protestantism.

I shall not dwell on this historical argument, because I think it is exceedingly dangerous to generalize from it and say that because Catholicism once persecuted in the past it will persecute again, and that the only thing at present which inhibits it from doing so is lack of sufficient power. But I do ask Catholics to be aware of the fact, with whatever charity they can muster, that this historical argument clings to the conventional Protestant image of the Catholic church, and that Catholics by their present attitude must help Protestants to eradicate it from their minds.

2. There is a second fact which weighs much more heavily on the Protestant consciousness when it ponders the problem of Catholic power. This is the accumulation of evidence from places where Catholicism holds overwhelming power *today*. And this contemporary evidence seems to the Protestant to point in a direction unhappily similar to the direction in which the historical evidence pointed. For in places where Catholicism is the overwhelming majority today, it is often true that Protestants are not only not allowed to evangelize or engage in public worship or sell Protestant translations of the Bible, but that they are frequently deprived of their civil liberties, sometimes actively persecuted, and occasionally killed.

I realize that every Catholic has heard this argument *ad nauseam*, and knows that he is about to be called upon to "say something" about what goes on in Spain and certain parts of South America. I realize that some American Catholics do not approve of what goes on in those places, and that a few of them have the courage to say so. But the Protestant remains distressed by the fact that so few say so, and equally distressed by the fact that very little seems to happen to change the situation. To the Protestant it seems quite evident that something is wrong when a church claims to believe in the rights of minorities in North America (where it is the minority), and does not seem to believe in the rights of minorities in South America (where it is the majority). Again, Spanish bishops cannot constantly state a policy which is at utter variance with the policy of the Vatican and escape being called to account. The conclusion the Protestant draws, whether rightly or wrongly, is that the Spanish policy and the policy of the Vatican are in accord.

Now, however tedious it may be to the American Catholic to have this issue dredged up again, he must realize that it is a *major factor* in American Protestant thinking. For the American Protestant has two immediate reactions: (a) he has a reaction of concern for his Protestant brethren in Spain and a quite natural desire to speak on behalf of their right both to physical safety and of their right to preach the gospel to every creature; and the Protestant also has (b) a very genuine concern about what the existence of the *present* Spanish pattern says about the *future* American pattern. This second concern is crucial for Catholic-Protestant relations in America. For well to the forefront of the conscious thinking of most American Protestants about "Catholic power" is the huge question, often expressed but lurking in the foreground even when unexpressed, "Would the same thing happen in America if Catholicism became as strong here as it is in Spain? Would the same thing happen if Catholicism in America, though still numerically inferior, became strategically superior in Washington?" This is the fear out of which grow the Protestant tactics which seem so offensive to Catholics, the cries of anguish about "Catholics in public office," the cries about "the absolute wall of separation between church and state," the statements of Methodist bishops or Presbyterian clergymen about "increasing Catholic power" which seem so rank and distasteful to the average Catholic.

And—just to get *all* the cards out on the table—the sense of Protestant equanimity in the face of all this is hardly cultivated when members of the Catholic hierarchy—American, Spanish, Italian, or whatever—make statements which say clearly that the Spanish pattern is the "ideal" pattern for church-state relationships, and that it is a pity that it cannot be normative everywhere. I shall quote one statement of the sort that worries Protestants tremendously. It is widely circulated in Protestant literature on Catholicism (I am sure more American Protestants have read it than American Catholics!) and it is cited as merely typical of many others that could be cited. It has particular weight for the Protestant since it was first published in Rome, in the Jesuit journal, *Civiltà Cattolica,* April 3, 1948.

> The Roman Catholic Church, convinced through its divine prerogatives, of being the only true church, must demand the right to freedom for herself alone, because such a right can only be possessed by truth, never by error. As to other religions, the church will certainly never draw the sword, but she will require that by legitimate means and worthy of the human being they shall not be allowed to propagate false doctrine. Consequently, in a state where the majority of people are Catholics, the church will require that legal existence be

denied to error, and that if religious minorities actually exist, they shall have only a *de facto* existence, without opportunity to spread their beliefs. If, however, actual circumstances, either due to government hostility or the strength of the dissenting groups, makes the complete application of this principle impossible, then the [Catholic] church will require for herself all possible concessions, limiting herself to accept, as a minor evil, the *de jure* toleration of other forms of worship. In some countries, Catholics will be obliged to ask full religious freedom for all, resigned at being forced to cohabitate where they alone should rightfully be allowed to live. But in doing this the church does not renounce her thesis, which remains the most imperative of her laws, but merely adapts herself to *de facto* conditions, which must be taken into account in practical affairs. Hence arises the great scandal among Protestants, who tax the Catholics with refusing to others freedom and even *de jure* toleration, in all places where they are in the majority, while they lay claim to it as a right when they are in a minority. We ask Protestants to understand that the Catholic church would betray her trust if she were to proclaim, theoretically and practically, that error can have the same rights as truth, especially where the supreme duties and interest of man are at stake. The church cannot blush for her own want of tolerance, as she asserts it in principle and applies it in practice.

This is not a statement from the dim past. It is a statement of *contemporary* Catholic belief. And it is the plentiful reiteration of this sort of thing that leads the Protestant to the conclusion that the Catholic position on tolerance and religious liberty can be stated in the following terms: *When we are in the minority we claim religious freedom for ourselves on the basis of your principles; when we are in the majority we deny religious freedom to you on the basis of our principles.*[1]
Whether this is an adequate statement of the Catholic position or not, it is the conclusion to which a high proportion of Protestants are drawn by the character of the Catholic evidence. Protestants are not happy with this conclusion, and it is at least encouraging to find the American Jesuit, Father George Dunne, saying of the *Civiltà Cattolica* statement: "The question here raised . . . needs to be honestly faced. It is no good merely to say that no American non-Catholic has reasonable grounds for being concerned when he reads such statements."[2]
Protestants *are* concerned when they read "such statements." It is this concern which leads them to go to such fantastic lengths to avoid losing a single isolated battle in a single isolated community

which they feel will advance the "march of Catholic power" dedicated to the ends described in the quotation above. Protestants refuse
to be soothed by the words, "it can't happen here." They not only
feel that it can, but they are afraid that it will. They do not, I am
sure, feel any animus against the Catholic children who don't ride
to parochial school on school buses. They do feel, many of them,
that the use of school buses for other than transportation to tax-
supported schools is simply one little further step in the process of
"taking over." I am not defending the Protestant attitude here (I
think we are much too hysterical about school buses), but simply
trying to explain what lies behind it.

3. Not only are Protestants disturbed by past Catholic history, and
by present Catholic practice in countries where Catholics do have
power. There is a third reason for Protestant fears about Catholic
power: Protestants observe that in places *in the United States* where
Catholics have considerable local or regional power, such things as
the rights of free discussion and the right of minority viewpoints
tend to be jeopardized, and even to disappear.

We may use as an example the incident in "Paper City," the town
of Holyoke, Massachusetts with a very high proportion of Roman
Catholics, which is reported in detail in the first part of Kenneth
Underwood's sociological study, *Protestant and Catholic* (Beacon
Press). A Congregational Church in Holyoke offered Margaret Sanger
the use of the church hall for a lecture on birth control. Underwood's book goes on to describe the types of pressures which were
brought to bear upon the church, its officials, the city government,
and all persons in any remote way connected with the event, to ensure that Margaret Sanger not achieve permission to speak anywhere
in Holyoke. Business men on the board of the Congregational Church
were warned that unless they rescinded their initial action, their
places of business would be boycotted by Catholics. Under this kind
of pressure the Congregational Church did submit and cancel the
invitation, and other halls in town were subjected to similar pressures
to make sure that no place would be made available. (The talk was
finally given at the eleventh hour in a union hall.) This kind of
thing could be duplicated in scores of communities where Catholicism has sufficient local power, politically and economically, to ensure that opinions conflicting with its own do not gain a hearing. The
multiplication of such local incidents causes Protestants to fear for
their own future, as well as for the future of political democracy
and the right of dissent.

But let us now look at the problem in broader terms. Many Protestants are quite willing to say, "I have no right to object to Roman Catholicism having rules for its own members. If Catholics want to abide by a bishop's decision not to see a certain play or read a certain book (or hear a lecture in a Protestant church hall) that is certainly their right and privilege. It is only when they begin to proscribe *my* actions, to insist that *their* rules apply to *me*, that I object to what seems a quite unwarranted intrusion into my own life."

Now in principle this seems like an admirable solution to at least part of the difficulty. It seems fairminded, democratic, and eminently reasonable. But having used this approach myself many times, I have found myself tripping up over a flaw in it, a flaw that worries me considerably because I am not sure how to cope with it. The flaw consists in the fact that in a society like ours, "rules for Catholics" end up becoming rules for everybody else as well.

Let us take another example. A given diocese decides that a new best-seller is immoral. Catholics are therefore forbidden to read the book. If that were the end of the matter, one could scarcely object. But very seldom is it the end of the matter. Catholics who own bookshops will be discouraged, or prohibited, from stocking the book, or at least from displaying it publicly. Non-Catholics who own bookshops will soon discover that if they do stock the book, Catholics will be told not to patronize them. The advertising departments of the newspapers will be told that advertisements of the book are offensive to Catholic readers and must not appear; if they do appear, the editor may be told that Catholics will be forbidden to read the paper, and that Catholic advertisers will withdraw their advertising. (This is where the shoe really pinches.) A magazine reviewing the book, particularly if it reviews it favorably, will find itself confronted by similar pressures. In these ways, the proscription against Catholics becomes a proscription against non-Catholics as well.

Now I, for one, am worried by what this kind of thing does to the lifeblood of a democracy. I am worried by the fact not only that the book is unavailable, but that there is no chance for the merits or demerits of the book to be publicly debated. I am worried by what it does to the soul of the non-Catholic bookseller who in the future must order his books in terms of the question, "What does the diocesan office think of this one? Can I stock it and still survive economically?" rather than in terms of the question, "Can my shop continue to contribute to the free flow of ideas and discussion which keep a democracy vigorous and alive?"

I grant that this kind of economic boycott doesn't happen all the time. But it does happen some of the time, and one has the uneasy feeling that it would happen more frequently if it could be enforced more effectively. I grant, too, that Protestants often indulge in their own methods of trying to make the whole of society conform to their own patterns of behavior, the 18th Amendment being a case in point. I grant further that the whole issue of censorship is a very complex one, and that I and other Protestants would certainly make common cause with Catholics concerning censorship of some forms of literature—pornography, for example. But these matters merit open discussion, rather than merely the attempt to suppress all discussion. How much more to the point it would have been in Holyoke, for example, if the Catholic churches had had a public meeting of their own, explaining *why* they were against birth control, rather than using all their undoubted power to prevent Protestants from having a public meeting to hear a discussion of reasons supporting birth control.

There is yet another way in which Protestant concern about the overall problem can be focused. Catholics sometimes argue that the church's "power" does not extend beyond the realm of faith and morals. They point out quite rightly that the Vatican, for example, does not legislate on the political opinions of American Catholics, and thus leaves a tremendous area for freedom of opinion, and even diversity of opinion, in matters not directly touching on faith and morals. In the previous chapter we saw instances of this diversity within American Catholicism.

Now this would seem at first sight to provide considerable solace for the non-Catholic, since the church will not legislate, even for Catholics, in matters outside the realm of faith and morals. My difficulty with the argument is simply this: "Faith and morals," rather than being restrictive terms, are actually all-inclusive ones. Surely there is no area in life which cannot be brought within the heading of faith and morals.

Once again, rather than avoiding "controversial issues," let us try to meet them head on. One of the most controversial of the immediate issues is the difference in attitude between Catholics and most Protestants on the matter of birth control. And this furnishes a convenient example of the way in which a very specific issue actually broadens out to include the most far-reaching issues. There have as yet been no infallible pronouncements on birth control, but there have been a number of encyclicals and other papal pronouncements which make the position of the Catholic church crystal-clear, and leave little room for the outsider to hope that the church will "modify" its position in any significant way. The teaching is that any artificial methods of birth control are strictly forbidden, and are condemned as morally wrong. There is *no* situation (such as the danger that conception might jeopardize the life of the mother) that can justify the use by a Catholic couple of artificial means to prevent conception. The reason for this is not the sociological one that Catholics want to out-breed everybody else, but the theological one that, according to Catholic belief, artificial methods of birth control are a violation of the "natural law," and the natural law is rooted inextricably in the whole fabric of Aristotelian-Thomistic theology. Starting with the Catholic theology of natural law, one comes by fairly easy and obvious stages to the proscription of artificial methods of birth control.

A Catholic is obviously bound by this teaching as long as he remains a Catholic, and the non-Catholic can have no legitimate complaint at this point. But the non-Catholic does have some legitimate complaints when the Catholic attitude is imposed on non-Catholics. I shall state five sources of tension concerning this matter, with the hope of clearing the air a bit.

a. Considerable harm is done to the atmosphere of the dialogue when the Protestant espousal of birth control is interpreted solely as an anti-Catholic measure. (Some examples of this were given in Chapter 3.) If to take a public position contrary to that of the Catholic church is to be a bigoted anti-Catholic, it could just as logically be argued that for a Catholic to be against birth control when Protestants favor it is to be a bigoted anti-Protestant.

b. Catholics seem unwilling to acknowledge that Protestants can have very positive and very theologically-oriented reasons for believing in birth control. It becomes a little tiresome to be told (as we are told again and again in Catholic polemics) that we favor birth control because we approve of lust, or because we advocate "race suicide" (a favorite term), or because we want to countenance willful murder, or because we are "anti-babies." The fact of the matter is that a positive Protestant approach to this matter has been developed, partly as a result of all the controversy, which makes such Catholic charges as the above irrelevant as well as being in questionable taste. This is not the place to spell out the position, but statements of it are easily available.[3]

c. Protestants also have many sociological and humanitarian reasons for being disturbed by the Catholic attitude, since it appears obvious, to the Protestant at least, that overpopulation, particularly in underdeveloped areas of the world, is fast become a problem of almost insoluable proportions. The "population explosion" is a fact, and while there can be no thought of "forcing" birth control practices on peoples or nations, it seems to Protestants that information should be available to all non-Catholics who wish to take advantage of it, and that suppression of such information is morally wrong.

d. Protestants are also disturbed by Catholic attempts to force Catholic practices upon non-Catholics in this area. The cause of Protestant-Catholic relations in a large eastern city was set back for years by an incident in which Catholics wanted to outlaw the giving of birth control information in *public* hospitals, by *non*-Catholic doctors to *non*-Catholic patients, in situations where the mother's life would be endangered by another pregnancy.

There is a further complication here in the fact that since the proscription of artificial birth control is not a matter of revealed truth (i.e. binding only on those who accept the Catholic revelation as valid), but a matter of "natural law" (i.e. a truth attainable to any person by the use of reason alone), some Catholic theologians argue that the proscription of birth control can quite legitimately be extended by civil law to non-Catholics as well as Catholics. This hardly makes the non-Catholic feel easier about the matter.[4]

e. Finally, Protestants are perplexed by what seems to them an illogical aspect of the Catholic position. Actually, the Catholic position does not outlaw "birth control," but only *artificial* birth control. Catholic couples are quite at liberty to engage in "family planning" and limiting the number of their offspring, provided they do this by "natural" means (i.e. abstention from intercourse during the period each month of greatest fertility) rather than by "artificial" means (i.e. the use of contraceptives.) The crucial importance of the distinction simply escapes the Protestant, who sees here a subtlety of logic which is tragically unworthy of all the controversy it produces.

By way of summary, we may say that Protestant concerns about Catholic power come to focus in three ways. The Protestant is disturbed by the evidences of Catholic power (a) in past Catholic history, (b) in present Catholic countries where Catholicism is the dominant force in the society, and (c) in portions of the United States where Catholicism has already achieved a high degree of local or regional power. In all of these situations he sees converging evidence to suggest widespread Catholic acceptance of what has come to be known as the "thesis-hypothesis" theory; namely, the *thesis* that Catholicism has the right to sole recognition as the religion of the state and must press for this recognition in every feasible situation, and the *hypothesis* that where this sole recognition of Catholicism is not possible or practical, Catholicism grudgingly, as a matter of expediency and only for as long as necessary, will accept the evil of other religions sharing some kind of recognition.

3. A Protestant rebuttal to the Protestant "attack"—an attempt to get the issues focused still more clearly

The full rebuttal to the Protestant "attack" must, of course, come from Catholics. There are signs that this is beginning to happen. In the interval, I propose to offer a rebuttal by a Protestant, but a rebuttal on behalf of Roman Catholicism. I do this, as a possible contribution to the dialogue, for the following reasons: (a) to point out to *all* readers that a person who has said the things that have been said on the last few pages can also say some other things as well, (b) to point out to *Protestant* readers that they must look more comprehensively at Catholic treatments of this issue than they usually do, and that they must be prepared to discover more than they initially expect to find, and (c) to point out to *Catholic* readers that there are further Catholic resources to be brought to bear upon the matter than they themselves may have realized.

This last is a point of some importance. It will hardly do for Protestants to solve the issue of "toleration" or "Catholic power" by telling Catholics in effect to stop being Catholics. If there is to be a breakthrough to new understanding about "Catholic power," it will come about not because Catholics give up their Catholic faith, but *because they exercise it more fully*. Catholics who themselves feel dissatisfaction with the position set forth in the last dozen pages must deal with the problem from within a Catholic framework, and it will be real gain if both Catholics and Protestants can be brought to see that there *are* specifically Catholic resources available for doing this.

The introduction of some further evidence

If it were absolutely clear that Roman Catholicism had already spoken its definitive word on the complex of issues under discussion, most Protestants (including, I think, this one) would be ready to close up the books and start fighting for survival. But some Protestants (including, I am sure, this one) are not quite ready to close up the books, and therefore do not want to start fighting. The reason for this is the recognition of a fact which is crucial for both Catholics and Protestants to bear in mind. That fact can be stated as follows: *We have not yet heard all that Catholicism has to say on the subject. There is another point of view which is gaining currency in contemporary Catholicism.* This point of view does not have as strong a voice, or as many voices, as the point of view we have been discussing, and it is not quite clear to the outsider just how much of a real hearing it has gained within the highest Catholic circles. But it *is* a voice, and it deserves a hearing. I shall try to give it a hearing in the following pages, in order to counterbalance the notion that the voice heard in the preceding pages is the only Catholic voice.

1. *Father John Courtney Murray, S.J.*

On the American scene, the principal exponent of this point of view is, as every person interested in Protestant-Catholic relations knows, Father Murray. Unfortunately, most of his treatments are printed in scholarly journals which are not easily accessible to the general public. (The re-publication of these in book form, incidentally, would be an invaluable contribution to the continuing dialogue in this country.) There is a very helpful summary of Father Murray's position, however, in John Bennett's *Christians and the State*, part of which I reproduce here:

> There is no anti-clerical or anti-religious motivation behind the American constitutional provision for Church-State relations and the Church need not defend itself against this doctrine as such.
>
> The Church in America, has, as a matter of fact, enjoyed greater freedom and scope for its witness and activities than it has in the Catholic states of the traditional type.
>
> It is important to emphasize the rights of the state in its own sphere, the freedom of the Church from state control, and the influence of Catholic citizens on the state.

It is impossible to separate religious freedom from civil freedom and there can be no democracy if the freedom of the citizen is curtailed in religious matters, for such curtailing can often take place as a means of silencing political dissent.

Error does not have the same rights as truth but persons in error, consciences in error, do have rights which should be respected by the Church and the state.

The Church should not demand that the state as the secular arm enforce the Church's own decisions in regard to heresy.

It does more harm than good to the Church for the state to use its power against non-Catholics.[5]

It must be agreed that this has a very different tone from what we have heard thus far.

2. *"Tolerance and the Catholic,"* with special reference to Father Léonard.

The position now under discussion is not simply a phenomenon of American Catholicism, however. It has received even more extended expression abroad. One of the most important collections of such expression is a group of speeches by French Catholics, available in English as *Tolerance and the Catholic.*

Father Congar, who has been one of the pioneers of Catholic ecumenism, shows how there is a new basis for Catholic-Protestant understanding, as a result of four groups of facts. First, he notes, there has been, particularly from the seventeenth century, a shift in the Catholic understanding of the role of the church from "direct power" to "directive power," with greater stress now on appeal and witness than on external authority. Second, he calls attention to the Catholic rediscovery of the importance of the layman living and witnessing in the world, so that pursuit of the monastic ideal is not the sole task of the church. This opens up a new ethos of possible collaboration between Catholic and non-Catholic. Third, he points to the solidarity of the Catholic and non-Catholic in the face of the evils of our day, where once again the destiny of both groups is drawn close together. Fourth, Congar cites the remarkable degree of convergence between recent papal documents and the shared concerns of all men.

The four groups of facts, as Father Congar calls them, suggest that a new situation has developed in the relationship of Roman Catholicism to the rest of mankind, and that they provide a real basis for cooperation. The two main concerns that must guide Catholics in this new situation are "that Catholics must remain them-

selves, and that they must avoid all double-dealing."[6] It is wrong
for Catholics to try to be less than Catholics, or to make concessions
that are a denial of their faith. There is a clear "totalitarianism of
the faith," for Catholicism claims to have the truth, but this does
not mean what non-Catholics often think it means, and Father Congar drives home an important point in this connection:

> The Church will never renounce the totalitarianism of the Faith,
> the intransigence and intolerance of truth; *but she can, without deny-
> ing anything of her true nature, refuse to exercise these except by
> spiritual means and the way of conscience.*[7]

The same conclusion follows a discussion of "papal power":

> In the Middle Ages a power was attributed to the Pope which he
> does not possess, and which everyone has since denied him, by the
> following line of argument: he who has the higher power also has
> the lower; if the Pope has complete power *in spiritualibus,* how much
> more, then, *in temporalibus.* This purely dialectical reasoning forgot
> just one thing, and that is that the spiritual is not a higher stage of the
> temporal but its own positive order . . . [Though] compulsion by
> physical force may be part of the power natural to monarchs, *it is not
> part of the spiritual authority of the Church. It does not belong to the
> Church because it has not been given to her.*[8]

It is Father Léonard's essay, however, on "Freedom of Faith and
Civil Toleration" which is the gem in this collection, and must be
basic reading for all subsequent discussion. Wide knowledge of
this essay on the part of American Protestants would be an inestima-
ble boon to the American dialogue. Father Léonard rightly recognizes that "tolerance" must be based on religious faith, and he states
the purpose of his article as pointing toward a position in which

> Religious freedom will no longer appear as an unavoidable but re-
> grettable concession, but as the very expression of the freedom of
> faith.
> A constructive toleration is not by any means a product of religious
> indifference; it depends much more on the respect that the Catholic
> Church has always shown for divine truth. It is because Catholicism
> is a dogmatic religion that it is the surest bulwark of human rights
> and freedoms, and in particular religious freedom, not only for itself
> but for the other Christian denominations, and even for the private
> consciences of all sincere men.[9]

Father Léonard, it will be seen, is quite unprepared to accept
the "thesis-hypothesis" theory, and he does not try to "justify" the

Spanish situation as normative. What happens in Spain represents "a theory or a kind of behavior that does not belong to the Church as such at all."[10] He is particularly concerned to speak to the real fear of non-Catholics, "who have the feeling that they are not faced with a doctrine but with a rather dubious kind of 'expedient,' that is always liable to be revoked."[11]

Father Léonard's illuminating discussion of "Faith: The Inner Testimony of the Spirit" should make an important contribution to removing that fear, and I shall quote several extracts from it, to make sure that their significance is not lost by paraphrase. The gift of faith is the result of God's grace. It therefore follows that

> If the believer's assent depends on an initiative of God's sovereign freedom, no human influence can be substituted for the intervention of grace. The Church herself, in the most strict meaning of the words, cannot give faith . . . Faith cannot be communicated as a fact of scientific observation, or as an elementary arithmetical principle; nor can it be imposed by the laws of society. Now, intolerance means the desire to put our own initiative in the place of God's freedom, to substitute our initiative for his. It means a lack of respect for God and an ignorance of the supernatural magnitude of faith. By this very fact it is not only to be condemned; it is bound to be ineffective.[12]

An important conclusion follows from this:

> The final justification of toleration comes from the fact that divine faith cannot be given or maintained as though it were a human conviction or a human law. And therefore the non-Catholic's freedom is not to be based on contingent circumstances but on the nature of faith itself, "and therefore [quoting from Pius XII] on something permanent, something valid at all times and in all places, whatever the balance of forces may be between Catholics and non-Catholics."[13]

On the relationship of all this to civil life in the state, Father Léonard disavows the notion that the state should sanction religious liberty only when it can give the Catholic church a privileged position:

> The State should promulgate religious freedom, not only as a lesser evil to be endured in a tolerant spirit, or as a relative good, so long as the "hypothetical" condition lasts, but as an ultimate principle, permanently established. This principle is not inspired by any superficial opportunism doing its best to adapt itself to the political changes of the modern world; it is a further application of the psychological structure of faith, its rootedness in the human person and his freedom,

and also of its supernatural transcendence . . . To be effective, religious freedom should be incorporated in a State's Constitution and
confirmed by legal statute . . . Even on the assumption that there
was to be a return to a time of triumph for the [Catholic] Faith, it
would still remain a sacred duty to support religious freedom.[14]

I do not think we can overestimate the significance of such statements as these, for Father Léonard is basing the case for tolerance
not on the "expediency" principle, which can at any moment be
revoked, but on the intrinsic character of the Catholic understanding of faith itself.

NOTE: After the manuscript for this book had been sent to the
printers, word was received from the publisher of *Tolerance and the
Catholic* that the book had been "officially withdrawn" from circulation, but that its case was "under review at the highest church
levels." This means that somewhere within the book are statements
held to conflict with official Catholic teaching.

Receipt of this word was naturally a great disappointment, and
there were several courses of action open: (a) One was to ignore
the fact and let the above paragraphs stand without further comment. But if the withdrawal of the book is a fact, and honest dialogue is to be based on facts, no good can come from the attempt to
suppress a fact. (b) Another alternative was to withdraw the entire
section on Father Léonard with no fuss and no bother. This would
have been the easiest thing to do, but it would have deprived readers
of an acquaintance with one of the best statements of a positive doctrine of religious liberty ever penned. Furthermore, there is no assur-
ance that it is Father Léonard's statements that have created difficulty
for the book. But even if this were the case, the point of view is one
that Protestant readers should make their own, and that Catholic
readers should ponder carefully, in the light of the fact that the status
of the book is "under review at the highest church levels." (c) Another alternative was to state that the book was in disfavor and leap to
the conclusion that this is "what always happens" to the creative edge
of Catholicism. I must say to Catholics that a good many Protestant
readers will probably draw this conclusion, and claim that the fact
of the book's withdrawal vitiates the contention of the above and
succeeding pages. I do not think it does that, though I must concede
that it tempers the enthusiasm of this section of the chapter. But
before any Protestant draws totally negative conclusions from the fact
that the book has been withdrawn from circulation, he is under obligation to read in its entirety the much more extended and more
fully documented treatment of the problem issued by the World

Council of Churches, *Roman Catholicism and Religious Liberty,* by de Albornoz, to which fuller attention is drawn in footnote 31 of this chapter.

If *Tolerance and the Catholic* is restored to circulation, we shall rejoice; if it is not, we shall be eager to know why, and to make the necessary adjustment in our appraisal of Roman Catholic thinking on this crucial point.

3. *Father Max Pribilla, S.J.*

The position which we are expounding has received expression in Germany as well. The Jesuit Max Pribilla has written a highly significant article on "Dogmatic Intolerance and Civil Tolerance."[15] Father Pribilla rightly rules out religious "indifferentism" as a basis for religious toleration. He then urges his readers to make a distinction between those parts of Catholic faith that are unchanging, and those that are no more than a particularized point of view appropriate to one situation but not necessarily to another. The church has taken many different positions on civil tolerance in the past, and there is no one pattern from the past which can be considered normative. Pribilla further calls attention to Canon 1351 (Canon Law as revised in 1917) which asserts that no one may be forced to adopt the Catholic faith against his will. He does not ignore the reality of the Inquisition, but after having mentioned it he comments, "But immediately after having made this concession, it is important to go on to say that the medieval inquisition is not an essential factor in the discipline of the Catholic church, but merely an historic phenomenon."[16]

But Pribilla realizes that a question will remain in non-Catholic minds: would not the recapture of the world by Catholicism lead to religious persecution and the re-establishment of the church as an institution making use of force to achieve her ends? Pribilla counters that since the Middle Ages the realization of the rights of conscience (including the conscience in error) has become much more pronounced not only in society but in the church as well. He feels that the church must leave it to God to judge the state of conscience of those who accept another faith than the Catholic faith. And he emphasizes that a Catholic understanding of toleration cannot be based on grounds of expediency. It will never do, he says, for the church "in one state to claim religious liberty for itself as being a right of mankind, and to refuse to grant it in another, depending on whether the Catholics are in the minority or the majority."[17]

Here, it will be seen, is another explicit rejection of the "thesis-hypothesis" theory.

Father Pribilla goes on to call attention to a remarkable but little-known statement of Gregory IX in a letter to the bishops of France (April 6, 1233), written at the height of medieval papal power. Pope Gregory said that Christians ought to have the same attitude of good will toward the Jews, that they would wish to have exercised toward themselves if they were in a pagan country. It is the application of this papal principle which must guide the church today in its attitude toward all non-Catholics.

Catholics may object to all this; will not such proposals appear to give error the same rights as truth? Father Pribilla counters that the objection does not hold. Religious liberty does not mean the protection of error, but it *does* mean the protection of the one who is in error. A person who is serving God according to his conscience must not have his right to do so threatened by any external means. St. Augustine is cited as having counseled Christians not to destroy pagan idols by physical force, on the grounds that it was more important to destroy the idols in the pagans' hearts by spiritual persuasion, and that the rest would then follow. This maxim, Pribilla feels, is as valid today as it ever was.

4. Catholic laymen: Jacques Maritain and Etienne Gilson

Pribilla's thesis that "dogmatic intolerance" is a guarantee of "civil tolerance" receives explicit and striking confirmation from other Catholic thinkers. And it is not only the theologians who are thinking along these lines but thoughtful Catholic laymen as well. Two examples follow.

Jacques Maritain addresses himself to the issue in a lecture given at Princeton University on "Truth and Human Fellowship."[18] He recognizes that zeal for truth has often been used for evil ends, and that therefore many people believe that to get rid of zeal for truth will help men to live in fellowship with one another. But for Maritain scepticism is not the answer: "The answer is humility, together with faith in truth."[19] He rejects the opinion that the best climate for democracy is relativism. This in fact becomes a form of intolerance since those who hold that there is no ultimate truth cannot tolerate those who disagree with them. Maritain counters,

> In reality, it is through rational means, that is, through persuasion, not through coercion, that the rational animal is bound by his very nature to try to induce his fellow men to share in what he knows or

claims to know as true or just. And the metaphysician, because he trusts human reason, and the believer, because he trusts divine grace and knows that "a forced faith is a hypocrisy hateful to God and man," as Cardinal Manning put it, do not use holy war to make their "eternal truth" accessible to other people; they appeal to the inner freedom of other people by offering them either their demonstrations or the testimony of their love.[20]

Maritain is quick to acknowledge that people who claim to know the truth sometimes persecute others, but he claims that this comes from our human egotism and will to power rather than from religion, and when it comes from the latter it is a religion that "has not been purified by genuine love." He condemns "the error of the absolutists who would like to impose truth by coercion":

> [Their error] comes from the fact that they shift their right feelings about the object from the object to the subject; and they think that just as error has no rights of its own and should be banished from the mind (through the means of the mind), so man when he is in error has no rights of his own and should be banished from human fellowship (through the means of human power). [21]

But he condemns the opposing error as well:

> The error of the theorists who make relativism, ignorance and doubt a necessary condition for mutual tolerance comes from the fact that they shift their right feelings about the human subject—who must be respected even if he is in error—from the subject to the object; and thus they deprive man and the human intellect of the very act—adherence to the truth—in which consists both man's dignity and reason for living.[22]

These are the terms in which Maritain very persuasively develops his thesis that commitment to truth and rejection of error do not mean the rejection of *persons* who are in error. For the basis of fellowship is not a fellowship of beliefs but a fellowship of those who believe.

> We can render judgment concerning ideas, truth, or errors; good or bad actions; character, temperament, and what appears to us of a man's interior disposition. But we are utterly forbidden to judge the inmost heart, that inaccessible center where the person day after day weaves his own fate and ties the bonds binding him to God. When it comes to that, there is only one thing to do, and that is to trust in God. And that is precisely what love for our neighbor prompts us to do.[23]

We find much the same position stated in an address given by Professor Etienne Gilson at Rutgers University on "Dogmatism and Tolerance."[24] Gilson is also opposing the notion (in this case ascribed to Bertrand Russell) that "a healthy relativism in philosophy goes hand in hand with liberalism and democracy in politics," and its obverse that "dogmatism in philosophy begets tyranny in politics."[25] Gilson argues,

> Let us suppose I succeed in convincing somebody that what I think is true. He will not accept it as true on the strength or under the pressure of my arguments. He will see, in the light of his own intellect, the very same truth which I had seen before him in the light of my intellect . . . The only way for the most dogmatic philosopher to secure approval for his own doctrine is to explain it to others with so much force and clarity that it will mean for all of them one and the same thing.[26]

Gilson rejects the notion that he may use political means in order to make someone else accept his own dogmatic conclusions. He too makes a basic distinction between ideas and persons. Error itself can only be denounced as false. But persons who err must be treated differently. Even though someone's ideas may be wrong, his right to express those ideas must be safeguarded. Why? Because "Tolerance is nothing else than a particular application to the needs of political life, of the moral virtue of friendship."[27] Force can neither make falsehood true nor make truth commend itself to those in error.

> This is precisely why free expression of error should be tolerated, not as an approval of error itself, but because we love our neighbor so much we do not want him to be a man who talks *as if* he knew the truth, but to be a man who knows it.[28]

Gilson drives his point home by contrasting his position again with that of Russell, who argues, "If it were certain that without Jews the world would be a paradise, there could be no valid objection to Auschwitz; but if it is much more probable that the world resulting from such methods would be a hell, we can allow free play to our humanitarian revulsion against cruelty."[29] Gilson responds in telling terms:

> Lord Russell invites us to live in a society where democracy is safe because there is a high probability that Marx and Hitler are wrong, although there remains a possibility that they may be right. Would

we not feel safer in a society where it was understood that truth cannot be proved by burning any number of heretics at the stake; that dictatorships, concentration camps and world wars are criminal in themselves; that even if the murder of a single Jew sufficed to turn the world into a paradise, there would be no justification for killing him? . . . Quite recently, Russell stated as the first of his ten commandments to save society from fanaticism, "Do not feel absolutely certain of anything." My own question now is: In what type of a society will there be more chance for political tolerance to prevail? Is it in a society whose leaders are not "absolutely certain" that mass murder is not sometimes permissible? Or is it in a society whose leaders feel absolutely certain, with Kant, that political murder is a crime? Against political fanaticism, a philosophical relativism is the weakest conceivable protection.[30]

5. *Summary.*

We have now examined a number of statements of a Catholic position on toleration and the use of "power." They come from a variety of writers, with a variety of backgrounds, from a variety of countries. I have expounded them at some length because it is the convergence of their independent testimony that is so striking. There are a number of things on which all of these authors seem to be agreed, and we can tentatively summarize the position in the following terms:

a. The position is not based upon expediency, nor is it merely a grudging concession that is made since Catholics cannot have their own way; it is an attempt to make religious toleration a matter of positive principle, and in this it is a conscious alternative to the "thesis-hypothesis" point of view.

b. The position asserts that there is no incompatibility between "dogmatic intolerance" and "civil tolerance," and makes this point quite convincingly.

c. The position makes a clear distinction between "error" which does not have rights, and "persons in error" who do have rights which must be respected at all costs.

d. The position not only advocates tolerance in positive terms, but explicitly repudiates intolerance, since the latter is a usurping by men of a judgment which can properly be made only by God.

e. The position distinguishes between certain things in the Catholic faith that are unchanging, and elements of Catholic practice (such as the Inquisition) that are no part of essential Catholicism and must be disavowed.

f. The position stresses that Roman Catholic statements which appear to contradict the principle of religious liberty must be judged and interpreted in the light of their historical context, and not treated in isolation from the specific situation to which they were speaking.[31]

What are we to say about the further evidence?

What will be the reaction of Protestants to the material just cited? On the whole I am afraid that the initial reaction will be one of amused rejection of the whole business. The effort will be described as "well-meaning" (the most pejorative term with which Protestants castigate fellow-Protestants in this area) but "naive." It will be asserted that the voices cited are not "typical" but merely "exceptional," that they are tolerated by the church because it is expedient to have a few people saying things like this in democratic countries, that they occupy no significant place in Roman Catholicism, that they lack any real support where it counts (namely in the "hierarchy" and ultimately at Rome), and that if the position were condemned tomorrow all the spokesmen would submissively accept the verdict and the position would be eradicated from contemporary Catholicism as fully as Modernism was eradicated in 1907.

In the light of these widely-voiced objections, I make the following comments in conclusion:

1. At the very least, the position is permitted. It has *not* been condemned and there is good reason, on the contrary, to believe that it is gaining ground. The espousal of the position does not render a Catholic suspect or heterodox. It is not "fringe Catholics" who speak for it, but recognized leaders of Catholic life and thought. In this area, as in perhaps no other area of contemporary Catholic thought, vigorous discussion is going on. For a Protestant to acknowledge only the existence of the other position is to be guilty of distorting the facts for partisan propaganda.

2. In addition to historical papal utterances which seem an embarrassment to the position, there are likewise papal utterances which can be urged in support of the position. Even Pius IX (scarcely to be remembered for his liberalism) said in 1854:

> The dogmas of the Catholic faith are in no way opposed to the mercy and justice of God. For while it is of faith that outside the Apostolic Roman Church no one can be saved, that she is the one ark of salvation, and that whoever fails to enter it will be lost in the deluge; yet we must hold it as no less certain that those who, through

no real fault of their own, are ignorant of the true religion, incur no guilt for this in the sight of God. And who will presume to delineate the limits of this ignorance, in view of the different circumstances of nationality, country, character and countless other things?[32]

In similar vein, Pius XII in the encyclical *Mystici Corporis*, (1943) said:

> Wherefore if any persons, not believing, are constrained to enter a church, to approach the altar and to receive sacraments, they certainly do not become true believers in Christ; because that faith without which it is impossible to please God must be the perfectly free homage of intellect and will.[33]

It cannot be said that the papacy is committed to the "Spanish line." And, as John Bennett has pointed out in a discussion of Father Murray's position,

> In December 1953, after this point of view had been strongly attacked by Cardinal Ottaviani in Rome in an address defending the Spanish conception of a Confessional Catholic State as the ideal, the Pope in a speech to a convention of Catholic jurists somewhat ambiguously made room for [Murray's] position. The fact that he said what he did in the midst of a trans-Atlantic controversy within the Church has encouraged American Catholics who hold this view to believe that the Pope is sympathetic with it. That is the most that can be said.[34]

"That is the most that can be said." But it *can* be said, and it must be said against those who assume that the issue is closed in the highest court of Catholic life. It is not.

3. Catholic practice, as well as Catholic thought, assumes no one pattern here. There are no *a priori* grounds for non-Catholics to conclude that Spain must be the pattern for Catholicism everywhere. There are different approaches to the problem in such "Catholic countries" as Belgium, France, Ireland, and Spain.

4. Catholic practice in Catholic countries can change, and change for the better. Protestants, for example, have been beating the drum about Catholic persecution of Protestants in South America for a good decade, and no drum-beaters have been more vigilant than *The Christian Century* and the action group, "Protestants and Other Americans United for Separation of Church and State." It is therefore particularly gratifying to be able to cite the following paragraph about the latter from the former:

Abroad, one of the most significant developments is the action of the Roman Catholic hierarchy in Colombia to curb repeated acts of violence against Protestants. This move is reported by C. Stanley Lowell, the Methodist minister who is a member of the staff of Protestants and Other Americans United for Separation of Church and State; he has just returned from that strife-ridden country. *The New York Times* of October 18 reported him as saying that "acts of violence are decreasing," and that he believes the Catholic hierarchy is determined to stop them.[35]

5. I recognize that the above considerations will not seem conclusive to those Protestants for whom it is almost an inner necessity to believe the worst about "Rome." But if they persist in refusing to take this evidence seriously, it seems to me that they are implying that such Catholics as espouse this position are either charlatans (i.e. consciously propounding a position in which they do not believe so that they can lull Protestants into a false sense of security), or else that they are dupes (i.e. they are being deceived by the church which is permitting them to speak merely until it is safe to silence them). Both implications are unworthy and deserve the moral censure of Protestants as well as the tired pity of Catholics. The duty of Protestants, rather, is to accept these voices for what they manifestly are—attempts conceived in integrity to carry on a discussion within Roman Catholicism which can have the most significant consequences for Catholicism in its relation to the rest of the world. We must listen to these voices, accept them gratefully, urge them to speak more loudly, and trust that they will be used by God.

And to those Protestants who still feel that this is perhaps "well-meaning" but surely "naive", I would urge a final consideration which seems to me at the farthest remove from naïveté: if we reject the witness of these voices, if we continue to insist that Catholicism "really believes" something quite different, then the sure and inevitable consequence will be to force all Catholics, of whatever persuasion on the toleration issue, to make common cause with one another in the defense of their beleaguered church, and to do so at precisely the worst possible rallying point from a Protestant perspective: namely in defense of the voices whose triumph would be a disaster for Catholic-Protestant relations, and whose triumph, by no means now assured, would thereby be hastened precisely by those who should least desire it.

5

Separated *Brethren* and
Separated Brethren

A look at the deeper issues

Two things have emerged from our discussion thus far that have a bearing on the discussion still to come. *One* of these is a recognition that if we start with issues raised on the American scene, a full consideration of the Catholic viewpoint on those issues will carry us beyond the American scene. The *other* thing that emerges is a recognition that a discussion of *immediate* issues (such as birth control or "Catholics in public office") can never be complete in itself, but can only point to the fact that there are *deeper* issues involved in Catholic-Protestant relations. The immediate issue of birth control, for example, raises the more ultimate issues of the validity of "natural law" theory in Catholic theology, the status of papal pronouncements, the degree to which matters of faith and morals extend to the details of Catholic (and non-Catholic) life, the problem of the relationship between church doctrine and civil legislation, etc.

The purpose of this and the following chapter, therefore is to push our discussion further in two directions, i.e. to make our appraisal of Catholicism at the same time wider and deeper: *wider* in the sense that our purview will be increasingly broadened to observe Catholic-Protestant relations in other parts of the world to see what lessons we can learn for the dialogue here at home, and *deeper* in the sense that we shall try to go beyond immediate sources of agreement and disagreement to the ultimate and deepest sources of agreement and disagreement.

In the achievement of this aim, our treatment must necessarily

be selective, and we can deal with only a few matters, taking them
as representative of many other matters. Our framework remains
that of the second chapter, namely a recognition that we are separated *brethren* (i.e. that we share a common heritage of faith in
Jesus Christ), but also that we are *separated* brethren (i.e. that at
certain crucial points we have grievously departed from one another
in the interpretation of that heritage). If there is to be a future to
the Protestant-Catholic dialogue in America, it will be because
people can recognize both of those facts simultaneously. Let us
therefore turn to see what we can learn from other parts of the world
about the deeper issues of Catholic-Protestant relationship.

1. Areas of increasingly shared concern

One thing is immediately apparent. There are a number of areas
in which Protestants and Catholics are discovering that they share
very deep-seated concerns, and that they have much to learn from
one another in these areas. Furthermore, the closer they are drawn
together at these points, the closer they come to a recognition that
they are both trying to serve the same Lord and Master. We shall
call attention to five of these areas of increasingly shared concern.

The fact that dialogue has already begun

In various parts of the world there is actual encounter and inter-
change going on between Catholics and Protestants. A good deal
of this is at the level of theological discussion which comes to grips
in a fundamental way with the issues that have kept Christendom
divided. Father Gerard Hughes, S.J., reports on a meeting of Protestant and Catholic theologians held in June 1959 at Maria Laach,
a Benedictine abbey in Germany:

> The meeting at Maria Laach is only one of many Catholic-Prot-
> estant conferences, which have been becoming more frequent since
> 1945. Some of the discussions are public; others take the form of three
> or five day meetings between small groups. Two Catholic periodicals,
> *Una Sancta* and *Catholica* deal exclusively with controversial ques-
> tions and contain articles from Catholic and Protestant writers. One
> result of this close contact is that old-style polemics are going out of
> fashion. German Catholic writers are no longer content to point out
> the dogmatic and moral defects of Luther and the Reformers, but
> attempt a much more positive appreciation and admit, too, the large

share of blame which Catholics must bear for the Reformation and their consequent duty of atoning for it. As far as Catholic writers are concerned, atonement consists in the heroic patience which they must exercise in trying to understand and appreciate the bewildering meanderings of the Protestant theologians, and in recognizing and resisting the temptation to write off all Protestants as obstinate heretics with whom discussion is useless. There are many indications that discussion is far from useless. Many of the questions raised between Catholics and Protestants on the nature of the Church, her essential visibility, the Scripture and tradition, the true Presence and the sacrificial nature of the Eucharist, are now being discussed in Protestant Episcopal Synods, in theological conferences, and in the many Protestant theological periodicals. Protestants are ridding themselves of that very restricting prejudice which tends to dismiss serious discussion of specifically Catholic teaching and practice as *a priori* suspect and a betrayal of Reformation principles.[1]

This kind of confrontation, becoming more and more common in Europe, is almost unknown in America. It presents one of the most important objectives toward which American Protestant and Catholic leaders can work, and must be at the foundation of all other attempts at Protestant-Catholic understanding.

The emphasis on Biblical studies

There was a time when Catholic reading of the Bible was at least not actively encouraged, and when Catholic scholarship concentrated on patristic studies or the interpretation of Canon Law. Recently, however, Catholic scholarship has entered a period of creative Biblical scholarship, and along with this, new emphasis has been placed upon lay reading of the Bible. Such new translations as that of Ronald Knox (Sheed & Ward) have been widely used, and widely used by Protestants as well. It has recently been proposed by an American Jesuit that a new translation of the Bible be made by and for both Protestants and Catholics. The fact that we share substantially the same Scriptures has long been marred by the fact that we have different translations of the same Scriptures.

Catholic and Protestant Biblical scholars now take quite for granted the help they receive from one another. (I have sought help on technical points any number of times from Protestant Biblical scholars, only to be told quite casually, "Father So-and-so knows that field best. Be sure to read his book.") Catholic scholars likewise have

easy access to works of non-Catholic Biblical scholarship, so the
traffic goes both ways.

A great deal of this impetus was given by the encyclical of Pius
XII, *Divino Afflante Spiritu* (September 20, 1943)[2], an encyclical
which the Protestant reads with joy, since it opens up so many doors
to Biblical research that the Protestant assumed had been permanently barred either by the Council of Trent or by the papal decrees
in connection with the Modernist controversy. Here is a notable example of the Catholic ability to embrace new attitudes after having
appeared to reject anything but the most dated attitudes.

There are extremely important consequences for the Catholic-
Protestant dialogue flowing out of this recent Catholic rediscovery
of the Bible. For one thing, it has been paralleled by a similar re-
surgence of interest in Biblical theology in Protestant circles, so that
both groups now have a common meeting ground—Holy Scripture—which they did not have before. Another type of convergence
emerges from a more careful examination of this phenomenon, and
can be expressed as follows: Catholic theology which very often
has a predominantly scholastic orientation, has become increasingly
dominated by a Biblical orientation, while Protestant Biblical study,
which at one time had been predominantly linguistic or historical,
has become increasingly dominated by a theological orientation.
And we can see the meaning of this convergence in yet another
way which can be put (in oversimplified fashion to make the point)
as follows: post-Tridentine Catholic theology tended to exalt tradition at the expense of Scripture, while post-Reformation Protestant theology tended to exalt Scripture at the expense of tradition.
And what is happening now is that Catholic theology is restoring to
Scripture a place of greater significance, while Protestant theology
is really beginning to take seriously the extent to which contemporary
understanding of Scripture is moulded and conditioned by tradition.

Now to the Protestant, the thing that is so exciting about the new
Catholic emphasis on Biblical study is based on the Protestant conviction that when men really expose themselves to the Word of God,
there are absolutely no limits that can be placed around what the
Holy Spirit can do with this fact. All of the great movements of
reform and renewal in the history of the church have grown out
of a rediscovery of the Bible, and there is every reason to believe
that the contemporary rediscovery of the Bible (both by Catholics
and Protestants) may create a new situation full of possibilities beyond our power to predict.

The liturgical movement

Increasing attention is being given by Protestants to the place that the liturgical movement occupies in contemporary Catholicism. It must be clear that the liturgical movement is not a Catholic device to make Catholicism more palatable to Protestants—a misunderstanding into which over-enthusiastic Protestant reporters tend to lapse. The liturgical movement is a movement indigenous to Catholicism itself, which has received explicit papal approval (particularly in the encyclical *Mediator Dei*) and which is endeavoring to make the Catholic liturgy more authentically a reflection of Catholic faith. Believing, for example, that the church truly is the "mystical body of Christ," and not merely a "hierarchy" doing things for laymen, members of the liturgical movement have been concerned to restore to the laity those parts of the liturgy which were once rightly theirs, and in which, for one reason or another, they no longer participate. Furthermore, there are a great many practices of individualistic Catholic piety that are quite appropriate in their place, but quite inappropriate during the mass itself, which is the action of *all* the faithful, and efforts are being made to relate the people more directly to what is happening at the altar. There is also emphasis in the direction of a wider use of the vernacular in the mass, so that the people (most of whom no longer know Latin) can really understand the meaning of the service.

As a result of the work of the liturgical movement there have been significant innovations in the liturgy: the changes in the services for Holy Week, inaugurated in 1956, have been described as "the greatest liturgical innovation in four centuries."[3]

The liturgical movement is a sign of hope as far as Protestants are concerned, in at least three ways: (a) it indicates that within the structure of Catholicism there can be creative adaptability and change—a fact many Protestants are either unaware of or stubbornly unwilling to acknowledge; (b) it demonstrates that the true meaning of the Catholic faith is found in *the church at worship*, rather than in the church as a "hierarchy" or "power structure"; and (c) it helps to draw Catholics and Protestants closer together in their common belief that the church is a *community* of worship, a fellowship of believers, even though the Catholic and Protestant understandings of what actually happens within the worship of the community may continue to be at great variance.[4]

The revival of Reformation studies

There was a time when Catholic treatments of the Reformation concentrated on Luther's "bestiality," or tried to establish that all the Reformers had acted from perverse motives. There is a different atmosphere today. It is a source first of astonishment, and then of delight, and then of humble gratitude, to read contemporary Catholic books about the Reformation which do not simply repeat the worst, but emphasize the best, and make a genuine effort to get "inside" the concerns of the Reformers. Naturally, a Catholic will not fully succeed in this attempt, any more than a Protestant can fully succeed in giving a comprehensive picture of Catholicism "from the inside." But some attempts can come closer than others, and some notable attempts are being made. Among these must be placed Father Bouyer's *The Spirit and Forms of Protestantism* (Newman Press). It is a tribute to Father Bouyer that his book has drawn fire from both sides. The first half is an astonishingly sympathetic account of the main emphases of the Reformation—this drew blasts from the Catholics. The second half is a trenchant critique of the inadequacies of these Reformation insights when nurtured in non-Catholic soil—and this drew the author into the range of Protestant artillery. But such a book is surely a more notable contribution to the dialogue than a book which excites nobody and offends nobody.[5] Similarly, Father Tavard's *The Catholic Approach to Protestantism,* (Harper & Bros.) is a genuine attempt to describe to the Catholic the fire of the gospel which inflamed the Reformers, and is a healthy corrective to earlier Catholic polemics.

Once again it must be noted that most of this has come from abroad. Both the books cited are translations from the French. Very little attention has yet been given to this subject by American Catholics.

Two things stand out, from the point of view of the Protestant, in this Catholic re-assessment of the Reformation: (a) there is a genuine willingness to acknowledge that the church drastically needed reform in the sixteenth century and that the responsibility for the rupture of Christendom is not all on one side, and (b) there is an increasing recognition that the concern of the Reformers was a genuine (if misguided) attempt to recover the rightful heritage of Christendom. The Protestant must be willing to grant the Catholic the parenthesis, for the sake of the rest of the sentence.

Naturally the way the Reformers went about it will seem "misguided" to the Catholic, else he would become a Protestant. But to have gotten the discussion to this stage is to have overcome what once seemed an unbridgeable chasm, and the Protestant reaction (beyond gratitude) might be a further re-assessment from the Protestant side of the same events. If we do not believe that our forefathers threw out the baby with the bath, we may discover that they did jettison a number of implements, the recovery of which might not only cleanse the baby more adequately, but even purify the bath water in the process.[6]

Catholic attention to contemporary Protestantism

Along with this concern about the Reformation, has gone an increasing Catholic concern with the whole phemonenon of Protestantism as such, and a genuine attempt to understand it rather than simply to run it down. This Catholic attention has been largely focused on the existence and meaning of the ecumenical movement in contemporary Protestantism, and it can be urged that current ecumenical concern both within Catholicism and Protestantism may well be the most important factor in the entire situation. We shall defer discussion of this crucial point until the next chapter, however, so that we can approach it after a realistic examination of some of the areas where there seem to be ultimate disagreements between us.

2. Areas of ultimate disagreement

Thus far it has been suggested that as Catholics and Protestants discover their common heritage as Christians, they are drawn closer and closer together. But it would be the height of naïveté to suggest that this is all that happens. For along with this very happy consequence comes another consequence, not only not happy but even tragic in its import. As we examine our common heritage we find not only that we are closer at some points than we dared believe, but also that we are farther apart at other points than we dared imagine. And the points at which we are truly separated turn out to be not peripheral but central.

Some would choose to ignore these ultimate cleavages for the moment. "Let us concentrate on where we agree," they will say, "and only look at the differences after we have gotten as wide a base as possible of common conviction." This approach will yield some happy short-term results for we will find more points in common than we had anticipated, but the ultimate fruit of this approach

will be an even deeper pessimism than before, for we will discover that the new agreements that presented such a happy augury
for the future will not be deep enough to encompass or resolve the
remaining—and basic—differences. The wiser procedure, therefore,
would seem to be to tackle both problems head on, both the agreements and the differences, approach each with candor, honesty,
and love, and offer the remaining enigmas to the Holy Spirit, by
whose breath the winds of healing can descend upon our ruptures
and divisions.

Therefore, rather than talking about minimal differences in the
pages that follow, where conceivably we could work out adjustments between ourselves, I shall deliberately stress what seem to
me the areas of maximal difference where, humanly speaking, it is
inconceivable that we can work out "adjustments." This will not
only clear the air of unwarranted optimism, but also help us to focus
our future discussion in the proper direction, namely to the further
clarifying of ultimate differences, rather than merely to bandying
secondary issues back and forth.

The problem of authority

I am increasingly sure that the fundamental cleavage between
Protestantism and Catholicism comes at the point of their different
understandings of *authority*. The issue is complicated by the fact
that while the Catholic view of authority is clear-cut and definite
(and by its content unacceptable to the Protestant), the current
Protestant view of authority is muddled and mixed-up (and therefore unacceptable to the Catholic). I am convinced that the next
big intramural task for Protestants is a lot of hard-headed re-thinking
about the meaning of authority in Protestant terms. The traditional
view of "the authority of Scripture" is no longer tenable in most
Protestant circles, and the development of a more tenable position
is still (as the World Council of Churches for so long was) "in
process of formation." In the meantime, the Catholic can be pardoned
if he seems less than impressed with the interim results.

But while it is fortunately not my present task to produce a Protestant doctrine of authority, I must at least suggest the basis from
which I as a Protestant find difficulty with the Catholic position. It
is my conviction, which many Protestants share, that the ultimate
authority over the life of the Christian and the church is the Word
of God made flesh in Jesus Christ, which Word we find revealed
to us in the pages of Holy Scripture. This Word of God stands over

us and judges and corrects us as individuals, but it also stands over and judges and corrects the life of the church. The traditions of men cannot for the Protestant be on a par with Scripture, but must stand under Scripture. The life of the church, then, consists of the ever-renewed attempt to hear the Word of God—to listen to what Jesus Christ is saying to his church through the pages of Holy Scripture, and to respond to that Word, not only when it is an empowering and healing Word, but also (and perhaps especially) when it is a judging and chastising Word. As a judging and chastising Word, it tells us that we have been faithless, and that only by submission to the Word made flesh, and only in contrition and repentance, can renewal in the life of the church and of the individual take place, as we open ourselves to the power of the same Holy Spirit who makes the Word of God a true and lively Word for us today.[7]

Now this submission to the Word of God, and its basic differentiation from Catholicism, can perhaps best be illustrated by the well-known phrase, *ecclesia reformata sed semper reformanda* ("the church reformed, but always *being reformed*"). In Protestant terms, the work of reformation is never done. It is always going on. "The Reformation must continue." For the church is always sinning, always corrupting the gospel that has been bequeathed to it, always forgetting that it has this treasure in earthen vessels, always making the mistake of equating the treasure with the earthen vessels. And —to put the issue directly—in Protestant eyes, Catholicism appears to commit this sin: it equates the treasure with the earthen vessels, so that the transcendent power no longer belongs to God, but is claimed by the church itself. To the Protestant, Catholicism seems to deny the Biblical injunction that judgment must begin at the house of God since all is well in the house of God, since in principle nothing can really go wrong there, since at the very heart and center of its life Catholicism claims to be unvulnerable to human error. The church need not be reformed in any basic sense, for it is already protected from error by the Holy Ghost. In a distinction Visser 't Hooft General Secretary of the World Council, has made, for Catholicism there can be reform *in* the church, but not reform *of* the church; here and there things can be tidied up, anachronisms removed, earlier practices relaxed or tightened, but basically and fundamentally the church is irreformable because the head of the church is infallible, and cannot err in matters of faith and morals.

Two case studies

The Catholic understanding of authority, then, comes to its clearest focus in the dogma of papal infallibility. Consequently we must take a Protestant glance at this dogma, not to score points, nor simply to reiterate that Protestants do not accept it (Catholics know that already), but to suggest, however briefly, why Protestants have such difficulty with the belief that is central to Catholic faith. We shall then consider why Protestants have a similar difficulty with an example of the exercise of papal infallibility.

1. *The dogma of papal infallibility.* I am sure that Catholics would assert that what is "central to Catholic faith" is faith in Jesus Christ, and indeed the Baltimore Catechism states that it is *he* who is "the head of the Catholic church." But no Catholic has finished saying what he means by asserting that Christ is the head of the church until he has spoken of the vicar of Christ on earth, the Roman pontiff, the infallible guarantor of the faith and morals of the Catholic church. We must try to explain why this is the great wall of division that separates Catholicism and Protestantism.

The dogma of papal infallibility has, of course, been a belief of Roman Catholicism for hundreds of years, but it did not become a formal dogma, which had to be believed, until so proclaimed by the Vatican Council in 1870. It is a Catholic belief which is particularly susceptible to misunderstanding, and is often "repudiated" by those who assume that it declares the pope incapable of sinning, making a mistake, or holding a wrong political judgment. Its content is, of course, nothing of the sort. The dogma is very carefully defined, and we should have the statement of the Vatican Council before us if we are to consider it fairly. That Council defined as a "revealed dogma,"

> that the Roman Pontiff, when he speaks *ex cathedra*, that is, when carrying out the duty of the pastor and teacher of all Christians in accord with his supreme apostolic authority he explains a doctrine of faith or morals to be held by the universal Church, through the divine assistance promised him in blessed Peter, operates with that infallibility with which the divine Redeemer wished that His church be instructed in defining doctrine on faith and morals; and so such definitions of the Roman Pontiff from himself, but not from the concensus of the Church, are unalterable.[8]

Thus it is clear that the dogma does not apply to every papal utterance or action, but *only* to those dealing specifically with faith and morals, when the pope is speaking *ex cathedra*, i.e. in his function as pastor and teacher of all Christians. But when he does so speak, he speaks "with that infallibility" with which it was the will of Jesus Christ that the church should be guided, and his statements are beyond the possibility of error. They are, as the definition says, "unalterable"; they can never be changed.[9]

Now what can be said, especially to Catholics, about Protestant difficulties with this belief? It seems to me that a great deal of Protestant energy is expended in dealing with what are only secondary aspects of the difficulty. Protestants, for example, have engaged in research which raises grave questions in their minds as to whether the dogma was indeed "received from the beginning of the Christian faith" as the Vatican Council states, and they find numerous examples of seemingly conflicting papal utterances which to them automatically discredit the notion of papal infallibility. I do not wish to deny the significance of these studies—but my point is that even if all the historical difficulties could be explained to the satisfaction of Protestant scholars, and even if the content of all papal doctrinal teaching could be harmonized to the satisfaction of Protestant theologians, the basic Protestant problem would still remain untouched: namely, the Protestant difficulty with the Catholic assertion that a human being can ever speak in the untainted accents of the Holy Ghost. Even if infallibility were a principle that had been defined but never formally exercised, the basic Protestant difficulty would remain—the difficulty that to affirm that a human being can be endowed with infallibility seems to be claiming for that human being something that can only be claimed for God Himself.

A clear Scriptural statement of the dogma would give the Protestant pause, but such a statement does not, of course, exist. It is inconceivable to the Protestant that it could exist, for it would go straight against the witness of Scripture, which asserts that the supreme sin is the sin of pride, the sin of trying to usurp the place of God. In Biblical terms, man can speak for God only in the acknowledgement of his own frailty, his own proneness to sin, his constant recognition that another word from the Lord may be needed to undo the harm he has done by claiming too unambiguously that he has an irreformable word from the Lord.

I am sure that it is difficult, if not impossible, for a Catholic to understand this feeling on the part of the Protestant, but I am equally sure that the Catholic must try to see at least that this *is* the source of Protestant difficulty. Thus—and I know how harsh this will sound to Catholic ears—the Protestant must record that to him the dogma of papal infallibility represents the ultimate expression of spiritual pride, i.e. the belief that a human being can be the perfect and uncorrupted transmitter of the word of God. This is indeed to mistake the earthen vessel for the treasure. The transcendent power no longer belongs to God; it has been claimed by men. Let Catholic readers be assured that no Protestant makes this statement gloatingly, as though he had scored a victory, but rather with heavy heart, for he is recording a disagreement of the most fundamental sort: the very place where the Catholic is surest that he hears the untainted accents of the Holy Ghost is the very place where the Protestant is surest that His voice is muffled and distorted.

That, then, is the basic cleavage, the awesome barrier, which I see no way, humanly speaking, of overcoming. The issue which separates us, finally, and seemingly irrevocably, is not sociological or historical or accidental, it is theological. It does not concern "abuses" that can be set right with good intentions, or practices that can be changed; it concerns a dogma that cannot be changed, that can never be modified without destroying the substance of what Roman Catholicism has become.

Beyond this basic difficulty, there are, as suggested above, other kinds of difficulties that the Protestant has with this central Catholic affirmation. I shall mention only one, both so that Catholic readers can get a further inkling into the Protestant mentality, and also as a transition to the next matter for discussion.[10]

Presumably the point of the dogma of infallibility is that it protects the church from error and assures that she will preach pure and unalloyed the faith once delivered to the saints. One would assume therefore that infallible utterances would be made whenever heresy threatens the church, so that the faithful would not be led astray. But as far as the Protestant can discover, the dogma has not in fact brought this about, but has even made the matter more difficult than it was before. For church historians and theologians are by no means agreed as to which are, and which are not, infallible pronouncements. There have presumably been a good many infallible utterances in nineteen hundred years, but there is no clear-cut agreement as to which utterances fulfill the conditions requisite for infallibility, and which do not. I cannot agree with such a statement as the following:

No one questions the fact that the following pronouncements are among those which may definitely be regarded by Roman Catholics as containing infallible definitions of the faith: the promulgation of the dogma of the Immaculate Conception in 1854; the Constitution of the Faith and the Constitution of the Church, both of which were issued at the Vatican Council in 1870; the decree *Lamentabili* and the encyclical *Pascendi* of 1907; and the promulgation of the dogma of the Assumption of Mary in 1950.[11]

I would *like* to agree with this statement because there would then be clear-cut material for examination, but many Catholics would dispute this list and assert that requisite conditions were not fulfilled in one or another of the utterances cited.

Save the last. It is, I think, beyond any doubt that if there is one definition within the two millenia of church history that is unmistakably an infallible utterance, it is the definition of the Assumption of the Blessed Virgin Mary, from the Apostolic Constitution *Munificentissimus Deus*, proclaimed by Pius XII on November 1, 1950. We shall consider this dogma briefly, since it will help to focus the area of ultimate disagreement more clearly still.

2. *The dogma of the Assumption of the Virgin.* The content of the dogma may be briefly stated:

. . . by the authority of our Lord Jesus Christ, of the Blessed Apostles, Peter and Paul, and by Our own authority We pronounce, declare, and define that the dogma was revealed by God, that the Immaculate Mother of God, the ever Virgin Mary, after completing her course of life upon earth was assumed to the glory of heaven both in body and soul.[12]

The place which the dogma now occupies in the structure of Catholic theology is indicated by the words that immediately follow:

Therefore, if anyone, which may God forbid, should dare either to deny this, or voluntarily call into doubt what has been defined by Us, he should realize that *he has cut himself off entirely from the divine Catholic faith.*[13]

This, then, is now infallibly declared to be a part of the Catholic faith without believing which no man may be saved. Catholics point out, quite rightly, that the dogma of the Assumption had been what is technically known as a "pious opinion" for hundreds of years, and that nothing new was added to the faith of the Roman Catholic church simply because it had at last attained the status of a defined

dogma. It is therefore hard for Catholics to understand the shock
that the promulgation of this dogma produced in the Protestant
world. I think the reason for the shock was two-fold: (a) because the
first unambiguously infallible utterance since the promulgation of
the dogma of infallibility in 1870 was a dogma that seems at the
farthest possible remove from the historic Christian gospel set forth
in Holy Scripture, and (b) because to the Protestant there is a
radical difference between a belief of this sort being defined as a
matter of pious opinion and not essential to salvation, and being
defined as so absolutely crucial and central that if anyone should
deny it or even call it into question, "he should realize that he has
cut himself off *entirely* from the divine and Catholic faith."[14] Thus
it is as great a sin for a Catholic to question the bodily assumption
of the Virgin into heaven, as to question the divinity of Our Lord,
the triune nature of the Godhead, or the resurrection of Jesus Christ
from the dead.

Now I want to try to make one point, and really one point only,
in commenting on Protestant difficulty with this dogma: we reject
it not because we want to believe *less* than the full gospel, but
because we want to believe *more* about Jesus Christ than we think
the Catholic now can. It is not because we are "liberal twentieth
century men," anxious to whittle away all possible doctrinal em-
barrassments, that we reject it, but because we are trying to be
evangelical Christians faithful to the gospel in all the scandal of its
particularity as it speaks to us through the pages of the New Testament. Let us see what this implies.

The Catholic, of course, is immediately ready with the rejoinder
that the dogma does not stand or fall on whether or not it can be
found explicitly in Scripture, for it is tradition that asserts that the
dogma is of the essence of the Catholic faith. (Most responsible
Catholic theologians do not try to base the dogma on Biblical
grounds, and when they do, their exegesis can only seem torturous
to the Protestant.) That it is based upon tradition is for the Catholic
sufficient evidence. In a very illuminating article on Catholic
grounds for believing the dogma, a Catholic theologian writes:

> If then the Assumption cannot be known either by historical
> evidence or by an explicit tradition, how can it be known? To this
> question the Bull of Definition gives a most explicit answer: we know
> it because the whole Church believes it, and this is a sure ground of
> certainty. We know it because the Church teaches it, and in her teach-

ing the Holy Spirit, and not merely human contrivance, makes sure that no mistake is taught, that none of the sacred deposit is lost, and no addition made to it.[15]

This forthright statement admirably serves the purpose of joining the issue squarely, for to the Protestant it can only appear that the dogma *does* involve an "addition" to the faith of the church. There is thus an irreconcilable difference between Protestantism and Catholicism at this point. For the Protestant, the touchstone in these matters is Scripture, and it is clear that neither Scripture nor even the first thousand years of the church's history give any indication that the dogma of the Assumption is something that can be called into doubt only at the price of cutting oneself "off entirely from the divine and Catholic faith." The Protestant sees the dogma of the Assumption, then, as a clear-cut and grievous example of what happens in the life of the church when tradition gains the upper hand over Scripture: importations come into the faith that are no part of the original proclamation of the good news of salvation. And on these terms the Protestant has to reassess the claim that tradition is normative over Scripture, and reject the claim more decisively than ever. For the one dogma in that tradition of which it is absolutely clear that it is an infallibly defined dogma, is the one which is to him at the farthest remove from what he believes to be "the faith once delivered to the saints."

Perhaps not quite "at the farthest remove." For another implication of the dogma worries the Protestant. He sees in it yet another step in the gradual elevation of Mary to a place in the life of the church that threatens to usurp the place that can only rightfully belong to Jesus Christ. Catholic theologians are already talking about the inevitable next step in the development of Mariology, which will be the doctrine of the *co-redemptrix,* Mary as co-redeemer with Jesus Christ of mankind. There seems to be a kind of ineluctable necessity about this next step, as unfolding from the implications of the Dogma of the Immaculate Conception (1854) and the Dogma of the Assumption (1950). The new dogma may not come for the space of another ninety-six years, but when it does, Protestants will have to say that the Roman Catholic faith has finally become another faith than the faith of the holy Catholic church. Even to consider the dogma of the co-redeemer seems to the Protestant not only to minimize, or simply to jeopardize, but actively to destroy, the Christian belief in the sole efficacy of the redemption procured for men by Jesus Christ in his cross, death, and resurrection. Thus the Mariological dogmas are not only introducing something "new," they are undermining something "old"—the New Testament claim of the sole efficacy of Christ's redemptive work.

So we come back to our starting point. The Protestant rejects this dogma not because he believes *less* about God's activity than the Catholic, but because he wants to believe *more*, i.e. to assert with full vigor and without possibility of diminution that the redemptive work of Jesus Christ by which our salvation has been procured, is a finished work that needs no addition made to it by anyone else. The addition of the dogma of the assumption thus seems to the Protestant to devalue who Christ is and what he has done. When the Protestant reads Catholic apologists who argue, for example, that the evidence of God's power over death is not sufficiently demonstrated by Christ's resurrection (because he was not a "mere creature" but was the God-man), and that therefore the dogma of the Assumption is needed to safeguard the belief in the power of God over death (since Mary *was* a "mere creature"), he can only feel that the age-old faith of the church catholic that Jesus Christ is "very God *and very man*" has been irrevocably undercut.[16]

I have spoken forthrightly on this matter. I hope I have not spoken with rancor. I am not happy to emphasize such a basic difference for it gives perilously heavy weight to the adjective in the chapter title. I cannot expect Roman Catholics to understand why Protestants feel as they do on this matter, though I ask them to make the attempt. On my part, I must not be willing merely to disagree: I must try to understand what the dogma can mean *to a Roman Catholic*, and I think I can get some inkling of this. I can see how (given Roman Catholic presuppositions) the dogma not only poses no problems for the faithful Catholic but is a source of aid and comfort to him in his prayers; for one of his own kind now stands very near the throne of grace, joining her prayers to his, and helping him to realize more fully and deeply the meaning of the communion of saints. With whatever differences we have, we are also called upon to sanctify our imaginations on behalf of one another and in the service of one another and if we can do this, we can still speak the truth to one another as we see it, for we shall be speaking the truth in love.

3. The importunity of dialogue

Where does all this leave us? It leaves us with what appears to be a most discouraging situation. We find that we have many areas of shared concern, and that some of these can broaden and deepen as we come to know one another better; but we also find that there are points of irreconcilable cleavage, and that these lie at the center of our affirmations rather than at the periphery. To the Protestant the authority of Jesus Christ means that no one else can speak for him in infallibly authoritative tones; to the Catholic the authority of Jesus Christ means that Christ's appointed representative, his vicar on earth, can and does speak for him in infallibly authoritative tones. The Protestant's faith in the God revealed in Jesus Christ makes it impossible for him to equate any human words with the words of God; the Catholic's faith in the God revealed in Jesus Christ makes it imperative for him to accept, as from God himself, the words which the pope pronounces as infallible truth.

Neither group can concede the position of the other without destroying itself. It would thus appear that a real dialogue is doomed before it starts, so wide is the impasse. I suggest, however, that precisely the opposite conclusion must be reached. It is *because* there are these basic differences, as well as areas of agreement, that we must come to know one another better. To deny this would be to assert that we are merely separated, and to forget that we are separated brethren.

There is one place where this level of dialogue is pre-eminently going on, and going on with such enrichment for all concerned that it makes despair over the impasse we have just discussed impossible. It is to a full discussion of this particular part of the dialogue, and the lessons it offers the American scene, that we must now turn.

6

Ecumenism: Source of Greatest Hope and Greatest Difficulty

The word "ecumenism" has become, and will remain, an indispensable word in Christian discussion. The Greek work *oikumene,* from which it comes, means "the inhabited world," and in modern Christian parlance ecumenism means concern for the church of Jesus Christ in every part of the inhabited world. Ecumenical concern is at the farthest extreme from preoccupation solely with one's own tradition, and ecumenical activity is the attempt to relate all the branches of divided Christendom more integrally to one another.

There has been increasing ecumenical concern in Protestantism for the past fifty years. All Protestants realize that the existence of 272 "sects and insects" is a shocking fact. The concern of Protestants that they come closer together, rather than drifting farther apart, has received visible expression in the formation of the World Council of Churches, to which all the major Protestant groups, plus the Eastern Orthodox, belong.

But even if the major Protestant groups should ultimately achieve some sort of organic union, there would still be three major divisions in Christendom: Protestantism, Roman Catholicism, and Eastern Orthodoxy. The ecumenical purview, therefore, has to be wide enough to include attention to these major rifts, as well as to the less awesome rifts within the Protestant sector itself.

It is only fairly recently that Roman Catholicism has begun to take an active interest in Protestant ecumenism, but this interest has become increasingly felt, and the purpose of the present chapter is to acquaint both Catholic and Protestant readers with the extent and involvement of Roman Catholicism in the ecumenical dialogue of our day. We will not have taken a real "look" at Roman Catholicism until we have examined Roman Catholic ecumenical concern.

That Catholic ecumenism is both a source of great hope and great difficulty will become apparent as the chapter unfolds. We may set the stage for this dual reaction by offering two images, each of which illustrates both the resiliency and the rigidity of Catholicism in this area.

The first picture has been sketched by Karl Barth, the Protestant theologian whom Roman Catholics seem to treat with deepest respect. Barth describes a meeting with a Catholic theologian:

> He held up one hand with his fingers outstretched and then—pointing with his other hand to each finger, one by one—he chanted, "The Pope forbids me this, the Pope asks me to do that, the Pope frowns on this, the Pope says this, the Pope says that." And when he finished, he smiled at me and poked a finger through the gaps between the fingers of his outstretched hand.[1]

This does not mean that the Catholic theologian was trying to out-maneuver the Pope, but rather that he still had ecumenical maneuverability within the context of his allegiance to the Pope.

The second picture was suggested to me by a friend of mine who said that Catholic ecumenists whom he knows resemble a steel ball encased in a sponge. There is remarkable resiliency, pliability, and even adaptability, until one's probes get to the steel ball in the center. Then there is only unyielding firmness.

That the finger can be poked through the gap, and that there is resiliency in the sponge, are both hopeful facts. That the finger can only be poked so far, and the resiliency ceases when the central core is reached, are both difficult facts. It is important to keep both sets of facts in mind. In the following pages, to be sure, we shall lay more stress upon the hopeful facts, both because they are less well known, and also because they will help us to deal more creatively with the difficult facts when we come up against them.

1. Catholic reaction to Protestant ecumenism:
some extended comments

Few things could be more salutary for either Protestants or Catholics than a realization of the degree of serious attention which Catholicism is presently giving to Protestant ecumenical activity. The American situation would improve considerably if this ecumenical concern began to be more actively shared by American Catholics. We shall look at the phenomenon in three areas: (1) the attitude of the papacy toward ecumenism, (2) some specific examples of Catholic ecumenism, and (3) the spirit of Catholic ecumenism.

The attitude of the papacy toward ecumenism

If one has a sensitivity to nuances, he can detect both an increasing *awareness* of Protestant ecumenism in papal utterances over the last thirty years, and also an increasing *openness* toward Catholic participation in it. It is not possible to tell this story in a few pages. Fortunately the story has been told elsewhere and continues to be told.[2] Here we shall simply call attention to a few of the highlights.

Since the sixteenth century the papacy has been willing to welcome back into the fold of the Roman Church the erring children who strayed away during the enthusiasms of the Reformation decades. But no particular theological attention was paid to Protestants as such until quite recently.

The first papal encyclical dealing specifically with ecumenism was *Mortalium animos,* issued in 1928 after the Stockholm and Lausanne Conferences. It was a distinct blow to Protestant hopes of significant Catholic involvement in ecumenical endeavor. After giving an impression of Protestant ecumenism in the late 1920s, the encyclical stated:

> This being so, it is clear that the Apostolic See can by no means take part in these assemblies nor is it in any way lawful for Catholics to give such enterprises their encouragement and support. If they did so, they would be giving countenance to a false Christianity quite alien to the one Church of Christ.[3]

These were harsh words to Protestant ears and would seem to have closed the Roman door permanently. But it is a sign of their ecumenical stature that Protestant leaders like Söderblom, Mott, Temple, and others did not let the cold water of *Mortalium animos* permanently dampen their concern with Roman Catholicism as a part of ecumenical endeavor. From the Catholic side, as Father Tavard has argued, the conclusions of *Mortalium animos* must be seen in the context of the Catholic appraisal of the "ecumenism" of Stockholm and Lausanne. The papacy detected, whether rightly or wrongly; a repetition of the cloven hoof of modernism that it had been at pains to expunge from the Roman communion scarcely two decades earlier. Subsequent events, however, have shown that the attitude of *Mortalium animos* is no longer representative of the attitude of the Holy See. Its interest, Father Tavard says cautiously, "is now mainly historical." A Protestant may offer the less cautious opinion that the document is dated, and remind Protestants that it is irrelevant to offer it as evidence that Rome has no interest in Protestant ecumenism.

Since 1928, Protestant ecumenical thought has deepened and broadened, and taken on a decidedly Biblical flavor. And almost in proportion to this, papal concern with the separated brethren increased. Pius XI, for example, indicated the new tenor of Vatican concern with reunion:

> For a reunion it is above all necessary to know and to love one another. To know one another, because if the efforts of reunion have failed so many times, this is in large measure due to mutual ignorance. If there are prejudices on both sides, these prejudices must fall. Incredible are the errors and equivocations which persist and are handed down among the separated brethren against the Catholic Church; on the other hand, Catholics also have sometimes failed in justly evaluating the truth or, on account of insufficient knowledge, in showing a fraternal spirit. Do we know all that is valuable, good, and Christian in the fragments of ancient Catholic truth? *Detached fragments of a gold-bearing rock also contain the precious ore.*[4]

During the war years the messages of the popes contained manifest statements of concern not only for the well-being of Christians in communion with the Holy See, but of all other Christians elsewhere, who, as Pope Pius XII said in his Christmas message of 1941, "without belonging to the visible body of the Catholic Church, *are near to us through faith in Jesus Christ . . ."*

A further step has been the recognition in papal utterance from Pius XI and Pius XII that Rome itself is harmed by the divisions of

Christendom and needs the reunion of all Christendom herself. Father Baum writes:

> According to Roger Aubert, it is only in recent times that the official documents of the Holy See have been ready to admit that the divisions of Christendom actually do harm to the Catholic Church, and that the whole Mystical Body will benefit from the perfect reconciliation of Christians. In former times the benefits of a reunion were foreseen only for the separated Churches. However, Pius XI and Pius XII are quite outspoken; they look forward also to the wholesome effects of Christian unity on the Catholic Church. "From the full and perfect unity of all Christians the Mystical Body of Christ and all its members, one by one, are bound to obtain a great increment."[5]

The Catholic Church was invited by the World Council to send official observers (not "delegates") to the first Assembly of the World Council of Churches held at Amsterdam in 1948, but to the disappointment of Protestants a statement from the Holy Office on June 5, 1948 refused permission to Catholics to attend.

After Amsterdam, however, a very important Instruction of the Holy Office, *Ecclesia Catholica*, was issued on December 20, 1949, which lays down the guiding principles for Roman Catholic relationship to Protestant ecumenical endeavor. The Instruction, which seems on first reading to be very rigid, is actually an attempt to make clear the conditions under which ecumenical discussion may proceed, a laying down of the ground rules, so to speak, by which the Catholic family must abide. The positive tenor of the document can be indicated by the following excerpts:

> The work of "reunion" belongs above all, to the office and charge of the Church. Hence it behooves bishops, whom "the Holy Ghost hath placed to rule the Church of God," to bestow upon it their special attention. They should therefore not only carefully and efficaciously keep this movement under vigilant observation, but also prudently foster and guide it unto the twofold end of assisting those who are in search of the truth and the true Church, and of shielding the faithful from the perils which readily follow in the tread of the movement.[6]

And even more clearly toward the end:

> The excellent work of "reunion" of all Christians in the one true Faith and Church should daily become more integrated as a distinguished portion in the universal pastoral charge and be made an object of concern that the whole Catholic people take to heart and

recommend to God in fervent supplications . . . All indeed, but mainly priests and religious, must be admonished and encouraged to seek to fecundate and promote the work by their prayers and sacrifices.[7]

Catholic ecumenists have taken heart at the Instruction. John Todd comments, "The reason for that instruction seems to have been simply the increasing importance of the Ecumenical Movement itself, and the increasing desire of Catholics to contribute towards the unity of all Christians."[8] Father Boyer, the director of Unitas, has called it "the great charter of Catholic ecumenism." And Professor Aubert writes,

It cannot be disputed that while remaining, as is their duty, unyielding on the matter of principles, and very prudent in the area of practice, the Roman authorities are here taking a less rigid attitude than has been characterstic in the past. Far from disavowing the activities which have been increasing in recent years, they urge the bishops to promote those among them which seem likely to produce favorable results.[9]

The dual impression which the Instruction makes on Protestants has been succinctly recorded by Oliver Tompkins:

The Instruction *Ecclisia Catholica* aptly illustrates the whole situation: on the one hand, the clear, persistent and reiterated claim of the Roman Church to be the Catholic Church and to offer no terms for reunion but submission and return; on the other hand it gives formal and official recognition, slowly conceded as the ecumenical movement has gradually taken shape, to the fact that fellow-Christians care deeply for unity in the Church of Christ, and that they must be taken seriously, in charity and in prayer.[10]

Visser 't Hooft of the World Council puts special emphasis on the second of these impressions: "The very fact that such a document has been published indicates clearly that the ecumenical movement has begun to exercise influence in the ranks of the clergy and among the faithful of the Roman Catholic church. We can only rejoice."[11]

An implementation to the kind of concern expressed in the Instruction was the presence at the World Council Faith and Order Conference (held at Lund in 1952) of four accredited observers from the Roman Catholic Church. In welcoming them, Archbishop Brilioth said:

That the Church of Rome has not found it possible to take active part in any of the gatherings which we have been used to call ecumenical in spite of the absence of so large a part of the Christian world, is a tragic fact which we have had to accept. That for the first time Roman Catholic observers have been appointed, by due authority, is an important sign that the great Church of Rome is not indifferent to what is being done in order to further a better understanding between Christians of different traditions, and that an amity of souls can exist in spite of ecclesiastical barriers that appear insurmountable.[12]

Observers were not permitted to attend the Evanston Conference in 1954, but two accredited Roman Catholic observers (one of them Father Weigel) were present at the 1957 Faith and Order Conference at Oberlin.

The activities of the new pope, John XXIII, in the first few months of his pontificate, have been such as to make Protestant hearts rejoice. Such matters as the excision from the Good Friday liturgy of the phrase, "perfidious Jews," are indications of a kind of good will which has been expressed in larger terms in the calling of an ecumenical council. While it is now clear that this council will not include non-Roman delegates, or be of quite the sort that the first enthusiastic press reports seemed to suggest, it is also clear that it will be concerning itself in a central way with the problem of the relationship of Roman Catholicism to the non-Roman branches of Christendom. We can underline Father Weigel's words:

> [Pope John XXIII] has made it abundantly clear that he looks on those outside our communion with very friendly eyes. He has taken the ecumenical movement churning in our midst very seriously indeed. He wants Catholics active in this movement, for he sees the finger of God stirring the waters.[13]

Catholic ecumenism: getting down to cases

The increasing openness of the Papal See to ecumenical concern and activity is manifesting itself in a variety of ways throughout the life of Roman Catholicism. I shall now very briefly describe some of the activities, and then some of the literature, of Catholic ecumenical endeavor. I do this with two concerns in mind: (a) to demonstrate to American Protestants that they are not thinking "ecumenically" as long as they are leaving Roman Catholicism out of account, and (b) to suggest to American Catholics that there is nothing "suspect" about interest in, and concern for, the movements which are at the heart of contemporary Protestantism. As we shall see, the impetus from the Catholic side is being supplied by European rather than American Catholicism, and the lack of widespread participation by American Catholics in this ecumenical encounter is a deficiency which Protestants can only hope the American Catholic bishops will seek to counteract in the future.

What kinds of things, then, are taking place in other parts of the world which are evidence of active Catholic concern with Protestant ecumenism?[14]

Perhaps the most significant single Catholic ecumenical activity is one located in Rome itself. In 1945 papal approval was given for the establishment of a center for Catholic studies, called Unitas, "to have as its special work the return of non-Catholic Christians to the Church, not simply by means of intensifying propaganda about the claims of the Catholic Church, but by sympathetic understanding, and by study of the positions, traditions and general circumstances of the other Christian bodies and their place in the Ecumenical Movement."[15] One of the most important of these activities is the publication of the journal *Unitas*, which appears in French, English, and Italian, and both the journal and the movement itself have had cordial reception within the World Council of Churches. The head of Unitas is Father Charles Boyer, S.J. who has done some of the most perceptive Catholic writing on Protestant ecumenical activity. The headquarters in Rome is a place where many meetings of Catholics and non-Catholics are held.[16]

Another important center of Catholic ecumenical concern is the Benedictine Priory at Chevtogne, in Belgium. This was founded in response to the wish of Pius XI that a group of Benedictine monks concern themselves particularly with Eastern Orthodoxy. Since its foundation, however, Chevtogne has broadened its scope to include ecumenical research and conversation with Protestants as well. Books and papers relative to ecumenism are published at Chevtogne, in addition to the ecumenical journal *Irenikon*.

> Chevtogne has indeed become a meeting-place for East and West, a place of reconciliation between Catholic and non-Catholic; it is a place of prayer and quiet, a place of study; a great library is consecrated to the work of reunion. Cultivating the traditions of the Western and Eastern Church within one community, it is a living example of the enrichment possible when the different Christian traditions unite within the one faith.[17]

In France, Le Centre Istina was likewise initiated with a primary concern for the relationship of Catholicism to Orthodoxy, but it has turned to a wider consideration of the whole ecumenical movement. The director, Père C. J. Dumont, O.P., has written extensively on Protestant ecumenism. The center publishes the journal *Istina*, and also a monthly bulletin on ecumenism, *Vers l'Unité Chrétienne*.

In Germany, a movement known as Una Sancta comprised of both Catholics and Protestants, has met regularly together since the first World War, and a journal, *Una Sancta*, is published quarterly. Karl Adam's important book, *One and Holy*, (Sheed & Ward) had its inception as a series of lectures given to Una Sancta groups at Stuttgart and Karlsruhe in 1947.

> The peculiarity of the Una Sancta movement is that it does not try to make converts of non-Catholics. It wishes rather to form an atmosphere of friendliness and mutual understanding. The dynamism of the whole effort is confidence in God, who alone can make of many one. If the Christians live up to their vocation of love and mutual affection, then God's power will take over.[18]

In addition to all of these activities (of which the above are the merest sampling), there is a large body of Catholic literature dealing with Protestant ecumenism. Most Protestants, and probably most Catholics too, for that matter, would be astonished not only at the sheer bulk but also at the high quality of this literature. Careful Catholic attention is given to all that is said and done within Protestant ecumenism. The quality of the writing is not harsh or polemical; it makes a genuine attempt to *understand* what is going on in ecumenical minds and circles, and freely acknowledges that the Holy Spirit is at work in the Protestant attempt to heal the breach in the divided bodies of Christendom.

I shall now mention some of the significant books on Protestant ecumenism by European Catholics. I have refrained from merely listing these in the footnotes, for I want the point to be driven home beyond peradventure of a doubt that Roman Catholicism is deeply committed to a serious and creative encounter with Protestantism on its ecumenical frontier.

Among the most important recent publications in England have been an appraisal by a Catholic layman, John Todd, *Catholicism and the Ecumenical Movement*, (Longmans); Father Henry St. John, O.P., *Essays in Christian Unity*, (Dent); and the very full treatment by Father Bernard Leeming, S.J., *The Churches and the Church*, (Darton, Longman & Todd), to which the present work is greatly indebted.

In Holland a Dutch Catholic priest, once a Protestant, Father

Van de Pol, has written a large work on *The Christian Dilemma,* available in English under the imprint of the Philosophical Library.

Some of the most significant books from Germany have been the previously mentioned Karl Adam, *One and Holy,* (Sheed & Ward); a pioneer work by Father Max Pribilla, S.J., *Um kirchliche Einheit,* first published in 1929; Laros, *Schöpferischer Freide der Konfessionen,* of which there is a helpful summary in Tavard, *The Catholic Approach to Protestantism;* and Thomas Sartory, *Die ökumenische Bewegung und die Einheit der Kirche,* which is shortly to appear in English.

In Belgium, the Dominican Jerome Hamar has written extensively on ecumenism, and one of his articles is available in English, "The Mission of Catholic Ecumenism," published in *Cross Currents,* an ecumenical journal printed in the United States.

But it is in France that Catholic ecumenical concerns seems particularly to flourish, and a number of the French books (though not all of the important ones) have been translated into English. The pioneer French writer on ecumenism has certainly been Père Yves Congar. His *Chrétiennes Désunis* first appeared in 1937, and was published in English in 1939 as *Divided Christendom,* (Bles). This huge volume is the presupposition of most subsequent French writing, and a number of quotations from it appear below. Congar has also written *Vrai et fausse reforme dans l'Eglise,* and his *Jalons pour une théologie du laicat* has been used by Protestant writers dealing with the theology of the laity.[19] Père Dumont, the director of Le Centre Istina, has published a selection of his articles from the journals of that organization, under the title, *Vers l'Unité Chrétienne,* recently published in English as *Approaches to Christian Unity,* (Helicon Press).

Two of the most significant French books, both of which have been referred to in earlier chapters, are now available in English. These are Bouyer, *De Protestantisme á l'Eglise,* which has been published in America as *The Spirit and Forms of Protestantism,* (Newman Press); and Tavard, *A la rencontre du Protestantisme,* now available as *The Catholic Approach to Protestantism,* (Harpers). Father Tavard has also published in English a very thorough historical treatment of the problem of the relationship of Scripture and tradition in Protestantism, *Holy Writ or Holy Church: The Crisis of the Protestant Reformation,* (Harpers).

Professor Roger Aubert, of the University of Louvain has also written a number of books on ecumenism. His *Le Saint-Siege et l'Union des Eglises* is an historical treatment of the attitude of the papacy to separated Christians. In 1953 he wrote *Problèmes de l'Unité Chrétienne,* to give Catholics some straightforward descriptions of non-Catholic Christian groups.[20] Much of the material in this book is repeated in *Unité: La Semaine de Prière pour l'Unité Chrétienne* (revised edition 1959), in which, before the prayers for each day of the Christian Unity Octave the author describes the groups for whom prayers are to be offered.

One of the fullest treatments of the World Council of Churches is contained in the large book of Canon Gustav Thils, *Histoire doctrinale du mouvement oecumenique,* (Louvain), in which it is suggested, among other things, that Roman Catholicism could engage much more directly and actively in close relationship with the World Council of Churches than it has yet done.[21]

That Catholics and Protestants in France are not merely discussing their problems at arms' length is indicated by the remarkable volume, *Unité Chrétienne et Tolérance Religieuse,* Editions du Temps Présent, to which outstanding Catholics and Protestants have both contributed, and in which there is discussion of such delicate issues as Catholicism in Spain and the St. Bartholemew Massacre.

The spirit of Catholic ecumenism

Thus far our examination of Catholic ecumenism has been devoted to the assembling of data. But more than this is necessary. We must gain some kind of impression of the *spirit* of Catholic ecumenism, and I shall try to communicate this, first by some comments on a single but very remarkable book, and second by giving a few further examples of the spirit of Catholic ecumenism to show that it is not limited to a single writer. The book in question is Père Maurice Villain's *Introduction à l'Oecuménisme,* (Casterman).[22]

Like many Catholic books dealing with Protestantism, this one contains a brief history of the ecumenical movement, an analysis of the various world conferences of the World Council, a description of its structure, and a section on the Church of South India. These chapters are factual and fair and show a wide acquaintance with Protestant literature, as well as a sympathetic appreciation of Protestant conviction.

Part II of the book is entitled "Getting to Know Our Christian Brethren," and has chapters on Protestantism, Anglicanism, and Orthodoxy (as well as a chapter on Catholicism by two French Protestant pastors). We shall use the chapter on Protestantism as illustrative of Père Villain's approach.

Ecumenical dialogue, he asserts, does not mean that each side gives speeches to show that it has the truth and that the other side is in error. The first task, rather, is to become thoroughly acquainted with one another, and this is a very difficult thing to do in the area of ecumenical belief. The way of achieving deeper comprehension will not come conceptually but spiritually. The conceptual approach always leads to an impasse, while the spiritual approach opens a door into the souls of the separated brethren and introduces us into a world which we had previously thought to be illogical and unstable, but which we now discover can have coherence and relative worth. The task, therefore, is to see things as much as possible from the point of view of the conscience of the separated brethren. Thus the Catholic must try to understand the inner life of Protestantism and not merely the exterior expressions of that life.

Villain then attempts to do just this. He sees Protestantism as an attempt to safeguard the direct dependence of the soul upon Christ the Savior. The Protestant is the man of the Word of God. Jesus Christ is this Word of God, a personal Word who comes to man through Holy Scripture. Scripture thus has a unique and definitive place; the Church, which is the guardian of Scripture, must nevertheless submit to Scripture, for it is Scripture that judges the church. A double conviction follows from this: the conviction of the transcendence of God and of the free gift of salvation: *soli Deo gloria, sola gratia.* Man does not procure his salvation—he has nothing to offer God—all he can do is receive God's grace. From this statement of the basis of Protestantism, Villain goes on to treat Protestant ethics, Protestant "pietism," and the Protestant neo-Calvinism represented by Barth, Maury, and others.

As I read these pages I find the lineaments of my faith accurately portrayed. I might want to change a phrase here or an emphasis there, but on the whole I cannot help feeling that justice has been done to my ultimate commitments, and that Père Villain has indeed followed the "spiritual" rather than the conceptual way.

The book next develops the meaning of "Spiritual Ecumenism." If we simply confronted a "problem," we would once more have the wearisome impasse in which the Protestant cried "Liberty," and the Catholic replied, "Submission to the Church," or the Protestant cried "Scripture," and the Catholic cried, ". . . and tradition, dogma and obedience to the Magisterium." The tragedy is that most of the statements of faith, confessions and catechisms, on both sides, have simply been conceived in these terms, and they reinforce the polarities. "Spiritual ecumenism," then (in Marcel's terms) confronts a *mystery* rather than a problem. Just as the mystery of the self is a mystery which cannot be explained but which explains everything, so in ecumenism, the mystery of Christ himself, and more precisely, the will of Christ, is the mystery in terms of which all must be seen and understood. The will of Christ is the unity of all Christians; it is this for which he prayed and continues to pray, and for which he died, and it is this unity which must be reestablished, at the time and in the manner in which he wishes.

There seems to be an impasse here, for Catholics feel that the unity already exists in the church of Rome; the Orthodox feel that Orthodoxy must be the organ of unity, and most Protestants feel that the form in which this unity will be established is not yet clear. In the face of these conflicting visions, the most important thing is to practice fidelity—fidelity to Christ and to the gospel as one receives them in his own confession, but an open fidelity, a fidelity of welcome and not of opposition. Therefore,

> Our first act will not be to expound or discuss, but to kneel together at the foot of the Cross of our common Savior, in an act of repentance: because we are all sinners before him, because we are all guilty, in our various ways, of the mistakes of separation committed by our forefathers . . . In this attitude of repentance, Christians are purified and discover the atmosphere—the only atmosphere—which is favorable to Christian Unity. This atmosphere can only be that of Christ's prayer in John: 17, or of his agony in Gethsemane, which is a continuation of it.[23]

Villain points out that true ecumenical prayer will not simply be prayer for individual Christians. The Protestant is not to pray only for Maurice Villain, but also for the Catholic church, the pope and the bishops. Similarly, Villain is to pray not only for the individual Protestant, but also for Protestant synods and Protestant pastors, even though he places his own trust and confidence wholly in the Catholic Church. For, at this crossroads of prayer, only one thing really matters, and that is "the unity which Christ wishes, in the time and by the means which he shall provide." We dare not give him plans or contrivances for unity—all we can do is to be open before him, ready to receive his grace. The basis of prayer for unity, then, will be found in the "praying Christ," and at this point both Catholics and Protestants *are* one; at this point they are reminded that they share the same baptism and are thus brothers. "From the fire of love springs forth light," was the way Abbé Couturier put it, adding, "so that from the light may spring forth the fire of love."[24]

The inspiration for this kind of approach was Couturier himself, who drew together his convictions on the matter in a pamphlet, "Prayer and Christian Unity," of which Father Tavard has given a helpful summary:

> A true union is possible, insofar as each side prays for the other and even devotes itself entirely and without reservation to the sanctification of the other. This is a "spiritual emulation" through which all Christians can remain faithful to their convictions, while they build up at the same time a community of prayer. The aim of this "emulation" should not be the suppression of this or that community of Christians—for a purely negative approach would create unity by voiding the problem of its meaning—but rather a growing together through which each will help all others to become better Christians, a "parallelaboration" through which the Church and the Churches would encourage one another to know and do the will of Christ. Such "parallelaboration" . . . being the result of a prayer one for another that respects the loyalty of each and sundry, will create on the face of the earth a spiritual power of cosmic dimensions that will some day be strong enough to break through human pride and reintegrate all Christians in the bosom of the one and only Church.[25]

"Spiritual emulation" for the Catholic in this situation will have two inescapable elements: (a) a profession of the full Catholic faith, and (b) a special sensitivity to the position of the separated brethren. Villain naturally does not offer a diluted Catholicism, but he does feel that the Catholic faith and the true concerns of the Reformers are not at odds with one another, for such things as the transcendence of God, salvation by grace, and justification by faith in Jesus Christ are also central to the Catholic faith.

The whole matter of relationship to non-Catholics, Villain avers, must be dominated by the theological virtue of charity:

> The basis of all our ecumenical action is the love of Christ, the anguish of the "great distress of separation," but its basis is likewise a sincere, profound and unselfish love of our separated brethren, and our recognition of them as *Christian* brethren. "One Lord, one faith, one baptism, one God and father of us all."[26]

In another chapter, Villain chastizes his fellow Catholics for creating needless obstacles along the path to Christian unity—such as giving the impression that Mary has become a fourth person of the Trinity, failing to distinguish between sacraments and sacramentals, etc. He sees that misunderstandings can be created quite as much by Catholic carelessness as by Protestant obtuseness.

One other chapter in Villain's book calls for comment. This is his discussion of "The Search for an Ecumenical Theology" (Part IV, Chapter II). He points out that both Protestant and Catholic theologies have been polemically constructed, even if unconsciously so. Catholic theology, for example, has been anti-Protestant, anti-Jansenist, anti-quietist, anti-Modernist, etc., ever since the Council of Trent. And the task of Catholic theology, if it is to speak relevantly to the ecumenical scene, is to rethink its positive position as if there had been no heresy. This will involve three stages:

(1) It will involve a willingness to incorporate the worthwhile insights of the Reformers. This would represent a distinct gain over conventional Catholic apologetics, which simply condemns Protestant doctrine by reference to the anathemas of the Council of Trent, and does not take the historical or psychological conditions of the time into account. Without approving of the defection of the Reformers, the Catholic should be able to understand the extenuating circumstances which made that defection seem necessary then; he can realize how corrupt the church had become in the sixteenth century; he can realize that the Reformers had no intention of "separating" from the church; and he can even realize, as Pope Adrian VI said, that the Roman Church had need of chastisement, especially on account of the sins of the clergy. (2) A second stage will be an attempt to expound Catholic doctrine constructively, and not simply in opposition to something else. This would mean a thorough re-examination of the way theology has been taught by the inheritors of the Counter-Reformation, for most Catholic manuals and catechisms are so negatively oriented that they imprison and debase much of what is greatest in Catholic thought. (3) After these steps comes the work of synthesis, the details of which are too lengthy to reproduce in the present discussion.

I hope I have said enough to indicate the breadth, the openness, the charity and the down-to-earth practicality of Père Villain's approach. If resultant dialogue could even begin to emulate the spirit set forth by Père Villain, and inspired by the Abbé Couturier, no limit could be placed around what might eventuate from it.

But we must not leave the impression that Père Villain stands alone. The kind of charity and concern that he exemplifies, and his passion for unity not so that Rome may "triumph" but so that the prayer of Christ may be fulfilled, is to be found in almost every writer to whom reference has been made in this chapter. Here is Père Congar:

> For us [reunion] is a matter of making it *possible*, not only by showing ourselves true children of the Church, but by treating our separated brethren as Christians who already possess in greater or less degree what we desire to see fulfilled in them, and who themselves secretly look for such a consummation . . . The expression "separated brethren" is no pious tag or empty formula, but the description of a real and profound truth which involves our whole outlook on the subject.[27]

After pointing out that knowledge is an important ingredient for correcting the present Protestant-Catholic impasse, he continues,

> But if knowledge is the foundation, it is charity that must build on it, edifying, in every sense of the word. We must arrive at the habitual practice of a genuine and supernatural love for our separated brethren. As we have said before, it is not a question of the victory of one system over another, but of helping souls to their fulfillment in the truth and in true Christian fellowship. We do not want to score debating points over our brethren, but to draw out that Catholicity which is already in them. And for this we need a sincere love for all that they have which is good.[28]

This spirit is manifested in the pastoral letter which the Dutch hierarchy sent out just before the opening of the first conference of the World Council at Amsterdam in 1948. To all Catholics this advice was given:

> During these days, pray for all those who take part in this congress [i.e., the World Council meetings] and for the many other non-Catholic Christians, who longingly look out for unity, who truly follow Christ and live in His love and who—although they are separated from Christ's flock—yet look to the Church—be it often unconsciously —as the only Haven of salvation. Especially pray for those who act as leaders of non-Catholic Christians, and who carry such a heavy responsibility because the simple faithful cannot attain the right insight by themselves.[29]

A similar spirit is evident in the *Principles of Catholic Ecumenism* drawn up by the Rev. Bernard Leeming, S.J., which are worth extended quotation, both to set an example for American Catholics, and also to demonstrate to American Protestants what the spirit of Catholic ecumenism is really like.

1. Catholic Ecumenism has a sincere fraternal affection for our separated brethren It looks upon them as brethren separated from us, not by their own deliberate choice, much less by ill-will, but separated by circumstances not of their own making. "Across all the imperfections of men," our own imperfections as well as those of others, Catholic Ecumenism tries to make this fraternal affection evident and felt

2. Consequently, our separated brethren are not theological adversaries to be refuted, but friends seeking with us a deeper love of Christ. Even if they do not agree with us as to the way in which Christ is best loved, we still love them because they love Christ, and because Christ loves them and makes them loveable

3. Consequently, Catholic Ecumenism not only acknowledges but rejoices in all the good possessed by our separated brethren: the undoubted blessing and reality of their baptism into Christ, not into any "denomination," and very many gifts of nature and of grace which God has bestowed upon them. We rejoice to see gifts of God not only in individuals but also in corporate groups . . .

4. Catholic Ecumenism especially rejoices that so many have engaged in the efforts to overcome divisions among Christians. We, too, accept very many of their theological principles which the ecumenical movement has thrown into clearer relief . . .

5. Catholic Ecumenism realizes the need of patience. Charity is kind, is patient, is long-suffering. The divisions have been existing for some centuries and cannot, save by a miracle of God, be healed quickly. Inherited attitudes, group ideas, historical associations—all these are intertwined with religion. Only with the patience of Christ can they be overcome, and not only by clever arguments or peevish confutations.

6. Catholic Ecumenism realizes that it is by good feeling as well as by good reasoning that our brethren will be brought back to the unity of Christ. The methods approved again and again by missiologists in dealing with non-Christian peoples and cultures are the methods which apply even more pertinently to dealings with separated Christian brethren. We do not try to convert non-Christians by showing them their errors, but by showing how the separate truths they hold ought to develop into the Oneness of truth.

7. Catholic Ecumenism gives the fullest credit for good faith, good will, honest effort to non-Catholic ecumenists . . .

8. If Catholic ecumenists sometimes call attention to ambiguities or what seems to them lack of grasp of fundamental and important principles, they do so in a spirit of helpfulness and a desire to support

those ecumenists whose appreciation of their principles is not complete or whose appreciation of them is not shared by others . . .

9. Above all, Catholic Ecumenism is convinced to the depths of its being that it is only through humility that reconciliation can come . . . Consequently, Catholic Ecumenism, *first, last, and always* prays. Only in the spirit of humble prayer can we do good for Christ and for His Church. Only God can overcome divisions so deep-seated and so long-standing. But the foolishness of God is wiser than men; the weakness of God is stronger than men, and because of this, and this alone, Catholic Ecumenism is full of hope, enthusiasm, and joyful zeal, and is never downcast by rebuffs, or annoyed by misunderstanding, or impatient because of delay. It relies on God and not on human efforts, though it strives to recoil at no labor, no effort, no humiliation to which God by His grace draws and inspires our weakness and frailty.[30]

2. A point of meeting: the week of prayer for Christian unity

If there is a common theme that unifies these examples of the spirit of Catholic ecumenism it is surely that work for unity must be enveloped by the atmosphere of prayer. We must pray for the unity of Christ's church, and we must pray for one another. We must also pray, as far as possible, with one another. The danger is always that this kind of concern will remain in the realm of lofty generalities.

Fortunately, there exists a means by which the lofty generalities can be given specific content. This means is "The Week of Prayer for Christian Unity," occurring from January 18 through January 25. The background of this observance is as follows:[31]

In 1907, a British Anglo-Catholic priest, the Rev. Spencer Jones, offered a suggestion to an American Anglican, the Rev. Thomas Wattson, concerning an Octave of Prayer for Christian Unity. The latter, the head of an Episcopalian religious community devoted to the task of Christian unity, helped to develop a series of prayers for the eight days between January 18 and January 25. Pius X gave it papal approval in 1909 and Benedict XV made the Octave an official prayer of the Catholic Church in 1916. (Wattson became a Roman Catholic in the interval.) The content of these prayers is quite unambiguous —Catholics are to pray for the *return* of the "other sheep" to the church of Rome. Specific groups are prayed for each day: Oriental schismatics on January 19, Anglicans on the 20th, Lutherans and other Protestants on the 21st, and so forth.

Now it was clear that such prayers could not be offered by the "other sheep" themselves, who were more than eager to pray for Christian unity, but not if it were defined simply as a return to Rome. Therefore, in 1935, the Abbé Couturier proposed in an article on "The Psychology of the Prayers of the Octave," that henceforth the Octave should be conceived as a convergence of the prayers of every Christian confession in full liberty and independence towards the Christ whom we love, adore and praise," and that the aim of this time of prayer should be full reunion, the precise character of which we do not know, save that God wills it, since Christ prayed for it. Couturier's plea was heard in many parts of Christendom, and the kind of concerns he stated have come to characterize the spirit in which the rest of Christendom participates in the Week of Prayer for Christian Unity, stress being put on full acceptance of the will of Christ, so that in relation to his prayer that all may be one, Christians pray "for the visible unity of all Christians such as Christ wishes and through the means which he will choose." In these terms, the Week of Prayer is recognized by the World Council of Churches, and special materials for its observance have been prepared under the supervision of the Faith and Order Commission, so that Protestants, while not praying for unity in Catholic terms, do pray for whatever unity among Christians may be "pleasing unto Christ."

It should be recognized that Catholics are not of one mind about the wisdom of Abbé Couturier's approach. Some feel that there should not be the slightest appearance of equivocation on the central fact that a united Church will be a church that gives its allegiance to the bishop of Rome. And certainly any Catholic, the Abbé Couturier not excepted, will see this as the ultimate goal of ecumenism. Even so, Protestants can pray the prayer of Abbé Couturier, that Christ's church may be made one, "in accordance with his wishes and through the means that he will choose." If we can pray this prayer, while our Catholic brethren are praying for unity in the terms which their faith dictates for them, at least we can say that we are united in prayer for the same goal—unity—even though our conceptions of that goal may differ. But we can say more than this. We can observe that both Catholics and Protestants will be engaging in a risk—the risk of prayer—which is that God might choose to answer their prayers in ways quite different from those that any of his children contemplate. Protestants, at least, can contemplate this risk with serenity, knowing that God's ways are not our ways, nor his thoughts our thoughts, and that any prayer worthy of the name must always conclude, "Thy will be done."

Couturier's vision for the Week of Prayer went further than the prayers themselves. He felt that during this period there should be special opportunity for meetings of Catholics and non-Catholics, to discuss matters of ecumenical concern, learn about one another, clear up misunderstandings, and so forth. Couturier himself conducted many such meetings, and there are many lessons to be learned from his experiences.[32]

A further activity of the Week of Prayer for Christian Unity has recently been proposed, this time from the Protestant side. The eminent New Testament scholar, Oscar Cullmann, who has worked closely with many Catholic scholars in Europe, has pointed out that during the Week of Prayer we must do more than simply pray for one another. We must also demonstrate actively that we have visible solidarity as Christians, even if we do not have visible unity. He therefore proposes that Catholic and Protestant churches collect offerings during the week to be used for the relief of the poor *in each others'* parishes, Protestants giving for the aid of the Catholic poor, and vice versa. Cullmann points out that this proposal does not compromise the doctrinal integrity of either group, nor does it imply a spurious unity which does not exist, but rather manifests the real solidarity in Christ which does exist. In a brochure dealing with the matter,[33] Cullmann deals effectively with the kinds of objections that will inevitably be brought against the proposal, and gives thrilling examples of instances in Europe where this reciprocal giving has actually taken place. This is a practical "next step" for improving relations between Protestants and Catholics in local situations—which is where the tensions are usually greatest. If properly arranged in conjunction with the authorities in each area, this could become a significant way of expressing Christian love across boundaries that for the moment seem otherwise insurmountable.

3. Protestant reaction to Catholic ecumenism: some brief comments

The picture of Catholic ecumenism that emerges from our study shows that there has been a gradual but perceptible increase of openness on the part of the papacy, that the resultant concern in the rest of Catholic life is astonishingly widespread, and that the spirit in which this concern is expressed is enveloped by fraternity, love, and prayer. We have also seen that there is a very significant point of meeting for each side, in the Week of Prayer for Christian Unity.

What are Protestants to make of all of this? At least three reactions are in order:

1. *Protestants are called upon to reciprocate.* We are the recipients of manifest love and we must return that love. The things we say and do are studied carefully; we must be willing to study carefully what Catholics say and do.[34] We are being prayed for; we must be willing to pray likewise. Where there are opportunities for discussion, we must discuss. Where there are books to be read, we must read them. Where there are misunderstandings of our faith to correct, we must correct them. Where there are no opportunities for this kind of exchange, we must help to create them. All of this represents our first obligation as Protestants; to receive gratefully what is being offered, and to give in return.

2. The second reaction is like unto the first, although it will initially sound quite different. *Protestants must have a realistic recognition of what Catholic ecumenism means and does not mean.* The Protestant must have no illusions that Catholic ecumenism means that Catholicism is going to "change" in any *basic* way. Protestants and Catholics are not going to draw up a list of convictions they share and then scrap the remaining differences "for the sake of unity." Protestants could never do this, and they can be very sure that Catholics will not. Catholicism could and probably would make numerous "adaptations" of its present structure to help Protestants feel more at home—a vernacular liturgy, a married clergy, communion in both kinds, and so forth—but Catholicism will not and cannot compromise its basic condition of reunion, namely recognition by the rest of Christendom of the supreme pontiff, the bishop of Rome, as the vicar of Christ on earth, infallibly guided by the Holy Spirit in the proclamation of matters of faith and morals. Every Catholic writer is clear on this point, and I will cite three examples (purposely taken from writers who have been at the forefront of ecumenical discussion) to make sure that there is no misunderstanding:

> Any "return," corporate or individual, must involve recognition of the Pope as the vicegerent of Christ. Once an individual has reached the point of recognizing this truth, he cannot stay outside Catholic unity, since he would in that case be refusing obedience to Christ in the person of his earthly vicar.[35]

The Catholic Church feels and knows herself as the Church of Christ in the emphatic, exclusive sense: as the visible revelation in space and time of the redemptive powers which proceed from Christ her Head, as the Body of Christ, as the *one means of salvation . . .* To admit even the possibility that the final union of Christendom could take place other than in her and through her would be a denial and betrayal of her most precious knowledge that she is Christ's own Church. For her there is only one true union, reunion with herself.[36]

There can never be a Catholic-Protestant church, or even a Catholic-Protestant fellowship of churches. This is the basic fact. It does no good to anyone to hope that this fact will somehow sublimate into something thinner . . . The Catholic must say to the Protestant that the [Catholic] Church was substantially right, and therefore any endeavor toward reunion will be a return to her unreconstructed, unreformed unity.[37]

There is no use disguising the fact that such quotations as these arouse the ire of a good many Protestants. "So," they bristle, "the gloved hand covers a mailed fist after all! The terms are really the same as they always were: total surrender!" I have occasional moments when I share this reaction, but I am sure that it is the wrong one. For one thing, Catholic ecumenists do not think of the matter in terms of "victory" and "surrender," as numerous quotations in this book should have made clear. They use rather such terms as "fulfillment", i.e. the fulfillment of all that is best in Protestantism, within the fullness of Catholicism. While to many Protestant ears this may seem little different from the words, "Naughty boys, come home and submit," the difference, I feel, is in the dimension of patience; for Catholic ecumenists are agreed that they must wait for Protestants to *want* to come home because the latter have finally discovered where home really is.

Protestants must also acknowledge the forthrightness and candidness of the Catholic ecumenists. They are not willing to let the discussion proceed under false pretenses. They are telling us at the start exactly how things stand. And this is a deed of love, not a deed of nastiness. To Protestants who resent what seems to them a kind of spiritual imperialism from the Catholic side, I would simply say, "Do you put it any less strongly from your side? Do you not insist that one of the conditions of reunion must be the repudiation by Rome of its post-Tridentine 'errors,' such as the dogmas of the immaculate conception, papal infallibility, and the assumption?"

Present Protestant conditions of reunion seem just as strict—and just as unpalatable to the other side.

"In that case," men of good will on both sides are bound to ask, "what is the point of prolonging this useless discussion any further?" And it is in answer to this query, that the third reaction must be offered.

3. *Protestants must realize that here we are not dealing simply with the will of men; we are dealing with the will of God.* However insurmountable the barriers may seem, it is the will of Jesus Christ that his children should be one. To fail to give this fact full weight would be to doubt the power of the Holy Ghost. We confront the problems of reunion and we can only say, "With men it is impossible." But that is not enough for the Christian to say. We must go on to say, "With men it is impossible, but with God all things are possible." Père Congar expresses this same concern in a wonderful image:

> Since [reunion] is something which of itself is quite beyond our power, and can only come about through the omnipotence of God, it must be for us, above all, an object of hope and prayer. Our sin and wickedness have entombed the unbroken unity of Christendom, and oppressed by the humanly insurmountable obstacles in the way of its restoration to us we begin to ask, like the holy women at the sepulchre, "Who shall roll away for us the stone at the door of the tomb?"[38]

We do not know how God can bring his order out of our present chaos. But we are not to doubt that he can do so when and how he wills. And this is the really important thing about ecumenical dialogue. It is our act of faith, our way of saying, "We will not close any channels through which the Holy Spirit might be pleased to work." We will remove all the barriers that we can. And where barriers remain that we cannot remove, we will not pretend that they do not exist, but will pray to God that by his power and might they may be annihilated. We will simply trust that God will use our ecumenical discussion for his own purposes.

We do not know all about those purposes. But we do know that they are good.

CHAPTER

7

Conclusions That Are Really Preliminaries

The aim of this book is not to conclude something, but to initiate something—a greater degree of responsible dialogue between Protestants and Catholics. Therefore a final chapter must emphatically not "draw everything together," and reach a series of conclusions. It must rather insure that everything is left fluid, and perhaps even a little disorganized, so that one can only conclude that we are in the preliminary rather than the concluding stages of discussion. Perhaps the best way of emphasizing the open-endedness of the discussion would be by asking that the second chapter now be re-read in the light of the intervening chapters.

To some Protestants it will seem a long journey from the bingo priest to the "principles of Catholic ecumenism," but they must not let the tangibility of the former blind them to the deeper reality of the latter, and it will be one of the marks of Protestant readiness for the dialogue to be able to make that journey without disavowing the bingo priest as a brother in Christ. To some Catholics it will seem a long way from the fundamentalist Bible Presbyterian minister in the funny-looking church across the street to the ecumenical vision of a Pastor Boegner or a Bishop Bell, but Catholics must not let the strident tones of the one deafen them to the ecumenical tones of the others, and it will be one of the marks of Catholic readiness for the dialogue to be able to believe that God is served even by the first as well as by the second.

1. An interim goal: the recognition that Catholicism and Protestantism need each other

But something more is needed than the recognition that each of us is, in his own way, serving Christ. What is needed is the recognition that *we need each other* if we are to serve Christ as faithfully as we ought, and I suggest this as a kind of interim goal that might guide us in the next stages of our dealings with one another.

A Protestant should have no difficulty accepting this thesis unless his sole concern is to keep fighting sixteenth-century battles in sixteenth-century terms. A Protestant must acknowledge that although he may become impatient with the majestic slowness of Catholicism, the very majesty of that slowness does provide a stabilizing force in Christendom that helps to counteract the sometimes unmajestic swiftness with which Protestantism can dart in this direction and that, casting itself upon every wind of doctrine. If Catholicism does not take to new theological fads with the eagerness that Protestantism does, it nevertheless finds ways in the next generation to incorporate within its structure and life whatever was of enduring worth in the new fads. The *continuity* of the faith, which in Protestantism is so often obscured by the proliferation of Protestantism into sects and churches, is maintained by Catholicism in ways for which Protestants should be more grateful than they usually are, and the great reservoirs of both piety and learning that characterize Catholicism at its best are reservoirs from which Protestants drink more deeply than they sometimes know.

But there is another, if less exalted, reason why Protestantism needs Catholicism if it is to be true to itself. For although Protestantism has the principles of correction and reform built into its very fibre (*ecclesia semper reformanda*), it is hard for Protestants to submit to correction and reform from within. And here the very existence of Catholicism, particularly a creative Catholicism, can provide something important for the total health of Protestantism, as John T. McNeill has shown:

> If we are farsighted we shall not pray, as our predecessors sometimes did, for the complete overthrow of the papacy . . . We need [Catholicism] as a wholesome stimulation to our morale. We are not, let us confess, so spiritually vigorous as to be able safely to do without the challenge of its adverse criticism and activity. Even the fact that

Protestantism is given a gloomy prognosis helps to keep us alert and forward-looking. The triumph of Rome would be a calamity; but its downfall in the near future would mean to us the loss of a helpful adversary. It would mean also the loss of not a little positive helpfulness in the realms of learning and piety.[1]

That Protestantism needs Catholicism I have no doubt, and I am sure that this conviction need pose no basic problems, sociological or theological, for Protestants. But can the other half of the initial statement stand? Can a Catholic truly assert that Catholicism "needs" Protestantism? I am not sure that this will be initially apparent to the Catholic at all. It may even sound like a suggestion that Catholicism "lacks" something essential that Protestantism must supply— and this notion the true Catholic will not accept.

But there are notions that the true Catholic *will* accept, and there has been an increasing note in recent Catholic thought that acknowledges that the full witness of the Catholic church to the world is weakened as long as Christendom is divided. We have already quoted Father Baum in this connection, and may cite him again, as he summarizes his argument:

> The reunion of all Christians, we conclude, will be of benefit even to the Catholic Church; it will reinforce her resistance to God's enemies and expand her missionary influence in the world. In other words, through the return to Christian unity the redemptive work of the Church will achieve a greater unfolding. While the Body of Christ is fully equipped to reconcile all humanity with God, this saving mission is prevented from its most perfect and complete manifestation by the persistence of Christian factions.[2]

Other Catholic theologians could be cited who speak in similar fashion.

I think the case can be made empirically as well, by asserting that Catholicism is the better off simply for having Protestantism around. To the outsider, at least, this is quite apparent. I doubt if many people, even Catholics, would claim that the Catholic church today is at its most vital in those areas where it completely dominates the culture. Surely the Catholicism of Mexico is less vigorous than the Catholicism of the United States. Surely there is a significant difference between the vitality of Catholicism in Spain and the vitality of Catholicism in Great Britain. The Catholic church in Colombia is not as creative as the Catholic Church in Germany. Catholicism, in its turn, seems to prosper from the stimulus of Protestantism.

I have heard some Catholics affirm a belief that in the mysterious providence of God it is a good thing *for Catholicism* that Protestantism exists. Protestantism has managed, with whatever defects, to preserve and utter at least some parts of the Christian gospel which Catholicism might otherwise be in danger of slighting. This is the point of Father Bouyer's *The Spirit and Forms of Protestantism:* the things the Reformers witnessed to were at the center of the faith. The church of their time had lost them, and it needed to recover them. Surely Catholics should be able to accept gratefully whatever dimensions of the gospel are proclaimed by Protestantism and incorporate them more fully into the life and pattern of their faith than they have done before. Without in the least degree compromising their belief in the Roman Catholic Church as the true Body of Christ, they should be able to acknowledge those fruits of the Spirit that are genuinely fostered in a Protestant ethos, and even learn from them.

Let me cite one historical, and one contemporary, example of this kind of contribution which Protestantism makes to Catholicism.

Roman Catholics and Anglo-Catholics sometimes claim that the justification for the Protestant Reformation of the sixteenth century is that it produced the Counter-Reformation. There is not a little truth in the statement, patronizing as it sounds to Protestant ears. For it is a fact that, at the very least, many of the distresses of Christendom were pointed up so vigorously by the Reformation that the Church finally had to take cognizance of them, and the Council of Trent was one of the results. The definitive statements of Catholic theology that the council produced are very clearly formulated in the light of the Protestant alternatives that the council rejected. Protestants, and perhaps some Catholics, would feel that this has been a mixed blessing at best. The point, however, is not at the moment the qualitative one, but a simple recognition that one of the major components in the development of modern Catholic theology has been the existence of Protestantism.

That may seem a somewhat negative contribution, and we have already noted Père Villain's plea that Catholic theology re-think its formulations from a different orientation. But our contemporary example is a happier augury of the healthy theological stimulation that can be exercised between Catholics and Protestants. A German Catholic, Hans Küng, has written a very full treatment of Karl Barth's doctrine of justification, as set forth in Barth's *Kirchliche Dogmatik,* IV, 1.[3] Küng takes exception to Barth's treatment of the Council of Trent in that volume, and proceeds to develop the astonishing and exciting notion that Barth—a Protestant of the Protestants—has developed a doctrine of justification which is, in fact, precisely what the Council of Trent really meant by justification, and that this is apparent once the historical situation in which that council worked is fully understood. Now the question which Barth properly asks Küng (after acknowledging that Küng has given a fair statement of his position), is whether or not Küng would have been able to give this particular interpretation to the Tridentine teaching if he had not first of all been exposed to the *Kirchliche Dogmatik*. I think the implication is a fair and interesting one: perhaps a Catholic theologian has come to a fuller appreciation *of his own faith* as a result of studying the works of a Protestant theologian.

Nor is this merely a case of Protestant wishful thinking, for John Todd, a Catholic layman, writes:

It is true that those Catholic theologians who have set about study-ing modern Protestant and Anglican thought seriously, are also those theologians who have produced some of the most worth-while theology from the point of view of the Catholic Church herself.[4]

So I think it is at least arguable that Catholicism needs Protestantism, just as Protestantism needs Catholicism.

But we must not allow the recognition of the need of Catholicism and Protestantism for one another to be the final goal. It can be no more than an interim goal. We must not settle for an acceptance of the present situation as though it were desirable. It is not desirable. It is an abomination and a scandal, for it is a rending of the seam-less robe of Christ, and a flaunting of the prayer of Christ "that all may be one." But as a step toward that time when in ways beyond our present knowing, by the mysterious workings of the Holy Spirit, we are drawn closer together than we now are, it is appropriate that we acknowledge that the existence of each group can be a genuine source of ministry to the other, and that as we are most characteristically and creatively ourselves, we shall have the most to contribute to one another's enrichment.

2. Next steps in the dialogue

It is tempting to go on from here to outline a Plan, or at least a Scheme, by means of which we might move through the stage of praying for one another, to the stage of talking with one another, to the stage of praying with one another. But no Plan or Scheme will do the job. The specific approaches that might be appropriate in one place, will be irrelevant in another. All that need be said at this juncture is that such things as the following need to be picked up, developed, changed, revised, and used wherever and whenever they can promote the dialogue:

(a) vigilant programs of caricature-assassination by each group *on behalf of the other,* so that the grosser stereotypes can be destroyed, and even, in time, some of the subtler ones as well; (b) reading groups and study groups under both Catholic and Protestant auspices, in which members of the respective communions can learn a few basic facts about one another; (c) face-to-face encounter between Catholics and Protestants as frequently and under as many varieties of conditions as the Instruction of the Holy Office will permit; (d) more readiness for frank discussion in the respective journals of the two groups, so that Catholics are more frequent contributors to *The Christian Century* and *Christianity and Crisis,* while Protestants appear with more regularity in *America* and *The Commonweal;* (e) a recognition that knowledge alone is not enough and that it must be encompassed by charity and prayer, with the result (f) that both groups give new attention and centrality to the Week of Prayer for Christian Unity, utilizing to the full the resources available to both groups and recognizing that prayer one week out of the year is not enough, so that a steady life of prayer can come to undergird all else that is done; and (g) a sense of openness on the part of all concerned, so that they truly believe that no doors are permanently closed to the Holy Spirit, and that in the valleys where He breathes, even dry bones can spring to life.

3. The particular challenge of the American situation

Something will be lost if no attempts are made beyond adaptations of what has been successfully tried elsewhere. For it may be that America will have its own contribution to make to the worldwide Protestant-Catholic dialogue now in progress. That contribution will consist in the new things which American Protestants and American Catholics can say out of the new situation in America in which these groups confront one another, i.e. the situation thus far unknown in Europe of a genuinely "pluralistic culture" such as we described in Chapter 3. The situation in America is not one in which either group now exercises overwhelming influence over the course of national life at the expense of the other. Protestants had this influence in the past and Catholics might like to have it in the future, but it seems much more likely that the two groups will co-exist somewhat as they do now, neither group making spectacular gains at the expense of the other. The co-existence can be peaceful or fretful, but co-existence it will be, regardless of the adjective attached to it.

This gives quite unprecedented opportunities to American Protestants and Catholics to learn to live together gracefully, and to make the lessons they learn available to the rest of the world. Christopher Dawson has argued that there is something providential about the American situation for the future of Christian unity, and that out of the experience of the American situation may come many of the insights that will illumine the next steps on the road to unity. This means that American Catholicism and American Protestantism are coming of age, and that as they leave adolescence and approach maturity things will be demanded of them that they yet know not of. This will take all of the resources of maturity that each group possesses, and it will have to be a maturity moulded by the highest reaches of authentic spirituality and grace.

And since neither group can attain maturity simply by willing it, or even by striving for it, my prayer for the Holy Catholic Church (of which I consider myself a member) will remain the ancient one:

Most gracious Father, we humbly beseech Thee for Thy holy Catholic Church. Fill it with all truth, and in all truth with all peace. Where it is in error reform it; where it is in want, furnish it; where it is right, strengthen and confirm it; and where it is rent asunder, heal Thou the divisions thereof; through Jesus Christ our Lord. Amen.

Amen.

PART

II

A CATHOLIC
LOOKS AT PROTESTANTISM

by Gustave Weigel, S.J.

1

Puzzlement

A Catholic in Southern Italy may have strange notions about Protestants because he has never seen one and any idea he has about them will derive from the preaching of his parish priest who himself knows little about the subject. For the priest Protestantism is something bad and for the layman it is something vague and alien.

A Catholic in England or America can hardly react in the same fashion. As he moves through the city streets he sees Protestant churches everywhere and he takes them quite for granted. Many of his friends are Protestants, or even members of his family group. In consequence the Protestant phenomenon is nothing alien to him. It does not disturb him nor does it excite strong reactions. Close as he is to the Protestant reality, he nevertheless knows little about it. When the spokesmen of his own church refer to it, they are usually negative. By his religious faith the Catholic cannot worship in assemblies outside his own church, but most American Catholics, for reasons other than worship, have been in Protestant churches for funerals, weddings, christenings, or meetings of one kind or another. The building holds no mystery for him and today most Protestant churches have an aspect not totally different from the Catholic Church where the Catholic himself worships.

This general situation was mine for many years of my life. Until I was almost thirty years old Protestantism was something visibly there but irrelevant to my existence. I had a mild curiosity about it and as a boy read some lives of Luther, but the theology involved hardly made the reading significant to a boy. I was quite content with my own church's evaluation of Luther. He was wrong and that is all there was about it.

Once I began the study of theology, Protestantism began to take on meaning in a more vital way. But as I met it, the main concern was the theology of the Reformers of the sixteenth century. Modern Protestants confused me because they did not seem to be in the same line of thought as Luther and Calvin. The liberal theologians did not even sound like Christians, and the fundamentalists sounded bizarre. Yet my curiosity was strongly aroused and I began to study the Protestant reality with diligence.

Protestants may not realize it—or maybe they do—but initially it is very confusing for a non-Protestant to look at living Protestantism. A Lutheran is a Protestant; so is a Christian Scientist. Episcopalians (begging the pardon of Anglo-Catholics!) are Protestants and so are the store-front church Pentecostals. Yet what have these different churches in common? When you ask the Protestant he cannot help you, because he doesn't seem to know. Even trained theologians are not too clear about the matter and they give the impression that the question is not important.

The Catholic is also confused because there is no authoritative spokesman for Protestantism. Tillich, Niebuhr, Mackay, Henry speak, but everybody knows that they speak for themselves. No Protestant feels any obligation to accept their doctrine. If some like it, they will adopt it. If they don't, they ignore it.

It is even difficult to form an image of the Protestant. By and large we think of Protestant worshipers as a sedate and dignified group listening to an earnest preacher. Yet one also knows that the "Holy Rollers" hardly correspond to such an image. One sees the zealous proselytizing action of the Witnesses of Jehovah which is so different from the courteous gentility of Episcopalians. And yet the only time I was rigorously baited was in an Episcopalian meeting!

Then of course there is the labyrinth of doctrines. Some churches have a great baptism day, hiring a swimming pool for total immersion of hundreds, or even playing a hose on hundreds with the aid of the municipal fire hydrants. Fundamentalists quite consciously believe that Jonah was singing psalms for three days in the belly of a whale and Unitarians do not believe that Jesus was God. Some have symbolic books with a doctrine summarized and accepted; others have no creeds nor do they want any. For some Protestants

Christ is truly and physically present in the Eucharist and for others he is not. Some baptize infants and for others this is an abomination. The ministers of some churches expect to be called "Father" while in other churches the same title is taken almost as an insult. The reality of Jesus is diversely conceived. Some will call him divine but they do not mean that he is the deity. Some think that the Bible gives an exact report of his life and work, while others believe that the man as he was does not even come through the accounts, because his defects and shortcomings are all blocked out. Some have a fine sense of doctrinal orthodoxy; others think that doctrine is unimportant and it is the brain-child of the theologians, not closely related to the message of Jesus himself. Some say that bishops are necessary for the Church; others say that they are not necessary but useful; still others think that episcopal institution is a corruption.

And so it goes. For the Catholic this is all very perplexing. It takes him some time to realize the basic truth about Protestantism, namely that it is not a church as the Catholic Church is a church. Protestantism is a principle to which Protestant churches subscribe without thereby forming even a sisterhood of churches. Certainly no single church is produced, and some Protestant churches like the Mormons and the Witnesses of Jehovah do not wish to be called Protestant and the Witnesses even refuse to be called a church.

Concerning the Protestant principle we shall speak later. Before dealing with that question we can discuss certain sociological characteristics of Protestantism which the Catholic can observe empirically. These traits may not have any root in Protestant theology but they certainly are a part of Protestant history. There is a specific Protestant piety. There is a Protestant morality. There is a Protestant stance. There is a Protestant fear. A Catholic sees these things because they are external and palpable. He can validly say what he sees—he is the world's authority on his own experience. However, he cannot hope to grasp the invisible part on which the visible things rest because this only a Protestant can perceive. I have become very very sceptical about "understanding Protestantism." Protestants have engendered this scepticism in me. When a Protestant with the best of good will and after thorough study of the subject, "explains" Catholicism, I feel nonplussed. His "explanation" does not fit the Catholic Church I know after many years of living in her. The Protestant is looking at my church from the outside and he does not know the inside story. This must also be the situation enmeshing the Catholic when he "explains" Protestantism. If the writer and reader of this study constantly keep this in mind, little harm can be done to either. Impressions are being ventilated. The Protestant substance in its objectivity may not even be touched by his kind of approach. The writer hopes to come to grips with it, but such hopes may easily be illusive.

2

Protestant Piety

The Catholic associates the notion of his religion with much prayer. He sees two kinds at work in his community. There is the sacred liturgy of the community in assembly met, and there is private meditation exemplified best in the religious orders and congregations. In these associations the practise of prayer is a principle preoccupation of the members, and the diversity of the orders has brought about a rich variety of prayer attitudes and techniques.

The average American Catholic is not conspicuously meditative but meditation for short periods is not alien to his life. Every parish church is open all day and some of the bigger churches are open day and night. You can go to St. Patrick's Cathedral in New York at any hour and find many men and women praying in the soft gloom. They do not do it by any prescribed rules but they do it some way. Some will do no more than read meditatively the prayers of a book of devotion. In critical moments of the Catholic's life he asks the prayers of his fellow Catholics and not a few will petition a religious community like the Carmelites to speak to God for them.

Private meditation is highly personal and when the Catholic then speaks to God he does so with utter spontaneity. He is also accustomed to use mediated prayer by addressing himself to a saint so that his own prayer be united with that of one certainly pleasing to God. In the religious orders meditation usually bypasses intercession by a direct appeal to God or his Christ.

Aids to this prayer life are found in books of devotion which are composed by prayerful souls. There is an embarrasing richness of

such works. Some are dull. Others are sugary. But there are many
with stimulating thought content and Catholic life produces these
books in every age and in every clime. There are many Catholics
who find no attraction in many of these works because their language
and attitude are so different from the pattern of concern which the
man of action follows. But it is extremely rare that the Catholic is
touched by none of them. The *Imitation of Christ* by Thomas
à Kempis is highly esteemed and much used by Catholics the world
over.

Those who pursue meditation seriously will also be assisted by
their spiritual director with whom they discuss their prayer life and
from whom they receive guidance. They will only be a small minority in the total community but, absolutely speaking, they are numerous. Not infrequently they will use the occasion of their periodic
confession for direction of their inner life of prayer.

But when the Catholic prays in public, his prayer is highly formal.
He uses prayers taken from the liturgy which are always sober and
short. There is a reserve in the Catholic when he prays out loud in
the assembly and the liturgical prayers are the best that the liturgy
of two thousand years has developed. Their tone is humble, noble,
and objective. The man who prays is clearly speaking to God and
nobody else.

The Catholic connects the idea of asceticism with the idea of
prayer. He abstains from meat every Friday. At stated times in
the liturgical year he fasts. A fast is also called for when he receives
the Eucharist, though this fast has been greatly mitigated by the
late Pope Pius XII. It is perhaps this principle of fasting which makes
Catholics go to Sunday services at an earlier hour than is usual
among non-Catholics, though late masses are certainly conspicuous
in present day Catholic churches.

Last of all, the high form of Catholic prayer is sacramental. In
the sacrament something more than words and feeling are aroused.
The sacrament is an action and even when the Catholic is incapable
of being very active himself, the sacramental act functions by its
own divinely infused power. The mass is an action, esthetically structured and requiring movement on the part of all. It is not a moment
for personal meditation but rather a symbolic enactment of the great
mysteries of salvation. Even the foreign Latin in use heightens the
sense of mystery. I have heard a story about an Orthodox priest
stationed among the Aleuts in Alaska. For a hundred years the By-
zantine Liturgy was there performed in Church Slavonic and the

priest thought it wise to change to Aleut. The parishioners objected. Their objection was expressed in this form: we do not want to pray to God in the language we swear in. There is among Catholics a current movement to have the liturgy performed in the vernacular language, but they can understand sympathetically the remark of the Aleuts.

The greater power of the act over the mere word is most clearly seen in the Catholic sacrament of Extreme Unction. The sick person, incapable of concentrated prayer because of his sickness and pain, enters into the whole act of anointing. There is a strong prayer-experience involved and yet the action is so objective. The sick person does not have to rely on his strength. The prayer is done and enacted in a definitive fashion. It moves *ex opere operato,* to use a theological tag which indicates that the power of the rite is in the rite itself.

This is the kind of conditioning with which the Catholic looks at the piety of his Protestant friends. He is well aware that piety is a Protestant thing no less than Catholic. Nor does this surprise him, because he takes it for granted that religion in any form brings forth piety.

In some forms of Protestant piety the Catholic is at home. When he enters an Anglo-Catholic church he understands everything he sees. There is the altar which is obviously an altar. There is the sanctuary light. Holy water stands by the church door. Confessionals are visible. When the mass—and it is called the mass—is celebrated, it is the mass he knows, even though the language is English. Yet he has a strange feeling. He asks himself why these things are found outside of his church. He usually knows too little Anglo-Catholic theology, with the result that he spontaneously, and erroneously, thinks that he is facing a mere imitation. He cannot believe that this is a genuine expression of the Protestant genius. I know that the Anglo-Catholics will agree with him, for they insist that their worship is Catholic and not Protestant. But this confuses the Catholic all the more. Why should a Protestant church want a Catholic liturgy? It is hard for the Catholic to understand the Anglo-Catholic position if he knows little about theology, and of course that is the situation of the overwhelming majority of Catholics. In a rather simplistic way he thinks Catholic is Catholic, and Protestant is Protestant, and if you are one, then you are not the other. High Church Protestantism, in consequence, is most bewildering for the average Catholic.

There is an explanation for this simplicism. It is beyond doubt true that Anglo-Catholic cultus forms are not the dominant pattern of Protestant worship in this country. The general pattern of service is evangelical and it has a different mood even though basically its visible structure is remotely derived from Catholic services. Today the liturgical movement within Protestantism has brought back into the churches much of the ancient paraphernalia of Christian cult. At least the minister today wears either a cassock and surplice, or an academic gown which of course is a cassock. This the Catholic unreflectively expects in worship. He is uncomfortably shocked when he sees the minister lead the community in prayer dressed in his street clothes. The Catholic feels that there is a strong distinction between the sacred and the profane, and the two should not be mixed. He is quite cold to the evangelicals' explanation that they are practising the Christian simplicity of the primitive Church. What shocks him more is the low church practice of receiving communion seated in the pews. For the Catholic, communion is a high moment in Christian life, the awesome coming of Christ to absorb the believer into himself. It is no time for melodramatics, but certainly the informality of the sitting position is hardly resonant with the solemnity of the event. A theology is at work here, and it is the theology of denial. Christ is not present in the sacrament and the mode of communion eloquently affirms that no adoration is to be given to what is only bread. In the Episcopal Church and recently in the Lutheran churches communion service is frequent but the Catholic always wonders why it is so rare in so many churches. Communion is certainly scriptural enough, and both Luther and Calvin believed in frequent communion but many of their descendants do not share their views in this matter. The Catholic's reaction is paradoxical really, because he does not believe that the Protestant sacrament is the true sacrament, and yet be the sacrament valid or invalid, he expects greater awe and reverence for the very idea of communion.

In an evangelical service preaching plays a most important role. From Protestant publications in our time I notice that it is no longer considered so central as formerly. In fact I have read protests from clergy and laity that there are some ministers who so insist on liturgical action that they are somewhat contemptuous of preaching. That of course is a domestic question within the evangelical bodies and would not normally be noted by a Catholic. But sermons are certainly being given; in church, on the radio, on television.

The Catholic hears sermons in his churches and cannot escape altogether the hearing of Protestant sermons. His reaction is quite uncomplicated. There are good preachers in the Catholic pulpit and these are good preachers in Protestant churches. There are mediocre and poor preachers in both camps—and these outnumber the good preachers no matter what be the denomination we consider. The Catholic, by and large, is no lover of sermons. He would rather listen to a good one than a bad one, but he is hardly displeased if on a hot summer's day, the sermon is dropped. He usually breathes a sigh of relief.

When the Catholic hears a Protestant sermon he notes a number of things. In most cases the sermon is on a moral theme, and could be heard without much, if any, change in a Catholic church. If he is an older Catholic he notices that the preaching style of the Protestant churches is changing, and as he sees it, for the better. The rather pompous, stylized tone is going away. The broad vowels affected earlier in the century have ceded to the normal pronunciation of everyday life. It used to be that on turning the radio dials to a sermon it was not necessary to ask if the speaker were Catholic or Protestant. The style gave the answer. A studied form of phrase and the use of a stilted tone marked Protestant sermons, but this is becoming rarer. Catholic and Protestant preachers are now quite straightforward in their approach to the topic, and the homiletic style is no longer artificial and fixed.

But it is revealing how the adherents of different faiths refer to their clerics. The Catholic used to say that his priest was a holy man; the Protestant spoke of his minister as a fine preacher; the Jew referred to his rabbi as a great scholar. Today the tendency of all is to refer to the cleric with the rather dubious compliment that he is a "regular guy."

One thing the Catholic does like in the worshiping Protestant community. There is a manly and stern piety manifested. Decorum and seriousness are palpable. The hymns sung may be a bit jingly and the words saccharine, but the Catholic has heard similar hymns in his own worship in spite of the fact that the liturgists are trying their hardest to get rid of them. The Camp Meeting still throws its shadow over an American evangelical service, though the Revival itself has become much more sedate. There is a world of difference between Billy Graham and Billy Sunday.

Of course Pentecostal worship simply amazes the Catholic. But then it also amazes most Protestants. It is not the bizarre activity of such services which surprises the Catholic, for he can see very bizarre things in some of his own churches. What frightens him is the lack of control which is by no means accidental to such prayer but a very principle. The Pauline insistence on decency in worship is a rule Catholics spontaneously respect, even if on occasions they do not live up to it.

In the same order of thought the Catholic reacts very badly to the spontaneous prayer spoken at Protestant gatherings. Certainly the idea of spontaneous prayer is unassailable but the way it works out frequently is uncomfortable. Some "spontaneous" prayer is evidently well prepared and rehearsed before the moment of pouring forth. In some cases it is written and read. When it is strictly *extempore,* there are many interspersals of *uhs* and *ahs,* betraying a conscious struggle in the man who is supposed to be uttering an overflow of thought and feeling. Those who are really masters at it, are frequently artificial and theatrical. And in spite of all its supposed spontaneity, it is remarkable how it usually comes out as a mosaic of King James Bible English, with *thees* and *thous* and *lookdowns.* Spontaneous it may be, but it is not the spontaneity of our daily existence but a labored attempt to achieve a studied biblical language expression. Then there is always the great danger that the man who is supposed to be praying to God is actually telling the audience what it should do. It is something like the man who knows that his conversation with X is being overheard and he takes the occasion to tell the eavesdroppers a thing or two.

As for the personal witness to grace received, it too can be grating on the hearer's sensitivities. Most experiences of most persons are not interesting nor highly significant. To be told of such experiences in public with an insinuated interpretation which is highly subjective and at times theologically or psychologically dubious, always makes me squirm. I remember once voicing this objection after having been exposed to such witness. The leader merely answered that Sister So-and-So's experience was very dear to her. I do not doubt it, but I could not help but feel that she should have cherished it in her own heart rather than embarrass the assembly with it.

It is in such moments that the Catholic becomes very grateful for the liturgical framework of public prayer. If he gives a blessing at table, he does not invent it with the great danger of becoming pathetic or irrelevant. He gives the ancient, consecrated formula, theologically sound and dignified. It exposes him to the danger of rattling it off like the multiplication table, but at least its content is not disturbing.

The Catholic also believes that the dearth of sacramental action in Protestant piety must impoverish it. Actually this was noted and stated by many Protestant military chaplains during the last war. When the soldier has been hit by a shell and in great pain, especially when there are hundreds in his situation, bible reading, or reflection is impossible from any point of view. What can the Protestant chaplain do for this man? He must have the impulse to imitate his Catholic colleague who in a brief, reverent action of symbolic significance understood by the tortured man receiving it, leaves him with the inner peace of faith in spite of his bodily suffering. Evangelical Protestants take a dim view of sacrament and sacramentals, yet these things are so eloquent and so in accord with human nature. To dismiss them all as magic is hardly a deep understanding of magic or of man or of God's condescension to him. Even the most severe Calvinist knows how telling the sign of the cross can be, and it is not a magical device when the Christian chaplain wears it on the lapel of his tunic. Catholics are favorably impressed with the Protestant insistence on the pure prayer of the heart but it is wise not to make it so pure that only an angel who has no passions can use it. The piety of man must be achieved in the human situation.

There is one image of Protestant piety which the Catholic admires and even envies. It is the image of the whole Protestant family gathered around the common table where father or mother reads the Bible out loud. This is the *lectio brevis et sincera* (short but heartfelt reading) so dear to Benedictine monks. It is, I am afraid, only an image because few Protestant families nowadays actually make it real. However, many Protestants individually do pore over the sacred text and make its message bear on their problems and life. This is undoubtedly genuine piety and true prayer according to the definition of St. Thomas for whom prayer was the elevation of the mind to God. There is here no question of polemic nor even merely study. It is an encounter with the saving Lord.

Perhaps this great insistence on the Book has kept Protestantism from writing other books. Some time ago a Protestant journal published an announcement of a collection of spiritual readings. The first section contained fifty books of devotion. There were some Catholic titles (including the two works of St. Augustine). The rest were well known Protestant tracts like Fox's *Book of the Martyrs* and Bunyan's *Pilgrim's Progress*. But there was nothing of the stature of St. Teresa's autobiography, the poetry of St. John of the Cross, the *Fioretti* of St. Francis of Assisi, de Sales' *Introduction to a Devout Life*. It was rich in polemical treatises, homiletic works, and biblical exegesis. Yet such books are not the most effective stimuli to devotion. It can be presumed that Protestantism by its history and theology wants to deal with the divine word rather than with the word of man. The Bible is enough for salvation.

I shall venture an essay at theory. My Protestant friends can tell me if there is any validity to it. It seems to me that Protestant piety is paradoxical. It is certainly a God-consciousness and a God-search. It has as its end immediate contact with God and his Christ. Protestantism makes much of the experience of the divine. Even fundamentalists do not believe that the mere letter of the Bible is the voice of God. They know very well that many read that word and come to conclusions quite different from those which they have achieved. They appeal to the Spirit speaking within the reader. It is the Spirit who speaks on the occasion of reading the text. There is much exegetical writing in Protestantism but the real impact of the Book is not from a scientific understanding of it but rather from an inner response to it which is not subject to scholarship. This inner response is the very heart of Protestant piety. It is a quasi-mystical experience.

What makes this paradoxical is the fact that Protestantism in most of its forms explicitly rejects the mystical approach to God. The fundamentalists in theory locate the revealing action of God in the biblical words. They say that the Bible is a simple book and it is only the pride of the learned which complicates it. This stand is not acceptable to any one who has made even the most superficial study of the Scriptures. How can an expression of the thought of men writing thousands of years ago in cultural situations so different from ours, be easily grasped in a translation? The fundamentalist rarely or never reflects on this phase of the Bible. The Book comes to him simply because he is rather simple in his approach to it. Even then his source of conviction is not the word in print but the word of the Spirit in his heart. Yet when he talks to you, he tries to persuade you that the *nudum verbum*, the mere word, says all that he believes. This kind of dialogue is of course distressing. But it is interesting because little by little the non-Protestant becomes aware that his Protestant friend is not relying on anything as objective as a printed statement but on a subjective experience. He disclaims mysticism and even speaks disparagingly of it, and yet at the very center of his own piety there is this quasi-mystical dynamism. This might explain why sacramental action is not so appealing to him. The sacrament is a material symbol of divine power. It does not claim to be that divine power unveiled. The Protestant wants to feel and perceive his God without veil and so the sacrament is not enough for him, for in the sacrament it is the symbol which is experienced, not God. He is very wary of the symbol because it is material. He fears idolatry and the symbol conjures up for him the idolatrous worship of those who know not Jehovah. He stands adamant in the persuasion that God must be experienced in himself, and he unwittingly discards the principle of divine incarnation.

Non-fundamentalists will say that I make too much of fundamentalism. They will point out that it is not dominant in Protestant life. Yet though this is true, the mystical élan is even more evident in broad Protestantism than in fundamentalism. The broad Protestant does not share the belief of the fundamentalist that the biblical word is the revealing action of God. He sees the word as a mere pointer to divine action which is to be grasped in a mysterious perception which is quite ineffable. This would seem to be even more mystical than the unwitting mysticism of the fundamentalist.

Such it seems to me is the paradox of Protestant piety. It is an effort to achieve mysticism in spite of the explicit rejection of the validity of mystical prayer. It has the aspect of great simplicity but actually is quite complicated. It is ambiguous about the use of sacraments because it does not want the reality of God mediated by things material. Its efforts are directed valiantly to the purity of the God-encounter, ignoring the fact that the encounter must take place in a material situation. As an effort one must recognize its nobility and valor but one cannot help but feel that this superhuman effort is involved in distressing frustrations.

It is strange that Catholics can feel close to different Protestant churches in some particular aspect, though in the totality of the other church's views there may be substantial opposition. So much of Episcopalianism is pleasing because there is a strong sense of tradition in that church. The Lutherans manifest a deep esteem for orthodoxy. They are not at all inclined to question the deity of Jesus of Nazareth. The fundamentalists take a strong stand on the reality of the supernatural which finds a resonance in the Catholic. Even the missionary zeal of the smaller sects is something appealing even though the Catholic feels that it is misdirected.

Protestant piety has its own structure. In its totality it puzzles the Catholic, but there are individual elements he understands and likes. He thinks that he can have the same elements in his own Church, but he sees Protestants devoted to individual elements more than Catholics. The usual result is that he urges his own people to a fuller Catholic expression of these elements. Then we see Catholics and Protestants doing the same things. Neither is really imitating the other but because of the example of one group, the other draws something similar from its own substance. It must be amusing to non-believers in this country to see the distinct and different churches engaged so often in the same type of action with quite different objectives. Still this cannot be avoided. The roots of Protestantism are in Catholicism and it would be surprising if there were no similarity at all in the approaches of the different churches to God and man.

One instance of this truth is the matter of Bible reading and Bible meditation. There seems to be a common Protestant persuasion that Catholics either may not or at least do not read the Bible. Of course this is quite erroneous. The Catholic liturgy contains many and lengthy Bible readings, and the language and illusions are always biblical. Many Catholics, following the lead of the patristic and medieval masters of the spiritual life, lean almost exclusively on the Bible. Four different Catholic English translations of the Bible have come forth in the last thirty years. What is surprising and delightful is that at the 1959 annual meeting of the Catholic Biblical Society an idea was aired and received enthusiastically, asking for a commission of Catholics and Protestants scholars to prepare a Bible translation which would be common to both churches, so that all English-speaking Christians would then have one and the same Bible.

It is of course true that the Catholics are not text-quoters as many Protestants are, but today the text-proof is no longer highly esteemed even in Protestant circles. It is also true that the *sola scriptura* idea, though admissable in Catholicism provided scripture and tradition are fused, will lead the Protestant to the Bible more directly and more exclusively.

However, it seems that the whole question of the Bible is not so divisive as once was thought. The flat fact is that in neither church is the Bible read enough.

3

Protestant Morality

American moral principles are to a high degree homogeneous. Protestants, Catholics, Orthodox, and Jews live basically alike. All are against murder, robbery, dishonesty, rape, adultery, and cruelty. We all stand for courtesy, kindliness, loyalty, and modesty. As the cynics say, we are all against sin; those who belong to a religious community and likewise those who do not. We all lament our current rash of juvenile delinquency and all are trying to do something about it. All are incensed with venality or partiality in our civil officials when it manifests itself. It may appear strange to some that the whole country was dismayed at the discovery that so insignificant a spectacle as the television quiz was rigged. It certainly was not strictly honest—but it was intended as entertainment and nobody was cheated in the whole business. Unlike other lands we frown on the licensing of prostitution, though it does take place in some American communities.

Yet there is a Protestant style of morality which distinguishes it from Catholic ethics, though the distinction is not substantial. "Rum, Rome and Rebellion" was the slogan used against the Catholics in the nineteenth century and the modest truth in the accusation was that the Catholics did not consider that the drinking of alcoholic beverages was immoral. They still don't. But today they are hardly alone in the matter. Of course Catholics agree wholeheartedly with Protestants that drunkenness is a sin but as they say, it is sinful because it is an abuse of drink rather than its legitimate use. Even the Catholic temperance societies never insinuate that drinking of itself and by its very nature is evil or contrary to the Gospel.

On the other hand, the Catholics show a nervous concern in the field of sex. They are against divorce, birth-control, literary or theatrical lack of modesty, exhibitionism, and sex activity outside of wedlock.

We might consider the Catholic's reaction to the moral emphases of American Protestantism. We have already mentioned the Protestant objection to alcohol. This is by no means universal but it still is a characteristic in the American image of Protestantism. As a rule Northern Protestants are not worried about the matter. In a social event organized by Episcopalians, Presbyterians, and Lutherans, there will be a modest place for a glass of wine or a cocktail. Northern Methodists feel an ambiguity about it. But in the South the puritanical spirit of evangelicalism has persuaded the civic communities to make stringent legislation about the traffic of demon rum. And yet bourbon whiskey comes precisely from this area! The Mormons are perhaps the strictest of all. In their communities not only is alcohol banned but even coffee and tea are proscribed. (But the church-owned Utah Hotel has a coffee-shop!) With this Protestant hostility to alcohol goes the resistance to smoking, though today it is not as strong as formerly. Even in the South I have been in Methodist meetings where ash-trays were available—and being used. But the southern evangelical more frequently than not, does not smoke—and yet tobacco is a major crop in the South.

Some of the smaller sects object to dancing, the theatre, and boxing. However, this is not general and these smaller groups have their counterparts in Catholicism. In general, drama, the dance, and sports are very much at home in Protestantism, no less than in Catholicism; and they were at home in Protestantism earlier.

The problem of drunkenness (something distinct from alcoholism) in the United States is of course a grave one. Yet it hardly seems objective to make of it a major concern of the community. In the Scriptures there are forthright condemnations of drunkenness. Some ascetic groups like the Nazarites never touched wine at all. But wine was the beverage of the people at large and our Lord took it. This seems so clear in the biblical books, and the explanations of some Protestant anti-alcohol campaigners whereby wine in the Scriptures means unfermented grape-juice, will not stand up in the light of sound philology. Because of this the Catholic wonders why so many Protestants give so much importance to this question. The impression is received that *a* social problem has become *the* social problem and the high imperative of the Gospel concerns drinking in a primary way. It has become a badge of American Protestantism, though not all Protestants wear it. Why? European Protestants do not share this persuasion. What makes American Protestants so nervous about it?

Along with this attitude to liquor the average American Protestant condemns gaming in all its forms. He is scandalized by the Bingo parties which loom so large in many Catholic churches. The Catholic agrees that gambling can be vicious, especially if it leads to general moral deterioration as it frequently does. However, petty games of hazard are not of themselves immoral and according to Catholic moral theology, they can be legitimate forms of recreation. The churches use them as sources of revenue, a custom employed in Europe by congregations both Catholic and Protestant. Again the Catholic asks why does the American Evangelical condemn all gaming on principle. It has perhaps to do with the mores of the American frontier in the nineteenth century where evangelicalism worked mightily against sin. At all events the Catholic is perplexed.

As has been stated, the Catholic is nervous in matters of sex. Here the Protestant is far more serene and open. There is of course a Protestant prudery just as there is a Catholic prudery, but I am not referring to either. It seems to the Catholic that the Protestant is not too worried about birth-control, obscenity in the theatre or in print, and exhibitionism in public. Here the Protestant stands for liberty while the Catholic considers it license. These different attitudes produce friction in the national community. The Protestant thinks the Catholic immoral because he drinks and plays Bingo—and it gives the Protestant satisfaction. The Catholic thinks the Protestant immoral because he will not fight birth-control and it makes the Catholic feel morally superior.

These attitudes to drinking, gambling, and sex are very conspicuous but somehow they are not too significant. The real difference between the two communities is their distinctive conceptions of virtue. The Protestant esteems the natural virtues while the Catholic makes more of the supernatural virtues. The Protestant thinks highly of truthfulness, sobriety, simplicity, reliability, and industriousness. The Catholic most esteems humility, mortification, penance, chastity, poverty, and abnegation. Both admire charity, but Catholic charity is warmer and more personal, while Protestant charity is more efficient and better organized. These remarks are of course generalizations and like all generalizations they must be taken in general but by no means universally.

The result of the different tempers of moral conception will be Protestant reserve, stiffness and gravity in contrast to the Catholic's tendency toward spontaneity, Baroque display and even Rabelaisian earthiness. Perhaps this is the meaning of the rollicking arrogance in Belloc's verses:

> Heretics all, whoever you be,
> In Tarbes or Nimes, or over the sea,
> You never shall have good words from me.
> *Caritas non conturbat me.*
>
> But Catholic men that live upon wine
> Are deep in the water, and frank and fine:
> Wherever I travel I find it so,
> *Benedicamus Domino.*[1]

There are theologies behind these differing façades. The Protestant tradition began with a concentrated gaze on Original Sin. The evil in man was excruciatingly recognized. Martin Luther had his gay and lighter moments but he seemed to be ashamed of them. John Calvin made of Geneva a very proper and prim community. Neither theologian put any saving value on works, but both insisted that faith brought forth good works. In fact, the absence of such works infallibly showed up a lack of conversion. Calvin especially despised the Catholic doctrine of mortal and venial sins. Sin was always sin and there should be no mitigation or toleration of it.

The doctrine of the total depravity of mankind must by its own logic produce a sour evaluation of human endeavor. True, few Protestants today would accept this doctrine except in some Pickwickian sense. But customs and attitudes outlive the dynamic ideas which brought them forth. Strangely enough, the Reformers did not think that sin could be avoided but nonetheless they had little patience with it. In fact they were fanatically intolerant of it. The merits of Christ hid human evil from the face of God, and union with Christ made a new man but he was always *simul justus et peccator* (simultaneously righteous and a sinner). This message should make for joy and it was conceived to do so. But it didn't. Sin and evil cloud the vision of Protestantism and a certain suspicion of things human is engendered. When the Protestant turns humanist, he becomes secularist as well.

In Catholic theology Original Sin is very much remembered.

Augustine and Thomas never forget it. Catholic ascetical training is a systematic effort to deal with an ever abiding concupiscence. But there is the belief that man can become intrinsically righteous in spite of the permanence of the stimulus toward sin. *Ex injusto fit justus* (the unrighteous man becomes righteous) was the doctrine of Trent in answer to Luther's conception of justification. Grace is not only the power in God but also a God-given power in man which works physically. Man with this grace can work righteously but he is called to make effort. The effort in as far as it is merely human is not saving but because it substantially derives from divine Grace freely accepted and freely used, it is salvific. The perduring effects of concupiscence will mar the perfection of the best act, but this is inevitable in the human situation. An understanding God will give the imperfection indulgence; it is venial. Even when because of concupiscence man sins gravely, this sin can be wiped out, not of course as an act but as a condition, by the forgiving Christ acting through the instrumentality of his prolongation, the Church.

Thomas Aquinas also changed the Augustinian doctrine of sin. With Augustine he taught that only action rooted in freely given faith and love leads man to God, his final end. But he also taught there was another norm of goodness which must not be overlooked. When a man builds his house, he is doing a good thing, and it is doctrinaire to say that he is sinning in building shelter for himself and his family. No one will accuse him of wrong-doing in this kind of an effort. The norm of judging is not the supernatural principle of faith and love. It is the natural norm of natural right action. Such action is not of itself salvific but it is not bad. Protestants are irked by the Catholic recognition of a natural scheme of things. They feel that this is a recession from the Gospel message. But the Catholic sees in the words of Genesis, which tell us that all that God created is good, a revealed truth which must not be summarily dismissed from our vision of things.

The Catholic conception of Natural Law whereby secular things are to be judged, has not always been properly understood—even by Catholics. The Natural Law is not a code of legislation written in heaven or in the human heart. It is rather the recognition that there is a moral dimension inherent in all reality. Creation is good because it is divine creation. Not only is creation good, it is also rationally constructed so that reason in the abstract has the capacity to see what the rational scheme is. Working in accord with this

scheme, man acts morally well, even though such moral rectitude
is not salvation. Man as man is called to live this way, and if he
does not, he upsets the scheme of things. This brings evil and suffering to himself and to his community.

The absence of the Natural Law theory in current Protestantism
produces a *malaise*. (Protestants in the past were staunch supporters
of the concept.) There are many moral questions to which the Protestant can today give no answer. More basic for this incapacity is,
of course, the absence of a living authority with the power of teaching and defining questions. It is not easy to give precise answers
to moral issues with a simple reliance on Scripture. The moral
question of the present is removed from the situation which the
Old and New Testaments envisage. Circumstances, as we all know,
alter cases. The Sermon on the Mount is rich in principles but the
application of them is not given in the pages of the Bible. "Thou
shalt not kill" is a simple command until we bring it down to a
concrete situation. Does it mean not to kill anything at all, not even
a stag, a lion, or a fly? Does it mean only not to kill human beings,
and if that be the case, is war or self-defense outlawed? Does it
forbid abortion as the Catholics say it does? Mere Bible reading
will not solve these problems. Even a reader of good will can only
come to a subjective certitude in the light of his knowledge of the
biblical texts.

The result in modern Protestantism is a complete anarchy in
moral judgment. Some believe that birth-control through artificial media is against the will of God while others think that there
may be Christian justification for it. Most Protestants are adverse
to divorce but practically they accept it, nor is there any other judge
in the matter than the secular magistrate. Some Protestants are
great lovers of animals and go to great extremes to protect the brute
kingdom but it is not easy to see what their principle of judgment
is. Instances of this ambiguity could be cited endlessly.

It seems to me that Protestants have only the vaguest of principles to aid them to make moral decisions. They look with distaste
at the power of Catholic bishops to declare a concrete action immoral, yet since there is no such authority in their churches, they
frankly do not know what should be done. In good Protestant
fashion every individual with the greatest sincerity possible makes
up his own mind. This is certainly an exercise of sincerity which
is a good thing, but do not we all know that great mistakes are
made in all sincerity? A simple Catholic youth does know what is

right and what is wrong in concrete circumstances. A Protestant may not agree with his norms of rightness, but he must certainly envy him for having answers to questions which inevitably face him and his Protestant comrade as well. I have met Protestant young people who are deeply worried about this lacuna in their lives. Even the well meant advice to see their ministers is not too helpful because they know that they do not have to listen to the minister. They are left to solve their problems by a moral feeling which they have developed at home and in their environment. But that is only a feeling. It is not a principle and young people want reasons for action. Feelings are not enough.

An interesting development is taking place. In the past the Protestants were strong advocates of Sabbath observance—on Sunday of course. Their tradition favored the Blue Sunday: no theatres, no baseball games, no picnics, no fun. They found the Catholics non-cooperative. But things have moved rapidly in this area. The Jewish community cannot look kindly on enforced Sunday observance, although as a matter of fact Sunday is no longer blue. The threat today is that Sunday will altogether lose its sacral character. Now the Catholics join the Protestants in an effort to preserve Sunday observance. In the past they were cold to Protestant efforts to keep the day holy in the Protestant fashion but today they warmly support Protestant campaigns, or try to enlist Protestant support for campaigns of their own.

What happened? Catholics were always for the principle of Sunday observance. They were willing to apply this principle much more broadly than Protestants. But now the principle is at stake and the Catholics are as militant as the Protestants were. This in general explains much Catholic action. They are always concerned with a principle and they object against or press for things not too significant except in as far as they point to a great principle. A Catholic bishop may ban a bathing-beauty contest. The matter of itself is hardly of transcending importance but the principle of Christian modesty is. The bishop is interested in that principle and he believes that in certain contexts this principle is at stake. Whether or not his evaluation is exact in every instance is not so important. What is important is that the chaos of subjectivism is avoided and objective principles are defended. If the evaluation has been mistaken, it will be changed in the light of reality.

As the Catholic sees it, the Protestant has too little moral guidance. It is of course true that every moral decision must be personal. No one can make it for another. Yet morality is an art and it has its rules. Rules beget conventions and the whole moral code of a community is an amalgam of universal principles and ephemeral conventions. It is hard to distinguish between the two and for this very reason society cannot permit that every Tom, Dick, and Harry make that distinction. The need of distinction is present but for the greater good of all the distinction must be left to a responsible minority of the community. This does not guarantee the infallibility of such decision, but it does guarantee that order will survive.

On the Protestant principle, it is most difficult to reach a consensus. Different preachers will advocate different kinds of action but they will be effective only in as far as they are persuasive. No one in conscience has to listen to the preacher. Concretely a congregation accepts certain patterns of action as obligatory. Yet even then the individual can leave the congregation without doing violence to conscience. If the congregation coincides with the general community, it will be very hard for the individual to reject the norms of the congregation because to do so means social ostracism. But here the motive for conformity will not be a moral decision but rather expediency, which is hardly a good moral motive.

One is always struck with the customs of some of the smaller sects. They will all wear certain styles of dress and do their hair in a prescribed way. This is also true of the Catholic religious orders wherein priests and sisters use a distinctive garb. But one feels that Amish dress is different from the dress of a Sister of Charity. The latter knows that by appropriate legislation her garb can be changed. Is there in the Amish community any built-in power to change its garb? Is the custom like the law of the Medes and Persians which cannot be changed? The original dress adopted was a protest against worldliness, but with time the dress is merely eccentric. Originally convention was opposed to convention but with time the convention becomes a principle. With time something accidental has taken on a sacral character forever.

To put it all briefly, a Catholic sees a distinctive Protestant morality but he cannot discover a working moral norm in Protestantism. There is indeed a fluid unity of Protestant moral views but there seems to be no moral authority capable of justifying the unity in fact.

4

The Protestant Stance

Every individual has his character. There is a personal style in his thought and action. Such a style I call his stance. What is true of the individual, is analogously true of a concrete community. Hence there is a Protestant stance.

Looking with Catholic eyes, one element in American Protestantism is its confident audacity. I suppose that many a Protestant on reading these words will be totally surprised. He takes it for granted that the shoe is on the other foot. To make my point, I must explain. The audacity referred to is not a bullying spirit, much less rudeness. It is a naive and energetic thrust forward from an idea sincerely conceived. From Luther's day onward, simplicity of soul and freedom of the spirit were always characteristic of the churches of the Reform. The Catholic on the other hand, is always led to test his ideas by tradition and authority. Corporate infallibility induces an awareness of personal fallibility as a limitation on thought and action. The Catholic makes his statements with caution and restraint lest he overstate something which might well be true. The Protestant is not so constrained. It is astonishing to see the security which fundamentalists manifest in their interpretation of the scriptures. They quote isolated verses in a sense which will not harmonize with others which they calmly ignore and serenely dismiss even when pointed out. They are so sure. They are not bothered by doubts or evidences against their positions.

Nor are liberal Protestants any different. They will proceed from postulates which are not carefully criticized, and carry on with an

enthusiastic assuredness which is incredible. It seems to derive
from an unconcern for tradition. Protestants of any school can
bring forth theories which are Arian, Nestorian, or Gnostic. Many
will not recognize their own positions under these labels because
they seem to be unmindful of the past. When it is pointed out that
their position is not new and that it has been rejected for centuries,
they remain unmoved. They seem to have no feeling of *malaise*
because their ideas have been rejected by the Church in ages long
ago. Their idea was vividly achieved in the present and with all
sincerity. No other recommendation seems necessary.

This attitude brings virtue in its train. Protestants are certainly
tolerant of diversity. In a Protestant meeting extreme positions can
be proposed by different speakers and no hearer shows distress. He
may inwardly dislike one or other of the positions, but in courtesy
and kindness he tolerates the champion of a disliked thought.

A generous tolerance is therefore quite proper of the Protestant
stance. It has its paradoxical quality. It is tolerant of diversity but
irritated by the theory of conformity. As many a Protestant has
said, he is tolerant of anything but intolerance, and the insistence
that the Christian faith must be doctrinally one is for him intolerance.
Any Protestant can sympathetically or at least objectively deal with
any Catholic doctrines in isolation. What annoys him is their fixed
place in the Catholic totality. Doctrines like episcopacy, physical
presence of Christ in the Eucharist, monasticism, do not annoy him
at all. He may not care for them personally but he is quite ready
for others to hold them. What he dislikes strongly is the statement
that these or other doctrines *must* be held by the Christian. The
"mustness" makes him bridle. If the theses are presented as free
choices, the Protestant has no quarrel with them. But they must
be free. There seems to be a lack of preoccupation for the demands
of total consistency. I must hasten to add that there are outstanding
exceptions. Paul Tillich certainly feels the need of consistency of
whole and parts, and this perhaps is the reason why his theology
is so distasteful to many Protestant thinkers.

Many Catholics glibly say that Protestantism is emotionalism.
Tillich in contrast says that it is the most intellectual form of
Christianity. This brings up the second factor in the Protestant
stance. It has an intellectuality. It favors scholarship and has always
produced it. Luther constructed his own theology in the light of
his age's improved knowledge of classical languages. Because of
the Protestant principle that the Bible alone is the definitive source

of doctrine, Protestants fostered literacy for all the people and developed biblical science. Many Protestants enthusiastically entered into the spirit of the Age of Enlightenment and later accepted the method of scientific positivism while the Catholics were very reluctant to admit these movements into their own thought, though they eventually did come to terms with them.

There is then a Protestant type of intellectualism and it is very dynamic on the American scene. To deny its reality is blindness or nonsense. However, to understand it amiss is also disastrous. Protestant intellectualism fits best into the framework of Kantian philosophy, and Immanuel Kant has rightly been called the Protestant Thomas Aquinas.

This kind of thinking has a number of facets. It makes much of the empirical approach to data. It is ultimately a scepticism. It overcomes its own scepticism by voluntarism.

The empirical approach of Protestant thought is most clear in the great philological contributions it has made to biblical understanding. The scriptural text has been carefully edited in the last five centuries and the great editors for the most part have been Protestants. Scientific exegesis until quite recently was mainly a Protestant endeavor. The best known histories of dogma come from Protestant pens. Catholics figure prominently in patristic studies but the Protestant effort has been neither mean nor insignificant. Walther von Loewenich insists that this is the essence of Protestantism: the direct approach to the Bible in the exclusive light of scientific exegesis. For him theological exegesis as something distinct from scientific interpretation is spurious.

Science works on postulates agreeable to an age. In different ages these postulates will be different. That is why Protestant thinking is different from generation to generation. The literal fundamentalist is still clinging to the postulates of the sixteenth and seventeenth centuries whereby it was supposed that honesty and commonsense in the presence of a satisfactory translation of the Scriptures could achieve their meaning adequately. This method was applied to any proposition in the whole book, because all texts were supposed to be effata of God himself. The higher and lower criticism of the text are not congenial to the fundamentalist, and if the title of the epistle says that it was written by Peter, that ends the question of authorship.

The eighteenth- and nineteenth-century postulates for scientific interpretation were far more sophisticated than the previous centuries allowed. Common sense approaches a text with a spontaneous readiness to believe what is said. The scientific approach comes to the words with a questioning and doubting mind. The proposition must be rigorously tested before it can be accepted in any way at all. Nor is it now presumed that the words are the very speech of God. By this method much less is derived from the text than in the previous way.

The twentieth century has further discovered that statements are not all alike. There is logical affirmation, mythical statement and symbolic assertion. The discovery of the literatures of the Near East also shows that there were stylized literary forms which we do not use in our writings today. History did not mean for Livy, Thucydides, or Babylonian writers what it means now, and it is a mistake to take their historical affirmations as if they were historical in our sense of the word. The result of all these recognitions makes modern exegesis quite different from what was offered in former times. In the current approach, fundamentalism is simply irrelevant.

Science, unlike mathematics or even philosophy, offers little certitude to man. It aims only at high probability, with which it is satisfied. All positions are relative to postulates and to the state of the data. Scientific statements are at best inadequate approximations to absolute truth, which is quite unknowable. The thing in itself lies beyond man's cognizance. This is of course Kantian and sceptical. Thesis and antithesis are both valid and we make a synthesis of them both only to give peace to our minds which are so ill at ease in the presence of contradiction. God is in a vague way knowable but he is really ineffable. The historical Jesus is now the great unknown. We had better not talk about him but rather take seriously the picture of him which the faith of the scriptural writers painted in myth and symbol.

There is here a despair of knowledge. A form of intellectualism has paralyzed the intellect. If it tries to make absolute judgements, it is ridiculed as illusory. There is darkness over the face of things and all is tohu-wabohu.

But the will can save us yet. We can take a stand, not in pure reason but in practical reason—which latter means the will with its moral dynamism. We make decisions and they can be life-giving. Religion is thus a call for decision. We make an act of trust on a meaning and power we do not see nor understand, and it is called faith. It is valid if it is scientifically criticized but of course it is not a scientific conclusion, nor even a scientific postulate. The intellect has failed us, but the failure is swallowed up in the triumph of will.

This brief description is not intended as a caricature. I sincerely believe most Protestant thinkers will see in it a rough outline of the basis of Protestant thinking. It fascinates and frightens the Catholic. His church makes much of intelligence and insists that the intellect can reach truth absolutely. His church is well aware that such knowledge will not be comprehensive but it insists that it is adequate. The Protestant, on the other hand, is amazed by this stand. For him relativism is the most man can expect from his knowledge and the formulation thereof. Certitudes do not derive from knowledge but from voluntary decisions.

This situation makes dialogue very difficult. Both sides can say "I think so and so." They can do no more. No dialectic in the older sense of the word is possible because there is no common epistemological ground. Epistemology divides Catholic and Protestant much more than the tenets of their respective beliefs. Agreement is possible in the realm of empirical phenomena. Both sides will agree that Jerusalem is in Palestine and that there are twenty-seven books in the New Testament. Things of this kind do not divide us. When it comes to the ultimate meaning of the phenomena, we are in conflict and there seems no way but the grace of God to get us out of it. A meeting of Catholic and Protestant is not so much the confrontation of Peter and Paul but rather of Kant and Aquinas.

What disturbs the Catholic is the danger that Protestantism will lose the substance of the Christian doctrine. Christianity is an historical thing with an identity which is precise. Any reform within it must be a recall to the substance found in the two thousand year old continuity. It is not a mere question of deriving a religious vision from the documents of the Church's infancy. The vision as it is contained in the Christian tradition is normative for the Christian. To be truly evangelical we must be simultaneously truly catholic. Evangelical and catholic are not words of opposition but words of total compenetration. The Christian meaning of the evangelical books is the meaning which the historical catholic church found there. To derive another meaning is no longer Christian. The new meaning may produce a new religion but it is not historical Christianity. Call it Neo-Christianity if you will, but do not label it simply with a tag which is proper to something else.

Apostolic succession is engrained in the Catholic. It means that he is now in the formal fellowship founded by the first Christian preachers and which continued unbroken through the centuries.

When a Catholic simplistically asks the Protestant: "Where were you before Luther?", he has a point. He is asking, to what historical fellowship did you belong. To the Catholic it is incomprehensible to be told that the Reformers stayed in the catholic Church while the Catholic Church in one single moment fell out of it by apostasy. As Chesterton wittily put it, it is hardly correct to say that in a violent storm Windsor Castle was blown away from one of its roof tiles. Protestantism is rooted in Catholicism and only by that reason can it claim continuity with the first Christian community. That claim, moreover, is justified only by the hypothesis of the validity of Catholicism itself. In their own way the Mormons see this. They justify their existence by an entirely new revelation made in our time, uncontained either in Protestantism or Catholicism. As the Mormon sees it, Protestantism derives from Catholicism which had already lost all authority at the moment of the separation. For the Mormon then, Protestantism could not be a channel to the revelation of Christ. Nor can Catholicism, but with this difference; Catholicism did have the authority up to the fourth century and then it became apostate. But the Mormon sees that the Protestant claim to possess Christian revelation must be derived from the Catholic Church. Nor can it be denied that the first Protestants left the Catholic Church.

In the light of these reflections the Catholic's concern with Protestantism centers on its capacity to retain the perennial Christian substance in its state of separation. Now, men like Paul Tillich have stated publicly that Catholicism has done a better job at conserving the Christian substance. In other words they see as the Catholic sees that the substance can become thin in the Protestant churches. What worries the Catholic most is that it may become so thin as to vanish. Perhaps the Protestant may be surprised, but the Catholic does not wish to see this. As long as the *vestigia ecclesiae* (vestiges of the Church) are in Protestantism, we are not altogether divided. There is ground for an ecumenical hope. However, should the scepticism and voluntarism of Protestant thought continue to grow, will these vestiges remain vital? Can we even talk to each other meaningfully if our epistemologies are so different?

There is then in the stance of Protestantism a peculiar intellectualism, an intellectualism not wholly unlike the intellectualism of current secularism. It is quite unlike Catholic intellectualism. The result is that Protestantism must feel nearer to the secularists than to the Catholics. And that from the Catholic point of view is most unfortunate.

The third characteristic of the Protestant stance is its abiding modernity. The Protestant is up to date. The cultural wind which blows at any given moment finds no breakwall in the Protestant spirit. Protestants usually accept it enthusiastically. When naturalism was the light of the times, Protestant theology was naturalist; when sociology was in ascendency, the gospel was the Social Gospel; when pessimism overcame optimism, Neo-Orthodoxy was pessimistic. When the spirit of the age is literalistic, then Protestants have a Puritan worship, but when symbol becomes meaningful to the people, Protestant worship is liturgical.

This readiness to adapt to the spirit of the times is undoubtedly an advantage for Protestantism. Every man is of his age and he wishes to be at peace with it. In the younger members of any generation there is an enthusiasm for the specific spirit of their own time. The men of the day will be prone to admire the flexibility of Protestantism. Every new movement makes the promise of being the wave of the future and all movements do influence the future in one way or the other. The language of Protestant theology is quite different in the present than it was in any period of the past. The Protestant feels no compunction in making such a change because the only past with which he is decisively concerned is the day of the infant Church, and this period he constructs quite freely according to the postulates accepted by his time. In accordance with his faith he wants to make his day like that far off day rather than like yesterday. Time and history do not cause the Protestant too much worry, for he does not see them as continuous or embodying an identity. He stresses the catastrophic and discontinuous nature of the historical process nor does his loyalty embrace every historical moment since the first Pentecost. He can easily admit that many periods were simply aberrations from the original thing, and even the original reality was not necessarily true to itself.

There are moments when the Catholic envies the Protestant's modernity. In the Catholic Church there is always a suspicion of current time. Catholicism adjusts slowly to any given age and this can produce impatience in the Catholics of the age. Yet when the Catholic reflects, he realizes that the tendency to modernity can be a luxury at once too costly and quite unnecessary. The Catholic cannot in consistency with his faith refuse allegiance to the Church of the patristic age, or of the Middle Age, or of the Renaissance,

or of the nineteenth century. He believes that there is and was only
one Church and the one he belongs to now is the same one which
he finds in the epistles of Cyprian, in the writings of St. Bernard,
in the verses of Dante, in the sermons of Bossuet, and the essays
of Newman. He will never dismiss these men as ultimately irrelevant. He will sift carefully what is ephemeral in their works
from what is the abiding faith of their time, which latter will be
his own faith. The Catholic must be conscious of the past just as he
is inevitably conscious of the present—and even of the future. The
whole action of ecclesiastical authority is always a break on modernism. This will not make the Catholic anti-modern but he cannot throw
himself into the now without caution and wariness. Changes will indeed come and there is evolution in dogma but novelty must not be
revolutionary nor reckless. To the man who is thoroughly modern
this attitude is necessarily treasonable. The Protestant easily escapes
his ire but the Catholic will be its certain object. The Catholic has
the consolation that modernity is shifting and uncritical; what is
wisdom in one modernity is folly in another. This consolation,
however, does not eliminate the malaise produced by being left
behind as the band-wagon moves away. We all like to get on the
band-wagon, even when it is not wise to do so.

Of course modernity always has its truth. It usually grasps onto
a valid insight of the moment. What makes the insight modern is
that a passion surrounds it and the union of passion and insight
usually produces a distortion of the insight. When the passion goes,
the insight still has its value but it has lost its modernity. Catholics
accept many things deriving from "modern" insights but they do
so after the insight has been freed from modernity and is in consequence no longer modern.

Where Protestant modernity makes its most significant gains is
in the area of communication. The Protestant speaks the language
of his day with ease and fluency. The concerns of the moment are
the starting point of his conversation. The result is that he is always
relevant, or at least seems so. In this context what he says seems
always to make sense. The fact that today's modernity contradicts
utterly yesterday's modernity is no disadvantage because yesterday's modernity is the butt of current modernity's scorn.

There are three elements proper to a good vision of reality. It
must be coherent with the data of experience. It must be a consistent unity in the light of logic. It must have an economical harmony of parts which will give it beauty. Plato distrusted the data

of experience, not because they were data but because the data came to men in the distortion of human experience. In consequence he put more trust in inner consistence and beauty. Consistence and beauty discipline experience so that experience does not have the last word. Plato was anything but a sceptic but he was profoundly sceptical of experience. He had a strange insight into what the Christian theologians call original sin (or what Freudians call the domination of irrational instinct over conscious achievement).

The nisus of Anglo-Saxon thinking has always been toward the primacy of experience. In the British tradition this is quite clear. Some wag has defined basic epistemological positions in terms of a baseball umpire—calling strikes and balls. The Scholastic umpire calls them as they are. The Kantian subjectivist calls them as he sees them. The Existentialist umpire insists that they are what he calls them. The Protestant by and large is a subjectivist with a strong leaning toward existentialism.

In our time Thomism has taken on a respectability it did not have fifty years ago. The influence of men like Jacques Maritain and Étienne Gilson is responsible for the fact. Yet it is interesting to see Protestants studying St. Thomas. Some go to him but do not stay long. The utter realism and sober objectivity of Thomistic thought simply baffle the Protestant reader. The rigorous logic of Aquinas rarely impresses the Protestant who so often is cold to metaphysics and logical structure. The result is that most Protestants find little in Thomism which gives them deep satisfaction. Those who study him with something more than rapid superficiality recognize that there is robust thinking in the Scholastic doctor, but it is not the kind of thinking they find profitable. Some will tell you in all simplicity that they found nothing in him. There are indeed others who can become quite enthusiastic in their study of St. Thomas, but for reasons which usually amaze the Catholic.

The whole point of this digression is to underline the modernity of Protestantism and to point to its root. Metaphysical consistency and logical beauty are not high values for the average Protestant. He gives pre-eminence to experience, which of course is not merely a discovery of the real but also an emotional reaction to reality. Empiricism is timely while metaphysical intellectualism is timeless.

In our day we see this working out in the realm of scriptural studies. Among Protestant theologians—conservative, neo-conservative, and neo-liberal—there is a heavy stress on being biblical. Everybody is doing biblical theology. Of course the word is absolutely ambiguous. If it only means that the scriptures are the privileged source from which the theologian derives his data and orientation, then the stress on biblical study is not at all modern. It has been the constant and admitted practice of Christian theologians for two thousand years. The theological writings of Origen, Chrysostom, Augustine, Bernard, and Aquinas are saturated with biblical quotations, references, and allusions.

But the modern cry for biblical theology does not mean primary or even exclusive reliance on Scripture. What is being advocated is the return to Hebrew terms and categories. In the attitude of not a few Protestant theologians, Greek is a curse-word. The telling blow in dialogue is to show that the other man has been guilty of using Greek and not Hebrew modes of thought and expression. Quite literally, the current Protestant theologian fears the Greeks, even when they bear gifts.

Actually what is referred to as Greek is often not Greek at all. It can at times be quite properly Hebrew. What the current condemnation of Greek means is the rejection of logical discourse resting on a recognized metaphysics with the result that we have clear and consistent terms and concepts. Certainly it is true that the Bible is not a source book for metaphysics, nor did metaphysics greatly engage the attention of the biblical authors. They were not victims of the obsession for clear and distinct ideas. They were certainly more kerygmatic than didactic.

But for understanding, the so called Greek way is superior. The Georgics of Virgil have a lovely charm but even though they are dedicated to the subject of agriculture, they are not a proper textbook for a school of agronomy. Undoubtedly there are insights you can get from the Georgics which are completely lacking in manuals of agricultural science, but these latter cannot be replaced by the former.

Admittedly there is a great danger in clarity. For clarity to be achieved, much of the data must be eliminated or distorted. Clarity is not a guarantee of truth. But clarity is necessary for accurate communication. One can suspect that the current enthusiasm for "Hebrew" categories derives from the unclarity of Hebrew modes of expression. Actually there is a metaphysic in a Hebrew pronouncement just as there is in the statements of the Greeks, but the Hebrew is quite willing to bracket his metaphysics. The modern theologian can then wittingly or unwittingly remove the bracket and insert one of his own. Reconstruction of the Hebrew statement is then easier and we need not worry whether the reconstruction is or is not a valid expression of the Hebrew writer's thought. That was never too clear and precise anyway.

Now you cannot proceed in this fashion if you believe that a statement is an affirmation concerning reality as it is. Such a belief is "Greek" and the rejection of the Greek may well be a suicidal scepticism with regard to the possibility of the intellect achieving the objective real.

In spite of the statement of Paul Tillich that Protestantism is the most intellectual form of Christianity, it is well known that Protestantism has always had a distrust of intelligence. Some Protestant divines have expressed this distrust quite forcefully. Yet the Christian theologian is necessarily engaged in the enterprise characterized by St. Anselm as *fides quaerens intellectum* (faith in search of understanding). It seems that the Protestant theologian is inevitably exposed to a kind of schizophrenia. Because he is a Protestant he is sceptical of intelligence and because he is a theologian he must believe in intellect. This kind of situation requires acrobatic skill.

Once more we have an attachment to modernity. As stated above there is passion in modernity. The passion has many elements of which two are resentment and hope. Modernity is a cry of revolt against the past. The sins of the preceding generation are finally brought to judgment—and they are severely castigated. But it is not from a pure love of justice. The dictamina of the past are resented because they were contrary to us. In substituting our insights for the insights of our fathers we have the hope that all the *aporiae* we inherited from our ancestors will wither away. They well may, but in disappearing they make room for the *aporiae* consequent on our ideas.

I wonder if Protestant complacency in modernity is not a sign of resentment against pure intelligence. Modernity gloats in showing that the intelligence of yesterday was really folly. For a man who distrusts intelligence this phase of modernity is most congenial. Intelligence is used to humble intellect. You can be as intellectual as you please, but you use intelligence to achieve freedom from it.

For the Catholic this whole position is impossible and he is faced with a heavy burden in consequence. He is often tempted to drop the burden in order to enjoy the freedom of modernity. The burden consists in respecting pure intelligence, not only in its current mani-

festations and achievements, but also in all that it has done in all
the eras of our cosmos. Hence there must be laborious essays at
reconciliation of past and present; effort at critical pruning of the
conquests of intellect; caution in the use of intelligence with an
ever high regard for it. This is a burden of which so many of my
Protestant friends seem to be free. But I personally feel no great
envy. After all I have found the yoke is sweet and the burden light.

5

The Protestant Fear

Fear is the feeling a man experiences when he foresees approaching pain or destruction. It is an experience all men know because the threat of pain and destruction is intrinsic to the human situation. Not all fear is panic. A certain amount of it is highly salutary, for it effectively turns us away from the evil before us. Because of fear men have increased their power and wrought great things. It is not a pleasant source of action, but it certainly is highly dynamic. Fear is constrictive and harrowing but the degrees of its *malaise* are proportionate to the size of the evil foreseen and to the degree of its imminence.

A man's fears tell us much about the man. The fear which a child has of the dark, which is really a fear of the unknown, is a sign of immaturity. Older people approach the dark without dismay. They even seek it out because it can be the occasion of peace. The fear which the citizen of a simple culture had of demons with which the culture peopled the world told us little about the world but much about the ignorance of primitive man. The fear which the paranoiac has of some ubiquitous "them" who are planning, plotting, and encompassing his ruin speaks volumes of the paranoiac's twisted psyche.

The Catholic, being human like the Protestant, Jew, Muslim or atheist, knows fear. He knows it in his individual existence as well as in his collective reality. His collective fear is more to our point than his numberless individual fears. The Catholics had an up-hill climb to make in the United States. The Protestant matrix of nineteenth-century America restricted the field of action for the Catholic. Today these restrictions are minimal nor highly visible. Most Catholics in the metropolitan East rarely become conscious of them.

One thing no Catholic is ever afraid of. He is not worried about the death of his Church. The very faith which makes him a Catholic also assures him that the Catholic Church will abide until the Savior come again. The Church may be exterminated here, there, or elsewhere. History has shown it abundantly in the past. Tunis is not Catholic—but it was so once. There are few Catholics in Sweden but it was a Catholic country centuries ago. However, the Church will exist and it will have tough vitality in the world unto the end. This is Catholic faith. When the Catholic doubts about it, he is no longer a Catholic.

The Catholic can be very fearful about the life of the Church where he is. He can see it threatened. If he loves that place, fear will make him sad. He does not wish to go into exile nor yet burrow into an underground existence. At the moment the American Catholic is not afraid of the suppression of Catholicism in the United States. He is afraid of the communists because if they should win the land, then Catholicism must return to the catacombs. He is not afraid of the Protestants who are still the majority because he does not find in them the desire or the power to liquidate the Catholic Church. Catholic fears concerning the Protestants center on the Protestant tendency to make of Catholics second-class citizens. This the Catholic resents quite bitterly and he is always afraid that the Protestants might at least regionally allow their tendency to bloom into full flower.

The American Catholic is not the only American with fears. The Protestant has his fears too. Looming large in these fears is the "Catholic threat." Some Protestants are quite paranoiac about it. They see that strange but powerful force, the "Hierarchy," gathered in secret council somewhere in the depths of the large cities plotting carefully the destruction of the faithful sons of the Reformation. They have unlimited funds at their disposal. Every Catholic obeys them and the Jesuits, clever rogues without conscience but with great learning and ability, are their expert instruments. Needless to say, this picture makes one's hair bristle.

I don't have to tell the balanced Protestant that this picture is the vision of a mind suffering from malfunction. The "hierarchy" is the sum total of Bishop Smith, Bishop Jones, Bishop Brown, and their two hundred colleagues. They are administrators of regional churches bedeviled with many problems and vexed with insufficient personnel and income. When you meet any one of them, just about the last thing you can imagine is that he is a conspirator. As for the individual Catholic, he is not listening all day long for a command of his bishop. The average Catholic is as much concerned about the Bishop as he is about the judge on the Supreme Court bench. Of course he holds him in reverence and is ready to obey his ecclesiastical directives but this produces no tension nor an abiding sense of expectancy. As for the Jesuits, well I am one and have been one for thirty-eight years. In my experience I have not found them either ruthless or diabolically clever. It is a very human group with all the diversity one finds in any group. I just cannot understand how anybody could see in them any threat. There are less than 8000 of them in this land of 180,000,000, and doomed indeed is the republic if so small a group can be a menace.

For the paranoiac these reflections are not sanative. They will be interpreted as wily attempts to narcotize the brave Protestants who in freedom follow the pure Gospel. Nor need we worry about the lunatic fringe of the Protestant community. Every group has its lunatic fringe nor should the collectivity be judged by it. But there is a Protestant fear of Catholicism to be found in the sane and sound Protestant. This fear is more significant and it should be considered. It seems to be characteristic of Protestants to see a danger for themselves in Catholicism. There are some historical justifications for this fear. The days of the Reform saw the death of Protestant martyrs. Traditionally Catholic cultures offer no welcome to Protestants but rather much hindrance. (But let Protestants not forget that many a Catholic was drawn and quartered on Tyburn Tree, nor is the Catholic decked with garlands as he walks into towns of the Bible Belt.)

Yet the facts of our American situation do not give grounds for Protestant alarm. Out of 180,000,000 there are some 40,000,000 on the active lists of Catholic parishes. In addition there are may be some 15,000,000 inactive, merely nominal, Catholics in the country. Both groups combined do not make up a third of the American population. Church-affiliated Protestants number over 60,000,000 and unaffiliated Protestants may well reach the total of 30,000,000. In combination the two groups make up a community of 90,000,000 members, more than one and a half Protestants to every Catholic. In addition there are some 25,000,000 Americans who belong to neither camp.

It is of course true that Protestant strength is weakened by the many divisions within it. But if there is an unequivocal question of Protestant versus Catholic, on that issue all Protestants will form a united front. Hence there is no chance of Catholics taking over even with the aid of the halberd-bearing Papal Swiss Guard. This is so obvious one wonders why the Protestants even worry about such an eventuality in any foreseeable future. There is a steady but small Catholic growth every year, but percentage-wise in the last thirty years Protestant church-affiliation has increased slightly more than Catholic church affiliation. In 1926 the Catholics on parish active-lists numbered 16 percent of the total population and Protestants formed 27 percent. In 1958 active Catholics were almost 23 percent of total population but Protestant church members were 35.5 percent of the whole. These statistics hardly give a clear picture because Protestant increase is largely due to the inscription of previously unchurched Protestants into determined church registers.

The real challenge to the churches is not the "taking over" by the Catholics but rather the high number of nominal Catholics and nominal Protestants which I estimate to be somewhere around 45,000,000—a group larger than Catholic church members. This large sector of the population is nearer to humanistic secularism than to Christianity, even though it will label itself with the Christian name. It has some weak bond with the Christianity but not enough commitment to identify itself actively and practically with any existent church.[1]

With all these data clearly before all the country, why is the Protestant afraid of the Catholics? Of course he has seen the ancient strongholds in New England and the Middle Atlantic States lost to him. Boston, Providence, New Haven, New York, Philadelphia, and Pittsburgh today have anything but a Protestant color. The rural areas are still in large part Protestant but the country as a whole is every day becoming more urban, and it is in the cities that the Catholics have their strength. This has produced a change and this change has frightened the Protestant.

The change was like the experience of an adult who is accustomed to ruling a group of children. He takes it for granted that he will command and that the children will obey. But the children grow up and the adult with a shock realizes that his once obedient charges are no longer children and they will not obey. In fact he does not even dare to command. He must now come to terms with people whom he still considers his inferiors, and there is resentment and a feeling that things are not right. What is more, the situation now demands that he adjust to changes which he can only deplore. He can fight a rear-guard action but he knows that in the long run this is meaningless. He can cheerfully make the best of it, but this is no easy task. As we have seen, the coming of age of the American Catholic community does not mean that the Catholics are "taking over." But their maturity does mean that the Protestants are no longer in charge. To the Protestant who was in charge for over a century, this new situation is itself distressing.

The Protestant fear shows up in restricted areas. There is no general effort made to keep Catholics out of positions of communal responsibility. No one is surprised or even much annoyed that the mayor of New York City should be a Catholic. We are quite used to that. State governors are frequently Catholics. Army generals, ambassadors to foreign countries, justices on the Supreme Court, congressmen and senators, members of the President's cabinet, presidents of state universities, scientists, and literary figures can be of the Church of Rome without giving Protestants too much worry. But there is one place which they try to close off to the Romans— the presidency. Obviously, this is because of the symbolic value of that post. If the Catholics can properly hold all the other posts, surely there is no reason why they could not hold the constitutionally limited post of chief executive. Yet logic here gives way to fear.

There is something degrading in the current Protestant baiting of the Catholic aspirants to the presidency. Other candidates are not humiliated by the inquisitorial scrutiny of Protestant groups. There is no objective need for it. If a pious Orthodox Jew were to run for high office, I doubt if it would occur to anyone that he might be a danger to the pork industry or that there would be a prohibition on lobsters. Sunday would still be our day of rest, even though the president might worship on Saturdays. We take it for granted that in Jewish religion there would operate principles whereby he could accomodate his religion to the national cultural patterns without violence being done either to personal piety or public responsibility. I say that we would take this for granted because it is reasonable to do so. Why should reasonableness suddenly be out of place if the presidential candidate is a Catholic?

What is more irritating is the implicit demand made by some Protestant groups that the Catholic presidential candidate declare that he is Protestant enough to refuse to be guided by "the Hierarchy." Imagine the howl which would make the welkin ring if some atheist group were to demand that a Protestant candidate declare that he owes no allegiance to the Bible!

Still it is not reasonable for the Catholics to become angry. The anti-Catholic prejudice displayed by many Protestants in the question of a presidential election is not something logically derived from Protestant faith. It comes from Protestant fear.

It is easier to recognize the symptoms of fear than to discover its object. Psychiatrists know that fear can be free floating without any definite object to which it is referred. Yet it might not be unprofitable to speculate on the causes of Protestant fear.

The king of England is a symbol for the English nation and for the whole British Commonwealth of Nations. This does not mean that the crown is to be relegated to the lares and penates of the British home. The king or queen has urgent tasks to perform, even if those tasks are not strictly of the administrative order. The President of the United States is a political figure with a political task to perform. But he is also a symbol. He is mightier in his symbolic function than in his political role. This latter he can share with many men who will work with him. However, no one, not even his wife, can share with him his symbolic action. He alone must bear that burden. There has never been a President who was not in some sense a Protestant. Many have not been deeply religious. Some belonged to no church. Yet they all had some willed link with Protestant religiosity. In consequence they manifested to the world that this was a Protestant land.

If a Catholic goes into this office, the world will know that ours is not a Protestant land. Of course in its constitutional substance it isn't. As a matter of concrete fact the nation is not controlled by the Protestant churches—and never was. Yet the culture of the country is Protestant just as the culture of Cuba is Catholic. Now cultures evolve and in their evolution they do not maintain the values which were their root. But it always remains true that the roots were such and such, and that these roots have an influence in the culture as it later develops. The Roman pagan of the fourth century felt that the imperial acceptance of Christianity was un-Roman and it made him angry. He wanted a return to the old Roman way. Julian the Apostate actually and pathetically tried to revive the way of the fathers. He failed because there was not enough vitality in the older forms.

It seems to me that every American Catholic should understand the situation of the American Protestant. America is becoming something different from what the nineteen-century evangelical knew. The evangelical and his Protestant brethren of all denominations cannot help but think that the de-Protestantization of the land is bad. They cannot help but believe that they have an obligation to keep things as they were. Since such is their belief, they certainly will do something about it. Protestantism is vague in its outlines, but all will agree it does not include Catholicism. There then comes the logical necessity of keeping Catholicism from running things—and the President is the symbol of running things.

If the Protestants succeed in making their desires dominant, history will praise them for their resolute energy. If they fail, as seems more probable, history will smile at their pathetic effort. If only Protestants would see that it is not a question of Protestant or Catholic, they might redirect their efforts. If the Protestants cannot run the country, certainly the Catholics can't. There is going to be a third force which will take over, and it will be neither Catholic nor Protestant. This third force already has a clear face, and it is the face of humanistic secularism. The growing power of humanistic secularism is not annoyed by the squabbles between Catholics and Protestants. Such squabbles are definitely to its advantage. The general body of the republic in the presence of the quarrelling Catholics and Protestants will say to them: a plague on both your houses!

Perhaps the Protestant fear is deeper than the one caused by the loss of dominance over the American scene. As I have previously stated, the Catholic by the faith which makes him Catholic believes that his church will endure until the end of time. I suspect that the Protestant has no parallel conviction. The intimations of mortality lie heavily on his thinking. Only recently we have heard Protestant prophets announcing the end of the Protestant era. They did not mean that the Protestant churches would suddenly disappear, but they certainly did mean that the Protestant principle would be embodied in new frameworks. To a Protestant not inclined to nice distinctions this message can only mean the end of the Protestantism he knows, and this thought for him must inspire fear. The Catholic simply rejects as credible that his church will die. His faith is bolstered by the memory of the unending chain of vicissitudes which have constantly threatened the very existence of his church but yet have been incapable of bringing her down unto death. The Protestant has no such background because he is young. Nor does he ignore the fact that gnosticism, arianism, nestorianism, monophysitism, lollardry, and other Christian denominations once thrived mightily but today are dead or dying.

Fear is not nice. Men in panic or in fright do things which they would never do in a period of calm serenity. The Protestant is not afraid of his Catholic friend and companion. On this level of living together there is usually no friction. The picture of papal forces deluging the country never includes the image of the Catholic next door. When that man or any one in his family is sick or in trouble his Protestant friend spontaneously rushes to his help. And it works equally as well from the other side. Neither Catholic nor Protestant can conceive the other to be part of a conspiracy against him. When the notion of conspiracy comes into awareness, the conspirators are always the faceless "they."

It is so unfortunate that a presidential election should bring out the notion of the "Catholic threat." And it does so with the signs of fright. We are a long way from the mud-slinging of the last century. Grotesque accusations are no longer hurled at the Catholics. Today every one cultivates the style of sweet reasonableness. But basic distortions of facts and doctrines are still the substance of accusations. In our moment two Catholic positions are being flooded with attention. The Catholics object to artificial contraception and their position on the relations of Church and State are declared un-American.

In both instances there is no great effort made to understand the Catholic position. In this country the Catholics as a plain matter of fact are not "outbreeding" the Protestants. Catholic birth rate and Protestant birth rate are not significantly different. There is no Catholic plan to overcome the Protestants by a victory through baby-cribs. It is well known that the Catholic Church considers continence, even in married folk, to be better than the perfectly good use of the marital right. The Catholic stand against artificial contraception is not inspired by a desire for an ever increasing population. All those who have read Catholic moralists will note that this phase of the question is hardly considered. Their stand is neither foolish nor machiavellian, and it was the general stand of Protestants themselves less than fifty years ago. Nor is the Catholic demographer blind to the problem of "population explosion," but he refuses to be carried away by hysteria. Procreation is a very complex phenomenon, an action with many dimensions. It is certainly more than an economic question, though it is also an economic question. Anyone, Catholic or non-Catholic, is stirred by an esthetic sense which finds to some degree repugnant the studied and contrived deviation of the pro-creative act. The whole thing has something sacred about it, and it should not be profaned. There is little possibility for non-Catholics to accept the ultimate Catholic argument which is the simple prop-osition that the illiceity of artificial contraception is so declared by the Church's magisterium. The added arguments from Natural Law will not move the non-Catholic, for by and large he does not believe in such a thing, and if he does he would hardly use the concept as the Catholics do. The moral judgment which the Catholic teach-ing organs pass on a current practice at best leaves the non-Catholic cold; at worst it makes him angry. It is against the anger that I make an appeal to non-Catholics. Let them only reflect that no matter what they think of the Catholic position, at least they can recognize that there is no perversity operating in Catholic judgement. Because my neighbor disagrees with me, I have no right to become exas-perated. Let us keep the proper balances needed for living together. If the majority of the community really want birth control, they will have it—either with the permission of positive civil law or without it. But the moral quality of the act is constituted neither by civil positive law nor even by subjective evaluation. That is another question.

One of the elements operative in the hue and cry about birth-control is the fear of the possibility of the Catholic Church's assault on non-Catholic liberty. This fear is very strong in Protestants. They will tell me that history has taught them that this fear is jus-tified. The confused historical evidences need not concern us here. It is, however, important for the Protestant not to remove the real or imagined threat by becoming himself a threat to the freedom of the Catholic. I sometimes feel that the birth-controllers are not only fighting for their own right to practise contraception but just as much to make the Catholic practise it, or at least give his moral approbation to those who do. If this were so, then there would be a deep insecurity in the hearts of the birth-controllers.

In the question of the relations between church and state, strange as it may seem, Catholics and Protestants do not differ on the basic principle involved. Both Protestant and Catholic agree that the state is not the last authority for action. They both agree that over the imperative of the state there is the imperative of God, and when there is a conflict between these imperatives, the imperative of God is final, so that the imperative of the state loses its obligational force. The Witnesses of Jehovah will not salute the flag nor will they permit blood transfusions, no matter what be the state law. The

Quaker and Mennonite will not bear arms. Actually our courts have recognized their right in so doing. Those who do not share their faith think that God does not command what the Witnesses and Quakers declare he does, but they will admit that if God did command it, then the Witness and the Quaker are right in their refusal to obey the law.

What separates the Catholic and the Protestant is the manner of knowing the will of God. The Catholic learns that will from the teaching organs of the Church. The Protestant theory supposes that there is a more immediate communication of God to him. When the Protestant objects to the Catholic's approach to the will of God, he is not offering a different doctrine on the relations of church and state. He is only objecting that the Catholic is Catholic and not Protestant. The average Protestant is perhaps annoyed with a Witness of Jehovah—but he rarely gets angry. Against the Catholic there is a tendency to get angry. Once more I think fear is playing a part in the emotional reaction.

When Catholics plan their own activities, there is little preoccupation with possible Protestant reaction. This may well be a mistake, but mistake or not, it is a fact. Our programs are not anti-Protestant and when there is a Protestant opposition, most Catholics feel a bit of irritation because they never intended to annoy the Protestant. Their objectives were beyond Protestantism. The Protestant can easily see in this fact his own nobility. It is a proof for him that he is tolerant and that this tolerance is recognized by non-Protestants. But this reflection may be deceptive. The Catholics go their merry way not in reliance on Protestant tolerance, but rather because they see a certain impotence in Protestantism. If Catholics had to rely on Protestant tolerance, they would be in dire straits. Wherever a community is made up largely of fervent believers in one or other form of Protestantism, the Catholics do not fare too well. In such a community the Catholic is marked with social stigma, victimized by social pressures to conform to Protestant mores, made defensive in all his actions. This is not a characteristic of Protestantism. It is common to any community with a large uniform majority. The Protestant will feel its effects if he lives in an overwhelmingly Catholic society and the Muslim will feel it in a large Hindu group. Presumed Protestant tolerance is never operative where zealous Protestants are the dominant majority with the power to make their way of life and vision normative for the community.

In America, nevertheless, there is a true Protestant tolerance operative but it derives not from Protestant faith but from Protestant indifferentism. So many Protestants say and believe that one church is as good as another, that each of us is going to God according to his own way. The stronger this belief is, the more tolerant the Protestant and less Protestant. I have known many Protestants who will go to any church on the relatively few occasions they attend services. They feel no uneasiness when they attend a Catholic mass. They seem to think that the mumble-jumble of ritual, be it in King James Bible English or in Church Latin, is innocent and to a degree soothing. They see little or no intellectual content in the functions nor is there a demand for commitment. If the Catholic, Episcopalian, and Orthodox eat fish on Fridays, there is no harm in it. In fact a bit of fish from time to time is a good thing. This is indeed tolerance but it springs from a lack of commitment.

This wide-spread lack of deep commitment must bother the convinced Protestant. But there is little he can do about it. The small sects can excommunicate those who are not orthodox in belief and behavior, but the bigger the church, the more difficult to deal with the indifferentists. The true believer in these circumstances can try persuasion (with dubious results) but he cannot appeal to authority. If the clergyman attempts anything like excommunication, the outcome will be either a schism in the congregation or the removal of the pastor. Any authority the minister has is a *de facto* possession due to his personal talents, but it is never his *de jure*. The congregation in general rules the official. His guidance is subject to the will of the group.

This arrangement makes for impotence. Impotence of itself does not make for fear. Where all are weak, the weak need not be afraid. But the presence of one strong group does arouse fear. The fragmentation of Protestantism up to the present unity movement knew this well. The particular type of Calvinism of Roger Williams had to face the more rigid kind of Massachusetts and he moved out of its orbit where like-minded men living on fervor and conviction could lead their lives in peace. In the nineteenth century there was no need for schismatic groups of small dimensions to leave home. There was enough indifferentism about to tolerate them and their schism merely concretized the congregational principle everywhere honored. When the sect became large, like the Mormons, it had to move.

It is not Catholic strength which frightens the Protestant. There is, as we have seen, not too much of it. The fearful thing is Catholic solidarity over against Protestant division. Protestant enthusiasm for

the Ecumenical Movement is an effective attempt to overcome fragmentation. However, Protestant ecumenism has to deal with a grave
problem. It wishes to unite warmly, effectively, and genuinely, but
it refuses to establish authority. It is all very well to say that the
authority of God is all the Church needs, but in a visible church the
invisible authority of God is not enough. Where there is no objective visible rule, unity is achieved only by vague formulas which
are understood differently by different members of the unity. This
is not effective union but only the application of paint on the cracks
of disunion. The divisions have not been healed; they have only been
ignored. In time of pressures the union which was so frail, can only
break apart.

An instance of this awareness of the weakness of Protestant unity
with its consequent fear is the group of Protestant and Others
United for the Separation of Church and State. They feel that they
cannot rely on Protestantism as such. They have invited non-Protestants into their union, and these outsiders are usually secularists.
Nor is the society much concerned with Protestant violations of the
principle of the impossible absolute separation of church and state.
They focus their attention on the Catholics. The Catholic is the en-
emy and of him they are afraid.

To sum it up, I believe that there is a double fear in American
Protestantism. The deeper one is the fear of the death of Protestantism, a haunting awareness of its own mortality. This fear makes the
Protestant nervously vigilant against any possible threat. The looming giant of Catholicism is always contemplated and always with
suspicion. It seems to be by historical tradition the main foe—not
communism, not nazism, not rationalism, not secularism, not naturalism, not neo-paganism. The Protestant naively believes that he
can come to terms with these lesser threats. American Protestants
often see great possibilities in Communist Russia. It is surprising
how many Protestant clergymen on their return from Moscow are
pleased with what they find there. Yet it must be no easy thing to be
a Protestant in the Soviet Republics. Is it possible that Protestants
breathe more easily because the Russian Orthodox Church (so much
like the Roman Catholic Church) has lost its power?

The fear of the Catholics is all the more uncomfortable because
Protestantism cannot live without Catholicism. The Protestant protest is not merely against idolatry and ungodliness. Historically it
has always been a protest to this or that feature of Catholicism, or
against the Church *in globo* with all its works and pomps. Yet if

Catholicism were to go, Protestantism would go with it. Catholic doctrine is necessary for the definition of Protestantism. If Catholicism were to go, the movement of Protestantism would be in all directions with no possibility of circumscription. The stabilizing interplay of centrifugal and centripetal forces within Protestantism would disappear because there would be no Catholic center of reference. There would take place a dissolving dispersion. The center of Protestantism is not within itself but in the Catholic Church.

Fear can usually be checked by courage, but the acme of fear is reached when it is realized that courage is not going to be enough. Then comes panic. When that comes, destruction, and unreason take over. It is because of this possibility that Protestant fear produces Catholic fear. The Catholic is not afraid for the survival of his church, but he can and should be afraid for his own personal survival.

The second fear of Protestants on the American scene is their possible loss of political and cultural dominance. As a matter of fact this dominance is already lost, but so many Protestants are unaware of it. The fear becomes dynamic especially on the occasion of presidential elections. The symbolic value of the presidency as an index of American religious commitment rouses Protestants to effort, and the effort is negative. They begin to harass the Catholic candidates with irrelevant guerilla attacks. An appeal is made to the unvoiced principle that America is a Protestant land. If it is, obviously there can be no Catholic president. But the hypothesis is not openly defended, though it is secretly believed. Yet the hypothesis is false both in constitutional principle and in actual fact. The Catholic is dealt with unjustly but the Protestant pays no heed to that. And then he wonders why the Catholics are not more friendly.

This second fear is less significant than the first but in America it can be more visible and more urgent.

6

The Protestant Principle

What idea lies behind Protestantism? This question has often been asked and has received many answers. Some Protestants reject the question. For them the reduction of empirical realities to ideas is suicidal. The flowing stream is the reality and its rushing movement allows no static ethereal surrogate to take its place. They give their message with the words, "Come and see." It is not an invitation to the mind to understand, but rather an invitation to an agent to act. In this act there will be a satisfaction which requires no intellectual formula and tolerates none. "O taste and see that the Lord is good!" (*Ps.* 34, 8; *Vulg. Ps.* 33, 9.)

Other Protestants will not take so extreme a position. They will not deny that there is an idea at the heart of Protestantism. They merely think that it is impossible to express it. I have heard Protestant theologians tell me this. The impossibility to convey this idea conceptually is for them no shortcoming. Like the previous class, they think that the proof of the pudding is in the eating. They do not forbid the search for the hidden idea but they do think that the quest will be frustrating and unnecessary.

By temper and training I cannot accept these positions. I suppose that my education in Scholastic philosophy and Scholastic theology just makes me incapable of this kind of approach. In this, most Catholics will sympathize with me, because Catholic intellectualism prizes ideas highly. Reality is always intelligible, and only in terms of ideas can it be understood.

We have often been told that the formal principle of Protestantism is the sufficiency of the Bible while its material principle is justification by faith alone. There is something in this double statement which gives it validity but one wonders if it really goes to the heart of the matter.

The principle has to be analyzed. St. Vincent of Lerins and St. Thomas Aquinas both taught the sufficiency of the Bible. But they were in no sense Protestants. It is a commonplace in Catholic theology that all revealed truth needful for salvation can be found somehow, somewhere in the Bible. Catholic theologians always look for Biblical support for their propositions. But the Catholics fuse the Bible with the Church. They find the Bible in the Church and the Church in the Bible. They object to the dichotomy of Bible versus Church. In Catholicism it is inconceivable to quote the Bible against the Church or quote the Church against the Bible. The revelation of Christ is given to us by the living Church and her primary privileged medium of instruction is the Bible. The two belong together nor must they be torn apart. It is not a question of the Bible over the Church or the Church over the Bible. The Bible is the word of God and the word of the Church. In his graciousness God gave his inspired writings to the Church as an accidental aid to her in her mission to teach all that he has commanded her. It was divine graciousness, because there was no absolute necessity that he give such a precious help to the Church. For a period she lived without the New Testament. If all the Bibles in the world were to disappear in some dreadful catastrophe, the Church by the power of the Spirit would still teach all that Christ commanded her but she would be without the singular instrument of the inspired word of God.

When the Protestants speak of the sufficiency of the Bible they do not mean what the Catholic does. In some cases they literally do not believe in the sufficiency of the Scriptures. Swedenborgians, Christian Scientists, and Mormons have other written sources in addition to the Bible, and they consider these non-biblical burdens to be necessary for salvation. Maybe Swedenborgians and Mormons will object to being called Protestants. Maybe Protestants in general will also object. I mean no offense to any one but as I see it, Swedenborgians, Christian Scientists, and Mormons are Protestants. People at large also think so. They are in the Protestant tradition and their stance is Protestant.

When the Protestant speaks of the sufficiency of the Bible, he means that the individual Protestant is free to interpret the Bible according to his own sincere understanding of it. Against this understanding no other proposition can prevail. By his own sincere understanding of the Book he must judge all things. He must judge his pastor; he must judge his congregation; he must judge the visible Church.

The task of understanding is conceived of differently by different Protestants. The orthodox followers of the Reformation believe that the Spirit in the believer enlightens the reader to grasp the authentic meaning of the text. The orthodox also believe in verbal inspiration so that every proposition is truly spoken by God in the plain good sense of the letter. Today the fundamentalists are the only ones who approach this position, though not even they are as forthright as their ancestors.

At the other end of the scale are the liberals who indeed believe that the Bible is the word of God in an accommodated sense but not in its literal structure. They do not see any difference between the biblical books and the sacred books of other religions. Bible, Upanishads, Sutras, Koran—they are all the same in constitution. The Bible has this advantage: it has universally valid insights which are definitively meaningful in the tradition of the West. These are religious insights and give valid religious orientation. Of course the Bible is no more inerrant than the Koran and to call it literally the word of God is unthinkable.

In between these two extremes there are many intermediate stands. The Neo-Protestant is neither a liberal nor a fundamentalist. The Bible for him is not revelation but rather the record of revelation. Revelation itself is God breaking into history, and the mighty deeds of God—not all of them, of course—for our salvation are recorded in the Bible. This is not by the way of scientific history but rather by the testimony of faith unto faith. Thus the Bible is a book in which we can find existentialist pointers to the saving God. In that sense it is the privileged word about God rather than the word of God. Following biblical pointers man encounters the revealing God immediately in the experience of faith.

Some Protestants are quite anxious to read patristic interpretations of the Bible and use them in their own understanding of the Scriptures. Others believe that the searching heart poring over the words is quite capable of getting all the religious nurture it needs. Others still restrict themselves to a most rigorous scientific examination of the books and their history; they make their affirmations only in the light of this fairly exact investigation.

As is clear, the sufficiency of the Bible is not a unitary concept in Protestantism. It is also clear that in some sense all Protestants give an ultimate value to the Scriptures. It is not altogether false therefore to say that the sufficiency of the Bible is the formal principle of Protestantism, but it certainly is an ambiguous statement.

Concerning the material principle of Protestantism, justification by faith alone, something must be said. In the hectic days of the sixteenth century the Lutheran doctrine on justifying faith was generally understood as a denial of all saving value to ethical action, of sacramental efficacy and of the possibility of truly virtuous action according to the norm of God's law.

We have come a long way since then and positions have been clarified. The Catholics always believed that the call to salvation and faith was initiated exclusively by God, and only from his grace could man receive the capacity for saving action. To die in God's grace was equally the exclusive gift of the saving God. That was the Augustinian doctrine as formulated by Caesarius of Arles at the second Council of Orange in A.D. 529 and it was made official by the Popes. The Council of Trent retained this position which is normative for all Catholic doctrine today. This is undoubtedly a strong affirmation that man is saved by God's grace achieved in faith. This is quite clear to all modern Protestant theologians who have studied the Catholic teaching. On this point there is no substantial difference between Catholic and Protestant theories on justification.

The Reformers' strong rhetoric against the value of works could be interpreted as a form of antinomianism. "Sin valiantly and believe more valiantly." Yet all the Reformers were against sin in all its forms and shapes. Calvin's Geneva was no place for sin or worldliness. Virtue was the strongly enforced law of the city. In the history of Protestantism we do not find antinomianism as a practice except perhaps in some exotic little groups not recognized as genuine by the mass of Protestants. In all Protestant communities it does make a difference whether you behave yourself or don't. Works are important, very important indeed. Catholic cultures are rarely as strict as communities where a strong calvinism prevails. Strangely enough, Catholicism always is more concerned with the faith of its members than with their works. For the Catholic the loss of faith is the greatest loss. With faith alive, pardon is possible. Where faith is absent, there is no pardon.

The Reformers were also understood to deny the freedom of the will. Mortimer J. Adler in his *The Idea of Freedom*, (New York:

Doubleday, 1958) has shown that freedom of the will is the tag not
for one question but for at least seven. No Reformer denied that man
could physically and psychologically choose between alternatives.
Calvin says that this is too obvious and too irrelevant for discussion. What the Reformers were saying was that an ungraced will
could not perform salvific good. This no Catholic denied or denies.
But the rhetoric of the Reformers was so shocking. They preached
the Catholic truth in so exaggerated a way, that it was easy to be
led to think that man was not truly a responsible agent. The primacy
of grace also brought up the question of predestination. Here again
outré rhetoric could lead the hearer to believe that he was damned
if he did and damned if he didn't.

With time the Calvinist formulas were understood in an Arminian
sense and I think it would not be rash to say that most of today's
Protestants don't believe in any predestination at all—though all
Catholics do. I seem to have the impression that today the average
Protestant seems to think it makes little difference what you believe
as long as you are decent and virtuous. About the only faith he seems
to demand is the one implied in the sincere effort to do the right
thing. Certainly the Protestant believers in the total depravity of
man are too few in our day to give current Protestantism their
specific coloring.

Once again we see that the material principle of justification by
faith alone is true of Protestantism but ambiguously. It is for this
reason that I do not like the two principles as exact rational reduc-
tions of the Protestantism which exists in our time.

Paul Tillich dealt with the question of the Protestant principle.
He sees it as a constant protest, not necessarily against the Catholic
Church alone but against any idolatry. For Tillich the protest is the
spontaneous consequent of the positive element in Protestantism,
which is man's total self-surrender to the self-revealing God. Because
God is God, the believing man will permit nothing less than God
take his place and assume his prerogatives. God is that which concerns man ultimately and God lies beyond the finite categories which
define all other things. God is perceived mysteriously at the point
where man reaches the very edge of empirical reality. There the
ground is seen and the Ground of Being is another Tillichian name
for God. The total surrender of the believer to the unconditioned
Ground of being, to Being Itself, makes man protest if anything else
usurps the ultimacy and absoluteness of the Ultimate Ground. Un-
definable infinity is the Divine, and all that is finite is not God,

though God is the ground of finite reality, in it and beyond it. Hence no church can speak in the name of God. No Bible is the ultimate word. No government can demand unconditioned obedience. Such demands are idolatrous and are in reality blasphemous.

Tillich is always fascinating. There is a sharp vision in his prophetic affirmations. When he speaks of things, he unveils unconsidered aspects of their reality. Tillich's principle does tell us a great deal about Protestantism, even though many Protestants refuse to see it.

In Tillich's thought the Protestant principle does not need a Protestant church for its exercise. Although he thinks it hard to practice it in Catholicism as it actually exists, he does not think it impossible —and he hopes that it will become more prevalent within it. In fact as far as I can grasp his thought, he thinks that the true Christian would be a Protestant Catholic. This is not an easy concept to assimilate.

Needless to say, fundamentalists abhor Tillich's view of the Bible. For them the Divine has been adequately expressed in the scriptural propositions. The Book in its propositions is the divine revelation, not merely a pointer to a revealing God grasped without concepts and without propositions. However Tillich is biblical in his own fashion, though he cannot accept either the way of the fundamentalist or that of the scientific philologist. To restrict the efficacy of the Bible to a microscopic analysis of its concrete, finite reality will give knowledge not of God but of something finite and human. This says nothing about God, though it can lead man to the strange awareness of God.

I think that it is true that Protestantism in any of its varied manifestations does rely on Tillich's principle. The Protestant has the courage to reject existing formulations of the divine will because as he sees it, God wants something different. Since God is God, then the errors concerning him must be refused. It is precisely here that I find the main difficulty. How can the Protestant avoid the admonition of Oliver Cromwell?:[1]

I am persuaded that divers of you, who lead the people, have laboured to build yourselves in these things; wherein you have censured others, and established yourselves 'upon the Word of God'. Is it therefore infallibly agreeable to the Word of God, all that *you* say? I beseech you, in the bowels of Christ, think it possible that you may be mistaken.

It seems clear enough that Protestants have pondered the words of Cromwell even when they did not know anything about that hardly gentle Puritan. Two words show up in the Cromwell message: *infallibly*, and *mistaken*. If the Protestant opts to be infallibly right, so that only infallibility can justify his faith and protest, then he had better become a Catholic. This is the Catholic stand. As a matter of fact, the ideal Protestant opts for the right to be mistaken. Infallibility makes the average Protestant's hackles rise.

The right to be mistaken is obviously no right. You can't have a right to be wrong. The man who is mistaken has rights because he is a man, not because he is in error. He has the right to be tolerated in his error because his fellows have no right to expect infallibility of man who is so fallible in all he thinks. The brachylogy used by Catholics: error has no rights; means error founds no rights. Neither error nor truth have rights, because rights are vested only in persons. But it is certainly true that the wrong can never establish a right in man.

The toleration of error is good ethics but it is bad ethics to make error the guide of the destiny of man. The Catholic Church is ineluctably bound to claim infallibility for herself because she claims to have the divine commission to teach all men the way of salvation. If she can make mistakes in declaring the will of God, how can she demand faith? "If the bugle gives an indistinct sound, who will get ready for battle?" (I Cor. 14, 8)

Protestants see this line of thought as well as Catholics. As Cromwell saw, many Protestants thought they infallibly understood the word of God. Because they believed it, they were willing to give up home, health and even life to remain true to their faith. But the tendency of current Protestantism is not in this direction. Today's Protestant seems to be proud of his fallibility and points to it as the best argument for his belief. It avoids the necessity of being certainly right. He will gladly say that infallibility is something devoutly to be wished, but alas!, it is impossible. You do the best you can with the utmost sincerity of which man is capable and then trust in God.

This is comforting doctrine. But it stems from or leads to relativism and scepticism. Much can be said in defense of these two epistemological positions, but no matter how you defend them, no man can accept them. He lives, loves and dies on inevitable conviction that there is a nucleus of knowledge which cannot be fallible. Discourse with the self and with the neighbor is possible only on the supposition that we do know some things certainly. We can only affirm our fallibility on the implicit supposition that we infallibly know reality in some of its parts. To look for the truth is an implicit affirmation that it can be found infallibly. Who will search for that which cannot be found? To find it fallibly is not to find it all.

This kind of thinking is as old as the hills. Augustine did it very nicely. In his own perverted way Descartes expressed it movingly. Many a thinker who did not like such thought admitted he couldn't get around it, but promptly added—why bother? We solve our problems much better by ignoring it. If we don't look at it, it may go away.

Of course it won't go away. Every generation of adolescents thrusts it out into the open. They are exasperated when their elders dismiss the issue as "meaningless." When religion is given to them on the admitted basis that the scheme may be altogether wrong or in many parts, with a forceful phrase they will tell you what they think of such religion. God is indeed what concerns man ultimately, not only ultimately but absolutely. A maybe-God and a maybe-Church is neither God nor Church, and using Tillich's Protestant Principle, I protest against them. The Catholic Church claims infallibility. This is no place for an apologetic for Catholicism, but if Yahweh is the Absolute who founded a Church to unite men to himself, infallibility is what it would necessarily claim.

It is clear that I do not think that the principle of Protestantism can adequately be expressed by the formulas we have been considering so far. Rashly but humbly I shall suggest another formula. It is rash because an outsider should not presume to tell the insider what his group is. But it is humble because the formula is offered as an outsider's view completely subject to correction by the insider.

Any formulation of the Protestant principle must substantially explain any of the many forms of Protestantism. It must explain not only Lutheranism and the Southern Baptist Convention but the Unitarians and the Witnesses of Jehovah, as well. These latter groups in the mind of the former are not really Protestant, but in the mind of outsiders, they are. All are in some way Protestant.

What do they have in common? It is hardly wise to say, nothing. There are common positions to be found in all of them. I submit that all of them have found God. This of course does not distinguish them from other religious groups. The Jew finds God in his solidarity with his people. The Catholic finds God in his church. The Hindu finds God in his culture. The Protestant finds God differently. He encounters God immediately. Lutheran faith is an *experience* of the saving God, produced in man by God himself. The empirical nature of the God-encounter is stressed in every type of revival-meeting where the effort is to evoke the vital realization of God's saving being. You may call it conversion, faith, decision for Christ, religious experience, "getting religion", the exercise of the religious sentiment, or any of the many names which have been given to the event. That evangelicals make much of it needs no saying. To read the conversion testimonies of Baptists is to see the experience described quite warmly. The Pentecostal forms his religious service so that the experience of the Spirit is rendered thoroughly conscious. Even sedater groups like the Presbyterians and Congregationalists rest their validity on the faith-experience of their members, though this experience is not hysterical nor flamboyant. It will be calm but nevertheless a deep awareness of divinity grasped in loving trust.

Jonathan Edwards in his day caused trouble because he insisted on the experience as a condition of membership in his Calvinist congregation. He failed because there were many who had never felt the experience, or at least did not feel it strongly. This will be true today as well as in the eighteenth century. But any Protestant knows that the experience is what he is looking for, even if he has not yet had it. The strength of his desire is proportionate to the strength of his religiosity.

The earmark of this experience is that it is not conceptual. It is a total response in a moment, not unlike a minor ecstasy. Thoughts go into the background; feeling and emotion fill the whole man. It is a gladsome feeling. As long as the man can live in the aura of this event, he is converted, i.e. changed. The proper function of Protestant religious service is to revive the conversion experience. The sacraments are dramatic recalls of the saving encounter.

Liberal Protestants believe in this experience no less than others. They are too sophisticated to look for it in the emotional atmosphere of an evangelist's revival but they do wish to see empirically the divine lying at the root of life and moral endeavor. Neo-Protestants certainly recognize the encounter as basic. Tillich sees man driven almost to despair by existentialist torment and in that moment he can apperceive the Ground of Being giving meaning and arousing hope for the man torn asunder by the split of essence and existence. For Tillich this is the moment of faith, and that alone can save.

Today the old theological quarrel as to the nature of Pauline faith is dissipated. Both sides now see what the question is. It isn't St. Paul. Faith in Catholic terminology means belief. Faith for the Protestant is lived encounter. That is why Protestants make so much of trusting faith; the intellectual phase of it, necessary indeed, is the least conspicuous element. For the Catholic faith as belief is the necessary condition for entry into the Church. The sacrament of baptism then truly makes the believer a member of the Church, thus one with Christ and through him one with God. Now God infuses into the new-born man the power to hope and love. This is an ontological event; not psychological. The Protestant sees faith as a vital experience, and all men of like experience with him are the Church no matter what the congregations think. This is a psychological moment; ontology is bracketed. To put it in shallow language, the Catholic because of the action of the Church has union with God; he does not have to feel it. The Protestant says that he feels his rightness with God; therefore he has it, and now is in the Church.

This immediacy in knowing God through a non-conceptual act of awareness is the first and supreme element in the Protestant principle. It is self-standing; it needs no other support. Protestants have always been disdainful of a reasonable apologetic for their faith. And quite rightly, for an experience is self-justifying. A stranger may doubt if I had it; may deny that I experienced what I say I did; but I am not shaken by his scepticism. I saw what I saw. (Of course that is precisely the point at issue in controversy: what *did* you see?)

The primacy of the God-encounter gives Protestants freedom. They insist much on their liberty as the sons of God. When there is dispute among Protestants, the less favored side always appeals to its Protestant freedom. In what does this freedom consist? Certainly not in license, nor yet to go counter to the experienced Lord. It is the liberty to interpret conceptually the initial encounter. That was illuminating; that was the teaching. It was non-conceptual but yet perceptive and therefore after the moment it is necessary to express in concepts what was perceived.

Since the encounter was the decisive starting point, the definitive criticism for any formulation of its intellectual content is from the remembered experience. Nothing else can be definitive, neither the voice of the congregation nor the bimillennial tradition of the Church. In loyalty to God as vitally met, the believer is necessarily free from the dominion of the visible congregation. It can excommunicate him from its fellowship, but not from the fellowship of the Church which is only the sum-total of those who had the faith experience. No man or group of men can exclude a believer from that mystical union. The believer can move on alone or form a congregation of those in agreement with him. The second alternative is necessary where it is possible, given the social dimension of faith. But where it is not possible, with courage and trust the believer must move on alone. But never can the congregation or the total Church impose doctrine or theory on the Christian which is not first judged in the definitive light of the coming of God to the believer in the grasp of faith. This is a double grasp: God seizing man, and man clinging to God.

To conceptualize the divine is not an easy thing. For the majority of mankind concepts are spontaneously accepted from the conceptual treasure of ambient community and culture. They have not the mental energy to form new conceptions. Hence for the majority of those who have the faith experience, strongly or weakly or only in desire, the conceptual description of their concrete religious community is satisfactory. But there will be some who can originate conceptions and these may not be satisfied by the commonly accepted idea-scheme as proposed in a written confession or in the customary thought-patterns operative in the group. They will make a new synthesis and its lack of agreement with the previous thought system is no argument against it. The new synthesis was not derived from the old; it was derived from the original faith experience. That and only that is definitive.

It has always seemed to me that the fundamentalist's deep displeasure with the liberals and Neo-Protestants is without logical justification. It certainly is true that liberals and Neo-Protestants have dropped the methodic and many of the working postulates of the early Reformers in their own explanation of the Gospel. But they did not drop the Protestant principle. They are using Protestant freedom and using it with all genuinity. If the fundamentalist expostulates that this Protestantism is not the Protestantism of the Reformers, the new men can easily retort that they are doing exactly what the first Reformers did when they rejected the previous tradition. If rejection of traditional conceptualization in the light of faith encounter was the right of Luther, Zwingli, and Calvin, why does it not justify the new men? Luther and Calvin were not infallible nor did they claim to be. It can well be said that the current theologians are not orthodox Lutherans or orthodox Calvinists, but they still are very genuine Protestants, no less and no more than the fundamentalists.

The Protestant freedom of the conceptualization of the saving experience of God in faith gives Protestants of every age and of every place the right to make new creeds and confessions. These do not have to be in accord with what Protestants did in the past. The Protestant who affirms that Jesus of Nazareth was divine but not the deity is perhaps a better Protestant than the believer who sticks with the doctrine of Nicea, Ephesus, and Chalcedon. (I personally believe that the Protestant who does believe with Chalcedon is right, but I do not think that he is a good Protestant when he refuses the right to another Protestant to deny this dogmatic thesis.) The fundamentalist sees it his way and he must be true to it; the Neo-Protestant sees in a totally different way and he must be true to what he sees. In Protestantism the encounter of faith is decisive; nothing else. One man's encounter is as good as the other's, and for him it is binding no matter what the others may say. The verbalization of the faith experience is subsequent to the experience and no infallibility is attached to it. For verbal formulization there must be freedom. This the first Reformers claimed and their later followers must have the same right. That by this method the Christian doctrine becomes suddenly or gradually something totally different from what it was in ages past is not an objection which one Protestant can validly make against another. On the Protestant principle this is inevitable. Even in Anglicanism where the Protestant principle is checked by the Catholic principle, the Protestant principle ultimately triumphs because as the eighth of the Thirty-nine Articles teaches, classical creeds of the Church are received because they are scriptural, i.e. what the Elizabethan divines thought was scriptural. This can only mean that the individual judges the Church by comparing her dictuma with Scripture—as understood in the light of the experience of faith. The cavalier attitude of most Anglicans to the Thirty-nine Articles is the logical prolongation of the Articles themselves.

Is the freedom the Protestant enjoys in his formulation of Christian faith absolute? No. If it were, there would be utter chaos and thorough dissolution in consequence. There is a vague limit and that is the biblical test. If a Protestant were to interpret his God experience so that its best formulation would be found in Koran, we would not say that he was a Protestant. We would only say that he was converted to Islam. The formulations of Protestantism must have biblical resonances. If no such resonance is found, we are beyond the Christian pale and Protestantism lies within it.

Yet the biblical test is negative and not positive. If a belief is utterly unrelated to Scripture, then it is not a Protestant belief. If a belief claims no scriptural warrant, it is not a Protestant belief. Thus far the test works very well.

Where a doctrine does claim biblical support, we have a Protestant position. That 99 percent of all Protestants deny that the thought is genuinely scriptural, still leaves the thesis Protestant. In making the claim that the statement is scriptural, the principle of biblical test is admitted. That is enough to make it genuinely Protestant.

The Bible does exercise some positive control of the expressions of Protestant belief. But it will never give a unified Protestant creed, much less a uniform one. The reason lies in the very nature of the Bible. In terms of neutral scientific investigation, the Scripture is one literary phenomenon next to innumerable others. Without a non-scientific postulate in its favor, the collection of Hebrew and Greek writings called the Bible is no different from any other collection of writings. For purposes of classification, the Bible is a collection of Jewish compositions where religion is the overriding concern. The bulk of the collection was accepted by the people of Israel as true description of their religious beliefs and practices. A smaller part of the book was proper to a group of Jewish sectarians of the first century of our era. They were called Christians by Greek-speakers who were translating an Aramaic word which can today be rendered as Messianists. Christians have always considered this small section of the Bible the important part, making it the key for the understanding of the whole. There are many authors of the different parts and it would be quite impossible to say how many there were. The compositions represent different periods of a tradition of more than one thousand years. All too frequently it is difficult to know the concrete situation confronting different writers. Our control of the history of Israel is today quite good but it is something less than thoroughly adequate.

In this situation it is obvious that different points of view will be presented: different themes discussed; different theologies implied; developments produced by later meditations; harmonizations effected by subsequent editors, and other things of like nature. There will be some central themes but their treatments will be various. Only the supposition that there is one growing message formally identical in all the parts will bring unity to the complete work. This supposition is pre-scientific or post-scientific.

We know that anti-Christian polemicists have culled passages from the total Bible and then put the excerpts in a continuous order. The result is of course uncomfortable for a modern believing Christian. The Patriarchs and the Kings were not the Christian's idea of good men. The Mosaic legislation contains things which are shocking if taken out of their historical and literary contexts. Every Christian on his supposition that these writings are God's word has a saving device for all this—but without this supposition, he would not try to find noble meanings in disturbing passages. To assert as the fundamentalists do, that just by reading the book one perceives infallibly that it is the word of God, is more than I can accept. The Bible is not only the occasion of edification but often of scandal. The liberals saw this quite clearly. They were not perverse when they dropped the fundamentalist understanding of Scripture; in sincerity and honesty they just couldn't go along with it any longer.

Great Jewish and Christian scholars went to the Bible with other norms of interpretation than the one suggested by the "plain sense." Men like Origen and Augustine were not deeply concerned with the literal meaning of texts, for which they indeed had respect. But they looked beyond the letter to get what they thought was the real burden of the words. This they did on the supposition that the Bible was a mysterious book, not a simple one. Because the Church told them that Bible was the word of God, they found a divine message but the man of common-sense or the scientific philologist simply cannot find their discoveries in the mere text itself.

If there is no objective decisive norm for the understanding of Scripture, then every reader in all sincerity will get a different message out of it. Every kind of thinking and interpretation proceeds from postulates, too often unrecognized. If there is no outer control, the Bible will be the base for innumerable faiths and theologies. All can truly say that they are biblical in their approach to God, but they are not using the same Bible. Every man's Bible is different from every other man's Bible. About the only way the Bible could unify believers positively would be on the supposition that it were a sacrament in the Catholic sense of the word, whereby it worked *ex opere operato*—by its own inner efficacy. But neither Catholic nor Protestant ever had such a conception of the Scriptures.

The biblical test for belief, then, is not an effective device for the validity of the belief, but it is distinctive of genuine Protestantism. Protestant faith does not derive from the objective meaning of the Bible but rather is itself an *apriori* demand that belief should be related to the Bible. This fundamental dogma was caused in no small part by the awe the Renaissance had for books of antiquity. The ancients were highly revered and if their wisdom was in print, presumably you had it. This was not a theological principle nor even a religious one. It was a mood of a period which enthusiastically discovered ancient literature and had printing to make its discoveries available. While the Catholics relied on the living Church, the Reformers relied on the Book. They thought they were more solidly grounded because a book is a hard public fact on which you can put your hands. This of course is true of the material volume but it is lamentably untrue for the formal book—the intellectual content which the writer tried to express semantically. Reading is not a mechanical operation. Good reading needs a high degree of resonance of the reader with the author of the printed word. Where there is no resonance, the reader does not get the author's thought but rather his own thought unconsciously stimulated by the material signs manipulated by the writer. The simple supposition that all you have to do is read the words of another man in order to understand him can hardly be maintained in our day when the psychology of communication has sufficiently bared the precariousness of the transmission of ideas.

Most of these observations are telling only against fundamentalists. The most conspicuous Protestant thinkers of our time do not fall into fundamentalist simplicism. They erect their theological systems with no illusion that they are reproducing the biblical conception of divinity and religion. Many believe that there is no unified scriptural doctrine, or if there is, it is humanly impossible to detect it. Either because of the stimulus of some scriptural loci or because of an original insight which can be related to scriptural expression, they work out a religious vision. There is no supposition that biblical propositions are dictated by God or any belief in scriptural inerrancy, even on the plane of religious ideas. *De facto*, the Bible is a religious landmark for western religiosity and it is a good point of reference, gladly accepted as a religious language and a religious point of departure. A toe-hold in the Bible gives the western religious man a good support, which if not better than any other, is at least better for us with our occidental conditioning. Biblical control is thus minimal and yet reasonable, giving the religious man fullest liberty in working out his scheme of divinity. That the resulting visions will not be uniform or even reconcilable is hardly a serious shortcoming. God's way with man is different with every man, although cultural pressures at a given moment in a given place will incline a man to a definite type of description for divinity. Protestantism must try to make divinity highly meaningful to every age. Past schemes must be demythologized and myths proper to the moment employed. There is here no fraud nor even disloyalty to the achievements of the past. God is real but ineffable. Theologies are necessary but never adequate. God will never be understood; he can only be met. This was true in times gone by and it is true now and will be true tomorrow.

Against this position no telling objection can be directed. It is a reasonable stand. One can truly say that this is not the idea which historical Christianity had of itself, but the Neo-Protestant will not be floored by such an observation. He knows its truth as well as the next fellow. He would merely say that we must not be stuck with the mistakes of our fathers, no matter how dear they are to us nor how much we love them. What was good in their conquests we shall retain; what was defective we shall gently and discreetly drop.

Liberals and Neo-Protestants are more genuinely Protestant than fundamentalists. These latter look more like seventeenth-century Reform Christians but the former are truer to the Protestant principle. Such a remark might surprise Protestants in general who might be inclined to opine the opposite. If such be the case, it merely shows the power which tradition has on all of us. If father did it, the adolescent is prone to hate it, but as the adolescent becomes a full adult he tends to agree with father, now dead and gone. The very foibles of father, intolerable when he was alive, now take on a lovingly humorous quality. Protestantism, secularism, Catholicism, and modernism all have a tradition and they follow it. The Catholic knows this is proud that it be so. The others either do not know it, or if they do, they try to ignore it. To be of one's time in the sense of not being of the past is quite impossible. The necktie is a useless thing, though once it was a necessary accoutrement. Slowly our American men are freeing themselves of its absolute necessity, but even today in the hottest kind of weather, the tie is indispensable for proper occasions.

To sum up these reflections, it can be said that the Protestant principle consists of three interrelated propositions. It is an affirmation that God must be experienced immediately in an experience which is non-conceptual and whose intellectual content is not central nor specific. Because it is primary, it is self-standing and self-justifying. The second proposition states that the conceptual expression of the vague intellectual content which will necessarily follow on the experience, is a task which the believer must perform in freedom. This freedom is not absolute. Hence the third proposition, which declares that there is a check, and that check is the biblical test. The conceptual expression of the epistemological content of the experience must be expressed in biblical terms.

As has been said, this essay at establishing the Protestant principle is one fallible outsider's effort. It was chosen because it seems to explain so many characteristic Protestant phenomena: its pluralism, its perpetual modernism, its inconsistencies, its dislike for metaphysics in favor of empiricism, its biblicism in myriad forms, its ambivalent attitude to tradition, its fluidity.

It will be noted that the Protestant principle as here formulated is wholly positive. The principle affirms: it does not deny. But it explains the denials of Protestantism if it be prolonged by corollaries.

Protestantism denies Catholicism. This is certainly beyond dispute if by Catholicism we mean the Roman Catholic Church (and in this sense I have always used the word). Yet today there is a great movement within Protestantism to affirm catholicism of itself. This claim rests on a conception of catholicism whereby it is equivalent to comprehensiveness. Both Luther and Calvin retained the notion of a universal Church incorporating all believers. They made that Church invisible and they refused to identify it with sum-total of the congregations. The congregations were the phenomenon but the Church was the epiphenomenon above the congregations. Obviously in this thought no one knows who is in the Church, though the believer trusts imperturbably that he is. But about his neighbor he can say nothing, though he thinks that he can make a shrewd guess. In this vision a Catholic can be in the Church if he has been revitalized by the faith encounter. Obviously a Lutheran, a Methodist, a Presbyterian, and an Anglican can be in the Church. Hence the Church rises above and beyond all denominational and congregational restrictions.

Today as a consequence of the Ecumenical Movement, there is a willingness to give visibility to the invisible Church. The churches are urged to unite so that this visibility will be ever greater. But the visibility and unity of the Church are subject to the Protestant principle. Protestant catholicism is simply a recognition that the Protestant principle legitimately has many forms. There is unity in the principle but no uniformity in the expression, because the expression is free and therefore necessarily tolerant of plurality of forms. Protestantism can tolerate a Catholic expression of faith, as long as this expression is in accord with the Protestant principle whereby such an expression is free and not binding on every believer. Anglo-Catholics are often watched with suspicion lest they be crypto-Romanists boring from within. But on principle they can be tolerated. As long as the Anglo-Catholic or the High Church Lutheran grants freedom to his co-religionaries in their expression of the faith, his own expression is quite tolerable. If the High Churchmen want the Mass, monks, nuns, seven sacraments, tradition, and hierarchy, they may have them. But they must admit that these things are not necessary to being a Christian. They may even insist that all these visibilities belong to the *bene esse* of the Church. That is a question of opinion. But they must not say that they belong to the very *esse*. The *esse* is defined by the Protestant principle.

The Protestant principle opposes Protestants to the Catholic Church because there is also a Catholic principle. The historical relations of Catholicism and Protestantism have produced injuries and resentments in both camps. I know an English Catholic whose family remained faithful to its Catholicism throughout the Reform to our day. The sufferings imposed on this family for four centuries are stamped deep in the consciousness of every new generation. The man told me that the word Protestant evokes in his mind the image of a man who is arbitrary, domineering, hypocritical, injust, persecuting, and unfeeling. I have heard Protestants speak in the same way about Catholicism. For every Protestant martyr in Bloody Mary's short reign, there are at least two Catholic ones during the rules of Elizabeth, James, and Cromwell. These things were real and they cannot help but poison the relations between the two parties.

Such a history alone could antagonize Protestantism to Catholicism. But it is not history which makes the opposition inevitable. The wounds of history can be sanated by study and understanding. What is more substantial is that the Protestant principle cannot tolerate Catholicism, whose own principle is so different.

I have essayed a formulation of the Protestant principle and I shall dare to do the same for the Catholic principle. It would run something like this: God, who spoke to Israel, historically became man in Jesus of Nazareth who left his living divine humanity to be truly prolonged in an organized visible society called the Church. If man wants God's salvation he must be incorporated into that society and by sharing its life, he shares the life of Christ who is God as well as man. The Christian man does not experience God immediately except in the special case of the mystics. What he does

experience is the sacramental symbol which by divine power
ontologically changes the sinner inwardly and totally. The truth
of God's revelation is the abiding possession of the consciousness of the society called the Catholic Church, and its divinely em-
powered organs will express it infallibly and adequately.

The two principles implicitly deny each other at every point.

CHAPTER

7

Envoi

Protestantism is a concern for Catholicism and vice versa. Concerns necessarily produce tensions. Yet in our country Catholic and Protestant must live side by side in an existence of fusion and common collaboration. It has not been perfectly serene, but all things considered, we have not done too badly. I think it is true that the individual Protestant does not hate the individual Catholic and the reverse can also be affirmed. The Protestant's bugaboo is the abstract Catholic—the little man who isn't there. In like manner the same situation exists for the Catholic.

But there is tension and this year of presidential election makes the tension more palpable than in other times. The tension is bearable, but it would be nicer if it weren't there at all. How can we deal with this tension?

We know the attempted solution of the past. Each side tried to annihilate the other by book, sword, and law. It didn't work. Both sides are still here. What is more, we are all rather ashamed of the efforts of our ancestors. My friend and co-author, Professor Brown, is pleased that there is now a monument in Geneva in expiation for the burning of Michael Servetus. I personally can draw little significance from the fact. An Athenian court in recent times exonerated Socrates from the condemnation fulminated against him by an earlier Athenian court more than two thousand years ago. These actions seem to me to be mere anachronistic gestures of modernity. Both Servetus and Socrates were condemned by the laws considered equitable for their time. With wisdom of hindsight we do not like those laws and judge them to have been either unrighteous or poor laws. Yet it is not inconceivable that the expiation monument in Geneva will be torn down in some future day and in its place a tablet be erected in severe criticism of us. The generations are so ephemeral, and their principles and prejudices do not necessarily survive them.

However, at this moment the average Catholic and the average Protestant are opposed to so drastic a solution of Catholic-Protestant tensions as the cruel and heartless extermination of the other party. What the Nazis did, makes Catholic and Protestant shudder. Pray God that this our common conviction survive in the future and become even stronger.

Something less than extermination is a program of gratuitous constant harassment of the other man. This is dreadful too. To be exposed all day and every day to repeated pin pricks is not fatal but it is a dreary life. To be incessantly humiliated publicly by petty socially organized devices of condemnation is soul-destroying. I imagine it is this that makes our American negroes so resentful of their situation in our midst. It makes me depressed when I think of what they must suffer.

Such action is of course persecution, though it is not bloody. Again I like to think that neither Catholic nor Protestant wants this to happen to the other. Hence there is perhaps no problem here.

The danger is fear. In the presence of threat to life or liberty, a man defends himself. No one feels guilty of sin when he uses violence against violence in self-defense. Our Lord gave us as an ideal not to return evil for evil, yet he himself when struck on the face protested vigorously. His rebuke of Peter for using the sword in the Garden of Olives may well have been against the uselessness of it rather than against any possible malice.

Fear may be aroused when there is no ground for it. Naturalists tell us that no snake attacks a man unprovoked. This truth is not consoling or fear-eliminating when I walk through the woods. Beyond all doubt I have no intention of attacking the snake or even annoying him. But he doesn't know that, and my approach is instinctively interpreted as aggression. He strikes and if the snake be venomous, I well may die, though the animal really had no murderous designs against me, nor I against him.

Something of the kind is with us. In our historical existences we have learned to look on each other with suspicion. Any sudden movement of the other, because of our habit rather than instinct, spontaneously brings the latent suspicion into flame. Aggression may have been farthest from the mind of the other, but because of our suspicious expectancy, the action will be spontaneously interpreted as aggressive. Then comes the effort at defense. With it comes violence. Our intentions are not directed toward aggression, merely toward self-defense.

This danger surrounds us constantly. It is not the danger from the other; it is the danger of panic. Against it our leaders must warn and instruct us. Panic is as destructive as malice.

We must not approach the task with a Pollyanna attitude. There should be no attempt to deny the painful conflicts of the past, much less white-wash either party's part in them. We must know that all these things took place without, however, concentrating on or exaggerating them. The scalded cat fears cold water and knowing the cat's reaction to water in general, we will bear it in mind.

We must therefore remember the neighbor in our actions. However, this must not be the overriding preoccupation in the formation of each group's programs of action. These obviously should be determined by the domestic needs and visions of the group. It is hardly wise to perform the tasks called for by the life of the group in such a way that to everything projected, there is one voice always warning: do nothing to offend the neighbor. If such were the concern of the policy makers, the chances are excellent that nothing at all would be done. Wisdom seems to counsel that both collectivities confront their own problems and seek the proper solution. But in the way the plans are carried out, charity would demand that we take into account the sensibilities of those outside of our fellowship. It is neither Christian nor prudent to stir them up when this reaction can be easily avoided. There is no need of Protestants calling Catholics papists, since this word has a derisive overtone in English, nor is it good Scripture to label the Pope as Anti-Christ. Catholics in their turn can avoid calling Luther an apostate friar and Protestants sectarians.

The main task required for our constructive co-existence is understanding. A beginning has been made. Catholics are studying Protestant reality with a spirit of objectivity. Much more must be done, and the fruits of these investigations must be transmitted to the pulpit from the seminaries. Harnack complained in the nineteenth century that *Catholica non leguntur* (Catholic writings are not read). This is not true today. Especially the more important Protestant seminaries are diligently reading Catholic work, and it is not too rare to find local congregations inviting Catholics to explain their own doctrine.

This is a beginning. It is not enough. I suppose that there are not many Protestants left who believe that Catholic priests have horns, but there are millions who think that Immaculate Conception is Virgin Birth; that Papal Infallibility is the personal sinlessness of the Pope; that Catholics are not allowed to read the Bible. So too Catholics are too frequently surprised that many Protestants have liturgical worship; that by and large they are not in favor of divorce; that most ministers believe in the divinity of Christ; that an intelligent man can be a sincerely believing Protestant.

There is still a widespread ignorance of the doctrines and practices of the other churches. It will be a slow action before there is enough information about for the essay of understanding to be commenced.

Optimistic readers will object that my preachment supposes that the division of the churches will continue. They believe that we must work to make one church of the many churches. From their point of view the necessity is here and the task not impossible. If we all put our minds to it and approach the job with good will, we can have one church in a very short time.

Regretfully I consider such thinking as utterly unrealistic. I do believe that with relative facility the multiplicity of Protestant churches can be reduced. In fact, unions are taking place in our time. The vast majority of Methodists are now in one church. The different forms of Calvinist churches can unite. Nor do I see why the Methodists could not join up with them. Even in such cases the task is not too simple, but there is nothing radical in these communities rendering the union impossible in principle.

But between Protestants and Catholics there can be no union except by the conversion of one collectivity to the other. In good logic there can be an Evangelical and Reformed Church, a United Church of Canada, the Union Church of South India, but there cannot be a Catholic Protestant Church. If I am not wrong, the Protestant principle and the Catholic contradict each other totally. They cannot coexist in the same man or in the same religious fellowship.

Many a Protestant, deeply interested in the Ecumenical Movement, is annoyed by the Catholic invitation to Protestants to come back home. As some have said, they do not want to go back but forward, and they invite the Catholic Church to do the same.

But the Catholic Church is like the Boston lady who saw no need to travel because she was already there. Once you persuade the

Catholic Church to enter into a genuine ecclesiological union with some other unconverted church, you will have no Catholic problem because Catholicism would be dead. (For the Catholic such a contingency is just as possible as the death of God.) If Catholicism drops the Catholic principle which includes the dogma of her own exclusive function to mediate between God and man, she would not necessarily be Protestant, but she certainly would no longer be Catholic. In like manner if a Protestant accepts the Catholic principle consistently, he will cease to be a Protestant.

It seems to me that this basic truth must be recognized by all who are interested in a pleasant and satisfactory coexistence of the two groups. That they will some day unite and become one church, is a pious hope which must be cherished—and as a matter of fact it will always be cherished. But this hope must not be the purpose of our coming together in amity. The amity might indeed result ultimately in ecclesiological oneness, but even if that does not come to pass, the purpose of the friendly relations would be achieved. It can be achieved. It is a goal which is noble and Christian nor is it beyond our human efforts. This purpose can be pursued without making ultimate union a condition.

There seems to be some ambiguity at work among those who are really striving to overcome the evils of our estrangement. There is what I consider an innocent duplicity operating in their well intentioned efforts. There is a Catholic school of ecumenical effort which in fact wants to bring all churches into the unity of one church. This Church for the Catholic is the Catholic Church based on the Catholic principle. However, they deliberately suppress in their own minds and in the minds of others this purpose, or they propose it in such a way that a non-Catholic might be led to believe that the Catholic colleague is not excluding the possibility of union on some principle other than the Catholic one. The phrases employed are vague. The Catholic will say he wants the union of all Christians according to the Will of God. Yet the Catholic necessarily believes that this union is exclusively within the Catholic Church, and the Protestant tends to believe that God's union will be over and beyond the unity of Catholicism.

Enthusiastically they come together. They pray in common. They hold friendly discourse. They produce a warm amity. Now if this had been their sole purpose, everything would be splendid. But both Catholic and Protestant may well have other ends in view. They want the amity to bring about one Church. This is not merely a pious hope, but the ultimate goal of the coming together. When this occurs, they are frequently working at cross purposes. The Catholic without saying so and perhaps without being fully aware of it, is making the meetings an instrument for the conversion of the Protestant who does not want to be converted. The Protestant finding so much good will in the Catholic, thinks that he can bring him over to his point of view. Neither of the two quite understands the situation.

There is a slogan for this kind of coming together: the greatest union possible in our time. It sounds reasonable enough but a few questions must be asked for the sake of clarification. Is the union you contemplate for the moment a united church or a non-ecclesiological union of charity? If it is the second, I would not quarrel with it, because that is exactly what I am pleading for. If it is an ecclesiological union, what is the church which will unify all participants in the coming together? Is it identical with the Catholic Church or is it some other church now inchoately present with a promise of evolution into a fully structured being? The Catholic must say that it is the Catholic Church as already existing and not some kind of future church which will transcend Catholic and Protestant differences. If he does not say and think this, he has already renounced the Catholic principle.

But must this question be brought up? Were it not wiser to shelve it, and in so doing produce a stronger amity and more collaboration? The important thing is to get together, and God will direct the union toward his own wise plan. This indeed is important and urgent. It should be done. But it can be done without the supposition explicitly or silently implied, that both parties are on the road to ecclesiological unity. That notion must be eliminated from the teleology of the meetings. The possibility that the meetings might by the grace of God result by way of consequence, not purpose, in one church need not be denied nor ignored, but the possible eventuality is not the goal of the effort.

In this way no one is deluded in the conversation. The Catholic has an advantage in such meetings. The freedom required by the Protestant principle gives the Protestant plenty of latitude in his beliefs and theology. The Catholic is much more restricted. The Protestant can approach the Catholic with much greater ease. However, the Protestant cannot escape annoyance when he sees his readiness to move over from his historical positions is not equally matched by the Catholic. He shouldn't be annoyed if he understands Catholicism properly, but the annoyance will arise just the same.

For ecumenical work the Catholic can follow only one tactic. He must ask the Protestant to be converted to Catholicism. He has absolutely no other choice. Yet this invitation is not what the Protestant wants. He may courteously listen to the invitation given, but there is nothing else he can do but refuse it, unless he has already lost faith in Protestantism. From his point of view he is not being invited to ecumenical discussion but rather exposed to a proselytizing campaign. I doubt if Protestants as a rule are interested in this kind of conversation.

If I do not interpret amiss, the current Ecumenical Movement is an effort to produce or educe the *una sancta* with no prior commitment as to the final form it will take. That it might finally be the Catholic Church, is not on principle excluded, but it is certainly excluded that one begin the dialogue already determined that it must. Since such are the rules of the game, I do not see how the Catholic can invite the Protestant to ecumenical encounter. The Catholic cannot play according to the rules which the Protestants have already set up, and if he doesn't, the Protestant has every right to complain that his Catholic host is not playing fair.

This holds equally for the Protestant. If the rules he has set up are such that the Catholic must collaborate on a basis which to him is irreconcilable with his being, the result will be frustrating paralysis. The lack of anterior commitment to what the *una sancta* is or will be is congenial to the Protestant principle but is a complete negation of the Catholic principle. Hence the Catholic cannot help but see in the Protestant invitation a request that he cease to be a Catholic. Of course we all understand that this is not the intention of the Protestant but it is the logical even though not the intended implication of the invitation to ecumenical meeting.

If this be so—and I think that it is—then Catholics cannot invite Protestants to ecumenical discussion, nor can the Protestant invite the Catholic. Before this is done, the rules of ecumenism will have to be changed. They well may be changed in the course of time, and then the situation will be different and it might well be that Catholics could then enter into dialogue face to face. There is no sense discussing this possible event because there is now no sign that the present rules of ecumenical conversation will be altered in any foreseeable future.

It might seem to the reader that I am cutting my own head off.

I want meeting and friendly intercourse and yet I have shown that it cannot be. I do not think that such is the logical consequence of my observations. All that we have been obliged to affirm is that our coming together cannot be ecumenical as the word is understood today. It can however be what one might call para-ecumenical, i.e. action along side of but not identical with the current ecumenical enterprise. It would proceed from a different starting point and tend to a different goal.

The starting point would be that Catholics and Protestants are here as a matter of massive fact, and that neither wants to become the other. The goal, therefore, will not be that they do become one church, though this is not a negation of the hope that at some day by God's grace they will. The purpose of the continuous symposium would be to eliminate or reduce the hostilities but not the differences existing between the two parties. As a result they could thus live in peace and security without the constant fear of raids and inroads. The Catholic would in Christian love respect the Protestant, not simply as another man but as a Protestant. The Protestant would return this same affection. This is not a church union; it is neighborliness of love and Christian charity. The whole supposition is that there is no union, experimental or achieved, in creed, code and cult. The utter altereity of the partners in charity would be the vivid awareness of the symposiasts.

Is such action in any true sense ecumenical? In order not to identify it with ecumenical effort in its present style, I have introduced the prefix, *para*. Yet the action would have ecumenical dimensions. First of all, it would bring the members of the churches together. A union would be established; not a church union, but a union of churchmen in terms of good will and mutual respect. In matters nonecclesiological, collaboration would be fostered and rendered fruitful.

It could also be pre-ecumenical. It could serve as a preparation of hearts and spirits for ecumenical conversation. It is hard to hold a profitable dialogue if both members are suspicious of each other. If they are friends and know each other, the talks are easy and pleasant. Understanding would be much more probable.

Still the value of the coming together here contemplated would be effective outside of the formal Ecumenical Movement. Protestants and Catholics today want much information about each other. The best man to give it to the Catholic is the Protestant, and vice versa. The best way to know something about the Mass is to attend one with a Catholic who can explain what is going on. Both Protestants and Catholics have a language of their own; it is a jargon borrowed from English. The trouble is that the English-speaker recognizes the word but does not know its precise jargon meaning. He must get a speaker of the esoteric language to translate for him. The words: "Believe on the Lord Jesus," do not mean the same thing to an evangelical and to a Catholic. For one it means to have full trust, and to the other it means to know. A conversation on the slogan can go all awry because the speakers don't understand each other.

I think that para-ecumenical dialogue would prevent the irritation of proselytism. I am uncomfortable when I suddenly realize that my Protestant friend is trying to make a Protestant of me. That he should desire such an event, I can readily understand. That he should know that I do not want to become a Protestant, I expect. An unwelcome gift is no gift. It is just an embarrassment.

And yet a missionary nisus is proper to Christianity. Catholics do not like Protestant missionaries working on their people, but they should remember that the Protestant feels an inner compulsion to make known the glad tidings as he has achieved them. The Catholic also has such a compulsion. Both sides should see this. However, both sides should also realize that good ends do not justify every and all means.

The missionary who stands out in my mind as admirable and worthy of all imitation was Father Matteo Ricci (1552–1610), a Jesuit who worked in Peking. He brought with him from the West not only his Catholicism which he wished to share with the Chinese, but also many secular goods of Europe. He knew astronomy, mathematics and mechanics. With clocks and astrolabes he attracted the intelligentsia of China. However, before he began his formal missionary work he became a Chinese. For years he learned the language and immersed himself in the culture of the people. Only when he was thoroughly naturalized did he make it known that he had something more to offer than clocks and celestial mathematics. He did not use high-pressure techniques to lure the Chinese into Catholicism. He did not attack Chinese culture and sensibilities. There was no hostility to Confucius and the other Chinese sages, for whom he had deep respect. All who were interested in Christianity could have their questions answered and their desire to know satisfied. He did not thrust his message on unwilling ears and hearts. It soon became evident what he stood for, but he was never aggressive and rude. He welcomed all who came for instruction, but he did not intrude. He even gave the Christian liturgy a thorough Chinese style.

Ricci can teach us much in what I call para-ecumenical endeavor. The respect, friendliness, and courtesy we need were splendidly exemplified in his method of giving witness. Like him we should be positive in our approaches of one to the other. We can profitably drop the polemics which marked our relations in the past. But we do not need nor do we want oily flatteries for each other. We'll only gag on such fodder. Straightforward presentation of our beliefs are in order provided we avoid the snide, bitter infighting which we all know too well. I do not think that men become angry when a man indicates difference of position, as long as he does not become angry or nasty about it. The dialogue is informative but it is not a debate.

Dialogue supposes a common basis of discussion. There is a large common substance in Catholicism and Protestantism. The jargons are different but the theology of the last thirty years has shown that when the jargons are correctly understood and adequately translated into the other jargon, there are large areas of agreement as a matter of fact rather than as a matter of principle. The Kingdom of Heaven, Jesus the Savior, the Church, are themes we both have. They are not conceived in the same way, but they are bridges which unite us. In the conversation on these subjects we shall eventually see that a point is reached where we can no longer walk together. At that point we stop the dialogue, because beyond it no dialogue is possible. But two sets of monologue for mutual information are still possible.

But must we resign ourselves to being divided forever? Can't we do something more than live with our separation? Certainly every Protestant heart and every Catholic heart longs for something better than the friendly coexistence of opposites. This is of course true and this desire has its firm foundation in the wish of Christ who wanted one fold and one shepherd.

As I see it, the only way to this consummation so devoutly to be wished is conversion. Compromise will never do. Nor will some rarefied theory of the comprehension of opposites produce what we are looking for. This is the fearsome conclusion I always reach, no matter how I try to look for another. The Catholic simply cannot entertain as licit the notion of converting to anything other than the Catholic Church. He can, of course cease to be a Catholic and become a Protestant, but there is then no continuity with his former faith. He has dropped that and taken on something essentially different. I would say that the change is almost as great as if he were to become a Buddhist or a Muslim.

The Protestant perhaps is not faced with this difficulty. Given the essential element of freedom in the Protestant principle, he can without violence to logic entertain the notion of becoming a Catholic. It will indeed mean that he will abandon the Protestant principle, but strangely enough, the principle itself permits this.

Professor Jaroslav Pelikan in his *The Riddle of Roman Catholicism* (Nashville: Abingdon, 1959) has dealt with this question. He thinks that the conversion of the Protestant to Catholicism solves no problem. His argument seems to be that the Reform was of God and when the Protestant becomes a Catholic, he must abandon the Reform altogether. He abandons something holy because the Catholic Church simply will not recognize the Reform as holy. It shows for Pelikan an abiding defect in Catholicism and a refusal to accept the will of God. If the Catholic Church would only admit the Reform as a holy thing in essence, overlooking all its accidental shortcomings, then conversion to Catholicism would be thinkable. It could even be group conversion.

Is this another way of saying that Protestants will become Catholics if Catholics first become Protestants? If it is, then we have made no progress. Instead of discussing the Reform it would always be wiser to discuss the Protestant principle. The Reform was itself an historical thing, full of ambiguities. Actually there were two sides to it. The Protestant Reform induced a Catholic Reform. Under the shock of the secession of many local churches, the Church pulled herself together. The period produced the Capuchins, Jesuits, missions to Asia and America, and the Council of Trent whose decrees are the marrow of Catholic life today. *Ecclesia semper reformanda est* (the Church must be constantly reformed) is an axiom which the Catholic can accept, but it must be reform coming from within and not from without. It must be edification, building up, but not destruction. The Protestant Reformers left the Roman Church. They did not think that they had left the Church of Christ but they certainly believed that those who stayed with the Pope were apostates. Their church was not the Pope's church. That much was clear enough to all. Now by elemental logic one of the two churches was not the Church. They condemned each other and disowned each other. If the church re-formed by the Protestants was the Church of Christ, then the Roman Catholic Church was not, nor is it now. If the Roman Church was the Church of Christ, then the church of the Protestant reformers was not and is not.

Nor is it satisfactory to say that both partially are, each in its own defective way. The Church always is one; it is not merely in the process of becoming one. Two churches living on diametrically opposed principles cannot in any sense be the one Church. The uniting Spirit cannot be saying yea and nay at the same time. He is with one or the other, but not with both.

This is the way a Catholic thinks. It might not be convincing to a Protestant who will use different categories and a different methodology. But the Protestant certainly can see that in Catholic thinking, the action of the church re-formed by the sixteenth-century Protestants is something outside of the Church. It is impossible to bring it into the Church either then or now. It was not of the indwelling Spirit who works from within and not from without.

The point I wish to make is that Professor Pelikan's desire that the Catholic Church accept the Protestant Reform as something lacking to her divinely willed completeness is not consistent with Catholic doctrine. Catholics have no difficulty in admitting that God sent the Protestant Reform to chastise the Church. But it was to chastise, not to reform. Only the Church can reform the Church. Under the lash of secession and the action of the seceders, the Church did strive mightily to make the lives of its members conform more to the life of the Head. There was conversion, the conversion of sinners away from their sinning ways.

Nor need the Catholic deny that in the Protestant tradition some of the truths of Christ were preserved and developed in a way that it will profit the Catholic to meditate. The Catholic can well see deeper dimensions of such truth than if he merely restricts himself to what Catholics have done in the matter. The Catholic does not have to deny all that is in Protestantism. He only denies the Protestant principle, or at least makes drastic distinctions on it.

This brings us back to the problem of conversion. It is easy to see that the Protestant will have deep affection for the Reformation, at least in its essence. It will be hard for him to see it as an unhappy error. Through its existence and operation he found God and Christ. It is dear to him and it must be shattering to think that it was not a divinely appointed instrument of grace. Yet Protestantism does not tell the Protestant that it is infallibly right. It leaves open the possibility of finding a better way. Protestantism really invites the Protestant to think about conversion.

Nor would the Protestant have to deny that his church was a channel of grace *for him*. God in his boundless mercy can use any of his works for the salvation of man, even a work whose inner structure does not have this purpose. In such a case, though not the cause of grace, it would yet have been the occasion God used to give freely the bounty of his soul-loving power.

To contemplate conversion, then, is an act of disloyalty for the Catholic, but not for the Protestant. He is free to give it thought and attention. It might be wise if he did so.

But I don't think that he will, at least not in great numbers. The Protestant who is riddled with indifference has no reason for conversion because he believes that one church is as good or as bad as another. The nominal Protestant just doesn't give the matter any thought. The committed Protestant is obviously satisfied where he is and any real or supposed freedom to consider conversion will be ignored by him. The more committed he is, the more he will be bound to his church, and the more the Catholic Church will be repellent to him.

After all this speculation, this is where we end. No matter how we approach the problem we always wind up by saying that in the foreseeable future there will be no united church. It requires conversion, and the Catholic by his religious faith cannot entertain this idea for himself while the Protestant sees no compelling reason why he himself should.

That is why para-ecumenical action is what we need in our day. It is to this that we must dedicate ourselves by the imperative of the faith operating both in Catholics and Protestants.

But even in this dedication we need to be prudent. False irenicism, of which Pope Pius XII spoke and which Ronald Knox translated as the spirit of appeasement, is a danger. It tempts both sides, but tempts the Catholic a little bit more. In our comings together the Catholic may readily see the Catholic truth toward which a Protestant proposition points. It only points, because it frequently stops deliberately before the target is reached. The Catholic in his anxiety to have sweetness and light all over the place may well tell the Protestant that his formula is satisfactory. The Protestant in good faith then believes that his truncated affirmation is acceptable to the Catholic Church. If on the basis of such belief he would become a Catholic he would be bitterly disillusioned and consider that he made a difficult step through deception.

Many Protestant assertions *by prolongation* can be made Catholic. It is good to remember this, but in the dialogue it must be pointed out that prolongation is needed. The Protestant is content with his position and usually does not want it developed into something else. He knows well what he affirms and what he denies. He will hardly be pleased when he is told that he holds transubstantiation because he holds some kind of real presence of Christ in the Eucharist. He knows what transubstantiation is and he has rejected it. To tell him that transubstantiation is another name for his own conception is neither candor nor truth.

Another fact to be remembered is that men are only men. They are not angels and much less gods. In Christian terminology we say that Original Sin works on them. Man makes mistakes in the intellectual order and in the moral order as well. He may have a good conscience while he is acting, but good conscience does not guarantee truth nor objective virtue. Passions are always at work and they confuse our judgement and make us unpleasant to our neighbors. It would perhaps be lovely if it were not so. But it is so.

Even when we try with all our might and main to produce para-ecumenical harmony, someone is going to rock the boat. We shall not be free of Protestants who annoy Catholics, and Catholics who annoy Protestants. I take it for granted that what I have here written is going to annoy some Protestants and I shall receive letters of protest, some angry and others hurt. I did not wish to annoy; just the opposite: but one's aim is higher than one's shot.

In a time like the present Catholics will have to be on their guard to control their exasperation. There will be anti-Catholic fears and resentments evident. This is unfortunate but to be expected. The more reasonable Protestants will be uncomfortable too, because they more than the Catholic will see the folly of it all. In the long history of Catholicism this sort of thing is of regular occurrence and the Catholic is vaccinated against it. But the Protestant who will not go along with some little anti-Catholic baiting will be suspect in his own crowd and that makes it harder for him.

Then there will be the Catholic who makes unhappy statements with the justification that he is being four-square and must tell the truth. His truth at times is of dubious texture but his nerve is high. Likewise as things are now, there are civic communities where the Catholics are in a palpable majority. There the Protestant will feel somewhat cramped. He will wisely get used to it. There is little else he can do.

Is the anti-Catholic professional lecturer still with us? He certainly has not been too conspicuous in recent years. I do hope that he stays under his stone though the warmth generated by the moment may entice him to crawl out again. Of this species the ex-priest was perhaps the least bearable. But here too the Catholics had better be careful. Because it is easy for the priest to become a Protestant clergyman, easier by far than for a Protestant minister to become a Catholic priest, Catholics almost take it for granted that the ex-priest left because he wanted to marry. It can be supposed that in many cases this was true, but it certainly is not true universally. The story goes that Alfred Loisy, the excommunicated Catholic modernist of the first decades of the century, decided that he would never marry precisely to still Catholic jibes against the married ex-priests. It is impossible to understand all the motivations in the fateful change the ex-priest makes when he becomes a Protestant pastor. Following the precept of the Lord, we had better judge not lest we too be judged.

Real as the tensions are between Catholics and Protestants, they are not as strong as they were sixty years ago. That is a consoling fact we must never forget. Things can get even better than they are now. We have a standing example before our eyes. In Germany evangelicals and Catholics have shown a high degree of amity in our time. Most symbolic of this new relationship was the 1959 *Kirchentag* of the Protestants in the Catholic city of Munich. Catholics invited Protestants to be their house-guests and Cardinal Wendel lodged a Danish Lutheran Bishop and his wife in the Episcopal residence. The Catholics of Munich did not fight the Protestant assembly, nor did they give it a cold reception of silence. They gave it every facility and were anxious that their Protestant friends enjoy all the graces of hospitality.

If Catholics and Protestants would only realize that the moment calls for a survival of faith in Christ who alone can save, they would be less prone to snipe at each other. We can easily be lulled into a narcotized sleep. In this country there is no campaign against religion and the churches. With us, atheist is now a dirty word, and the Atheist League changed its name to the Tom Paine League. American society is quite literally forcing Americans into the churches. Everywhere we are told that religion is American. There is no need to sneer at the statement but there is need to ask if Americanism is our religion. One gets the impression that to be a good American you must belong to a religious congregation; it matters not which one, as long as it is one of the three socially accepted faiths: Protestantism, Catholicism, Judaism. Will Herberg has written acutely and profoundly on this phenomenon.

No man can be genuinely religious if his motive is Americanism. America cannot be the judge of divinity because America itself is under divine judgment. We are so hurt that other nations are unimpressed by our good actions and good intentions. We fail to recognize the ambiguity of our efforts and there is a feeling of profound righteousness in our souls. We hear no cries to repentance because we have no awareness of sin. Our faith is not in Christ, and him crucified, but in our goodness and power. We are the chosen people and this is God's country. We are saved because we are Americans living in the land of the free and the home of the brave. Near the Catholic altar stands the American flag and you find it next to the altar in the Protestant churches. Is the flag protecting the altar or is the altar speaking sternly to the flag?

The ever spreading religion of Americanism is a genteel secularism. Unlike all other forms of secularism, it has not fought religion. It has done much worse; it has absorbed it. The great Christian slogans have been kept. But charity now means humanitarian giving; faith means trust in American ideals and effort. God is not our judge but our leader and helper. We do his will when we advance the American way.

This is neither Catholicism nor Protestantism. Catholics and Protestants desirous of relaxing tensions between these two groups must be wary lest they melt away the tensions by fusing both religious visions into a starry-eyed Americanism. In both groups what we need is a strong prophetic voice warning the people against the worship of Moloch.

Difference is always an occasion for tension. There are tensions between the male and the female, between the young and the old, between Catholics and Protestants. Tension is not altogether bad. It makes the steel spring move the clock. We can live with our tensions and get some good of them. But in God's name let us not needlessly exacerbate our frictions.

NOTES TO PART ONE: A PROTESTANT. LOOKS AT CATHOLICISM

Chapter 2: Preliminaries That Are Really Conclusions

1. Jaroslav Pelikan, *The Riddle of Roman Catholicism* (Abingdon), deals with the problem perceptively in Chapter XIV.

2. With whatever difficulties conflicting Protestant Christologies may raise for Catholics, it is encouraging to note that from the Pope on down, contemporary Catholics can recognize this bond of union with contemporary Protestants. Referring to the Pope's Christmas message of 1941, and quoting from it, Dom Aelred Graham comments: "What makes non-Catholic Christians near to us of the Catholic Church is not simply that common brotherhood in a human nature which we share alike, but something much more significant, a 'faith in God and in Jesus Christ.'" (Graham, *Catholicism and the World Today*, [McKay], p. 200.)

3. This is no mere euphemism, for the Protestant Reformers (on a Protestant reading) were not a bunch of dissidents separating themselves from Christendom, but a group of men trying desperately to bring Christendom back to the New Testament gospel it had so long forsaken.

4. Cf. the Instruction of the Holy Office, of December 20, 1949, discussed in Chapter 6 below.

5. I am aware that the Instruction of the Holy Office referred to above explicitly tells Catholics not to accept all the blame for the necessity of the Reformation. But there is a considerable difference between acknowledging no blame, and sharing the blame with Protestants.

6. Cf. further Chapter 7 below.

Chapter 3: American Catholicism and How It Got That Way

1. The story of Catholicism in America has been told a good many times. The following are a few of the sources which are easily available and readable. Herberg, *Protestant, Catholic, Jew* (Doubleday), Chapter 7, is the best brief treatment and is well documented. Ellis, *American Catholicism* (University of Chicago Press), is a somewhat fuller treatment, with helpful bibliography. The advantage of Herberg is that the picture is presented by a non-Catholic. The advantage of Ellis is that the picture is presented by a Catholic. Shuster, *The Catholic Spirit in America* (Dial Press), is an early attempt to paint the picture. Cf. also, more recently, Maynard, *The Story of American Catholicism* (Macmillan). A full treatment is Putz, ed., *The Catholic Church, U.S.A.* (Fides); the Intro-

duction, and Ch. 1, 2, 3, 8, and 20 are particularly illuminating on the history. Cross, *The Emergence of Liberal Catholicism in America* (Harvard University Press), shows very clearly the divergences of opinion within American Catholicism. Weigel, *Faith and Understanding in America* (Macmillan), Ch. 4 and 5, helps to complete the picture.

2. Herberg, *Protestant, Catholic, Jew* (Doubleday), p. 151.

3. Ellis, *American Catholicism* (University of Chicago Press), p. 19.

4. Cf. the fuller treatment of this point in Herberg, *op. cit.*

5. "The Ideologists and the Missing Dialogue," *Christianity and Crisis*, June 8, 1959, p. 82.

6. Herberg, *op. cit.*, p. 174.

7. Two helpful Catholic appraisals are *Catholicism in America* (Harcourt, Brace), a symposium edited by the editors of *The Commonweal*, and Putz, ed., *The Catholic Church, U.S.A.* (Fides). A non-Catholic appraisal is contained in Scharper, ed., *American Catholics: A Protestant-Jewish View* (Sheed & Ward).

8. Father John Tracy Ellis has been active in discussing this with his fellow Catholics. Cf. the concluding portions of his *American Catholicism*, and even more fully his essay, "The American Catholic and the Intellectual Life," in Putz, ed., *op. cit.* Father Walter Ong has also made the point in a number of challenging ways in *Frontiers in American Catholicism* (Macmillan). Thomas O'Dea, *American Catholic Dilemma* (Sheed & Ward), is centrally concerned with the problem. For a non-Catholic appraisal, cf. Cross, *The Emergence of Liberal Catholicism in America* (Harvard University Press), Ch. VIII, "Intellectual Life and the Church."

9. Brogan, *U.S.A., An Outline of the Country, Its Peoples and Institutions*, London, p. 65.

10. Ellis in Putz, ed., *op. cit.*, p. 317.

11. *Ibid.*, p. 355.

12. For a readable and well-documented account of this episode cf. A. R. Vidler, *The Modernist Movement in the Roman Church* (Cambridge Univeristy Press). The relevant papal documents of rebuttal and condemnation are the Decree of the Holy Office, *Lamentabili* (Denzinger, *The Sources of Catholic Dogma*, Herder, para. 2001–2065a), the encyclical *Pascendi dominici gregis* (Denzinger 2071–2109), and the "Anti-modernist oath," from the *Motu proprio* "Sacrorum antistatum" (Denzinger 2145–2147).

13. Just to keep the record straight I would say the same thing about American Protestants *vis-à-vis* Catholicism, save that I would change the statement to read that Protestants are *mis*informed about Catholicism. If Catholics need to clear up vast areas of ignorance and a few areas of misinformation about Protestants, Protestants need to clear up vast areas of misinformation about Catholics in addition to a good many areas of ignorance.

14. Clancy, "A Roman Catholic View of American Protestantism," in *Christianity and Crisis*, June 8, 1959, p. 86.

15. O'Dea, *ibid.*, p. 81.

16. Clancy, *ibid.*, p. 87.

Chapter 4: Beer, Ballots, Birth Control, Bingo—and All That

1. The statement itself, attributed to Veuillot, is almost certainly apocryphal; cf. Pribilla, "Intolerance Dogmatique et Tolerance Civile," in *Unité Chrétienne et Tolérance Religieuse* (Editions du Temps Présent), p. 165. Nevertheless, it states with startling accuracy the image most Protestants have.

2. Dunne, "Religion and American Democracy" (The America Press), n.d., p. 41.

3. The fullest and most up-to-date treatment is Fagley, *The Population Explosion and Christian Responsibility* (Oxford University Press). Cf. also his briefer "Christian Approaches to Responsible Parenthood," *Christianity and Crisis*, January 25, 1960, pp. 211–215.

4. Cf., for example, the argument of Father Connery, "Religious Pluralism and American Morality," *America*, February 21, 1959, and the quotation from it cited in Scharper, ed., *op. cit.*, p. 181. There is a complication presented by the situation in Massachusetts and Connecticut, where there are statutes forbidding doctors to give birth control information to anyone. Protestants occasionally try to get these rescinded, and Catholics of course vote for their retention. This leads to Protestant statements about Catholic "imposition" of Catholic practice on non-Catholics. Actually, Protestants should bear two further things in mind in these situations: (a) the statutes were put on the books not by Catholics but by Protestants themselves, and a Catholic cannot easily be expected to vote for the removal of a law in which he believes, and (b) Protestants should note that in no state are Catholics taking action to initiate the enactment of such legislation, even though there are a number of states where they could probably achieve this if they so desired.

5. The quotation is found in Bennett, *op. cit.*, pp. 265–266. I used this admirable summary in my contribution to Scharper, ed. *American Catholics: A Protestant Jewish View* (Sheed & Ward), pp. 85–86, and make no apologies for repeating it here. It should be re-read in the context of Dr. Bennett's very important chapter "A Protestant View of American Roman Catholic Power," in *op. cit.*, pp. 252–268.

I have given the sources for some of Father Murray's articles in Scharper, ed., *op. cit.*, p. 103. For further American statements, cf. Bishop Wright, in Putz, ed., *op. cit.*, p. xxi; Ellis, *American Catholicism*, p. 155, and "Church and State: An American Catholic Tradition," *Harpers*, November 1953; Archbishop McNicholas cited in Ellis, *op. cit.*, p. 155, and Father Dunne's comment that *Civiltà Cattolica's* statement does not represent the viewpoint of American Catholicism, Dunne, *op. cit.*, p. 42.

6. *Tolerance and the Catholic*, p. 193.

7. *Ibid.*, p. 197, italics added.

8. *Ibid.*, p. 198, italics added.

9. *Ibid.*, pp. 98–99.

10. *Ibid.*, p. 99.

11. *Ibid.*, p. 103.

12. *Ibid.*, p. 107.

13. *Ibid.*, pp. 108–109.

14. *Ibid.*, p. 121.

15. This was originally published as "Dogmatische Intoleranz und bürgerliche Toleranz," in *Stimmen der Zeit*, April 1949, pp. 27–40. This was unavailable to me at the time of writing and I have based my comments on a French translation which appeared in *Unité Chrétienne et Tolérance Religieuse* (Editions du Temps Présent), as "Intolérance Dogmatique et Tolérance Civile," pp. 147–172. This book, incidentally, is an important contribution to the Catholic-Protestant dialogue on toleration.

16. *Ibid.*, p. 158.

17. *Ibid.*, p. 164.

18. Published as "Truth and Human Fellowship" (Princeton University Press, 1957), 32 pp.

19. *Ibid.*, p. 4.

20. *Ibid.*, p. 7.

21. *Ibid.*, pp. 9–10.

22. *Ibid.*, p. 10.

23. *Ibid.*, pp. 24–25.

24. Published as "Dogmatism and Tolerance" (Rutgers University Press, 1952), 14 pp. I am indebted to Professor Herbert Slusser of the College of St. Thomas, St. Paul, Minnesota, for first calling this to my attention.

25. *Ibid.*, pp. 3, 4.

26. *Ibid.*, pp. 4–5.

27. *Ibid.*, p. 9.

28. *Ibid.*, p. 9.

29. Russell, *Philosophy and Politics*, Cambridge, p. 25.

30. Gilson, *op. cit.*, p. 12.

31. After completing the above section, I discovered the very important book *Roman Catholicism and Religious Liberty* by Dr. A. F. Carrillo de Albornoz, published under the Protestant sponsorship of the World Council of Churches. On the basis of much fuller documentation, Dr. Albornoz comes to substantially similar conclusions. His work is required reading for Protestants and Catholics.

Albornoz offers rich documentation to support the following points:

(a) Real and sincere doctrinal division among Roman Catholics exists on this matter.

(b) Many Roman Catholics defend universal religious freedom as "thesis."

(c) This position is held, not only by individual theologians but also by outstanding members of the Roman Catholic hierarchy.

(d) Such a doctrine is not only different, but directly opposite to the theory of "thesis" and "hypothesis."

32. Cited in Flew, ed., *The Nature of the Church* (Harpers), pp. 33–34; the full text is in Denzinger, *op. cit.*, para. 1646–1647.

33. *Mystici Corporis*, para. 101, cited in *Tolerance and the Catholic*, p. 95. The whole of Father Léonard's essay referred to above can be understood as a commentary on this papal utterance.

34. Bennett, *Christians and the State* (Scribners), p. 267.

35. *The Christian Century*, November 4, 1959, p. 1268.

Chapter 5: Separated Brethren and Separated Brethren

1. Hughes, "German Protestants and the Coming Council," *The Tablet*, September 19, 1959, pp. 780–781.

2. Excerpts are in Denzinger, *op. cit.*, para. 2292–2294. The full text is in "Biblical Studies," Catholic Truth Society.

3. In Putz, ed., *The Catholic Church, U.S.A.* (Fides), p. 302.

4. I have reported on this a little more fully in Scharper, ed., *op. cit.*, pp. 65–67, and given some bibliographical references there.

5. I have dealt with this book in more detail in "A Step Forward in Catholic-Protestant Understanding," *Christianity and Crisis*, April 1, 1957, pp. 35–38.

6. There remains an unresolved problem here, for Catholic scholars tend to think that it was the abuses within the life of the church that led to the "revolt," and that since these abuses have now been cleared up, Protestants should have no trouble returning to the fold. The Protestant concern, however, was not, and is not, with the relatively peripheral instances of immorality, etc., but rather with a different conception of the very heart of the gospel itself. This will become clearer in later portions of the present chapter.

7. Cf. further Robert Johnson, *Authority in Protestant Theology* (Westminster Press).

8. Denzinger, *op. cit.*, para. 1839.

9. It is not directly germane to the present point, but it is germane to the over-all issue, to add that there is a kind of "practical infallibility" which flows from this. A papal encyclical is not an infallible pronouncement, but to all intents and purposes the faithful are expected to treat it as such. Paragraphs 19 and 20 of *Humani Generis* (1950) make this clear.

10. Cf. the full discussion from a Protestant perspective in Mac-Gregor, *The Vatican Revolution* (Beacon Press), which contains an annotated bibliography of Catholic and Protestant sources.

11. Hudson, *Understanding Roman Catholicism* (Westminster Press), p. 173.

12. Denzinger, *op. cit.*, para. 2333.

13. *Ibid.*, italics added.

14. In one sense Protestants should have been prepared for the latter point, for Catholic belief has more and more tended to place all dogmas on precisely the same level. Cf. the following excerpt from

Mortalium animos (1928): "All true followers of Christ, therefore, will believe the dogma of the Immaculate Conception of the Mother of God *with the same faith* as they believe the mystery of the august Trinity, the infallibility of the Roman Pontiff in the sense defined by the Oecumenical Council *with the same faith* as they believe the Incarnation of Our Lord." (Italics added.)

15. Leeming, "The Assumption and the Christian Pattern," *The Month*, March 1951, p. 144.

16. The fullest treatment of Catholic dogmas about Mary, from a Protestant perspective, is Miegge, *The Virgin Mary* (Westminster). Cf. also Schlink, ed., *Evangelisches Gutachten zur Dogmatisierung der leiblichen Himmelfahrt Mariens* (Chr. Kaiser Verlag). The Danish theologian Skydsgaard discusses this and related issues in *One in Christ* (Muhlenburg). One of the most vigorous dissents is contained in Torrance, *Conflict and Agreement in the Church*, Volume I (Lutterworth), pp. 156–162.

Chapter 6: Ecumenism: Source of Greatest Hope and Greatest Difficulty

1. Karl Barth, cited in *Look* magazine, July 21, 1959, p. 21.

2. Cf. *inter alia*, Roger Aubert, *Le Saint-Siège et l'Union des Eglises*, which takes the story as far as 1947: Leeming, *The Churches and the Church* (The Newman Press) esp. pp. 164–182; Tavard, *The Catholic Approach to Protestantism* (Harpers); Todd, *Catholicism and the Ecumenical Movement* (Longmans); and the article by Oliver Tompkins in Rouse and Neill, ed., *A History of the Ecumenical Movement* (Westminster).

3. Cited, in Tavard, *op. cit.*, p. 107. The text of the encyclical is unfortunately not given in Denzinger.

4. Cited in Baum, "Ecumenical Attitudes," *Apostolic Perspectives*, December-January 1959, p. 5, italics added. The entire issue of this Catholic journal is devoted to articles on Christian unity. Father Baum's article is part of a book, *That They May Be One* (Newman), which unfortunately was not available to me at the time of writing.

5. *Ibid.*, p. 7. It is not fair perhaps to let this statement simply stand by itself, for, whenever it is made, the point is also made that Rome herself is the one true church, and that even now she lacks nothing *essential* in fulfilling her role of the one channel of salvation for all mankind.

6. Cited in Todd, *op. cit.*, p. 27.

7. Cited in *ibid.*, p. 28.

8. *Ibid.*, p. 27.

9. Aubert, *Problèmes de l'Unité Chrétienne*, p. 17, my translation.

10. Tompkins, in Rouse and Neill, ed., *op. cit.*, p. 693.

11. Cited in Aubert, *op. cit.*, p. 100. Cf. further, Leeming, *op. cit.*, Chapter VI, and also Appendix II where the Instruction is translated in full.

12. In Tompkins, ed., *The Third World Conference on Faith and Order* (SCM Press), p. 106.

13. Weigel, in Scharper, ed., *American Catholics: A Protestant-Jewish View* (Sheed & Ward), p. 233.

14. Fuller descriptions are given in Todd, *op. cit.*, Ch. 1, 3, 6; Villain, *Introduction à l'Oecuménisme*, pp. 191–200, and Weigel, *A Catholic Primer on the Ecumenical Movement* (Newman), Ch. II.

15. Todd, *op. cit.*, p. 31.

16. Cf. further, Leeming, *op. cit.*, Appendix III.

17. Todd, *op. cit.*, pp. 36–37.

18. Weigel, *op. cit.*, pp. 31–32.

19. Cf., for example, Kraemer, *A Theology of the Laity* (Westminster).

20. This book also contains a helpful appendix by Père Dumont on the 1952 Lund Conference of the World Council of Churches.

21. For appraisals of such material as the above, cf. 't Hooft, "Notes on Roman Catholic Writings Concerning Ecumenism," *The Ecumenical Review*, i, 1956, pp. 191–197.

22. Père Villain is also the author of *L'Abbé Paul Couturier* (Casterman). Couturier, a remarkable Catholic ecumenist, has been the inspiration of much that characterizes Villain's approach. I am indebted to Mr. and Mrs. James Breedon for initially calling my attention to these two books.

23. Villain, *Introduction à l'Oecuménisme*, pp. 146–147, my translation.

24. *Ibid.*, pp. 149–150.

25. Tavard, *op. cit.*, pp. 139–140. The full text of the pamphlet is printed as Appendix IX in Villain, *L'Abbé Paul Couturier*, pp. 354–372.

26. Villain, *Introduction à l'Oecuménisme*, p. 158.

27. Congar, *Divided Christendom*, pp. 247–248.

28. Cited in Todd, *op. cit.*, p. 109.

29. Cited in Leeming, *op. cit.*, Appendix V. Prominent use is made of this prayer in Aubert, *op. cit.*, pp. 20–21.

30. The full statement can be found in *Unitas*, XI, No. 2, 1959. Cf. also Leeming, "Ecumenical Conclusions," *The Heythrop Journal*, No. 1, January 1960.

31. The full story of the background is contained in Aubert, *La Semaine de la Prière pour l'Unité Chrétienne*, pp. 5–13.

32. These conferences would, of course, now be carried on under the terms of the Instruction of the Sacred Office, of December 20, 1949. Villain, *L'Abbé Paul Couturier* describes numerous such meetings which Couturier himself conducted.

33. Cullmann, *A Message to Catholics and Protestants* (Eerdmans).

34. An outstanding example of this reciprocal concern is Jaroslav Pelikan, *The Riddle of Roman Catholicism* (Abingdon).

35. The Abbot of Downside, in the Introduction to Todd, *op. cit.*, p. xii.

36. Adam, *One and Holy*, (Sheed & Ward), p. 93.

37. Weigel, *A Catholic Primer on the Ecumenical Movement* (Newman), pp. 50–51.

38. Congar, *Divided Christendom*, cited in Todd, *op. cit.*, p. 46.

Chapter 7: Conclusions That Are Really Preliminaries

1. McNeill, in Ferm, ed., *The Protestant Credo* (Philosophical Library), pp. 118–119.

2. Baum, "Ecumenical Attitudes," *Apostolic Perspectives*, December-January 1959, p. 7.

3. Cf. Kung, *Rechtfertigung; die Lehre Karl Barths und ein Katholische Besinnung* (Johannes Verlag Einseideln), 1957.

4. Todd, *Catholicism and the Ecumenical Movement*, p. 6.

NOTES TO PART TWO: A CATHOLIC LOOKS AT PROTESTANTISM

Chapter 3: Protestant Morality

1. "Heretics All" in *Sonnets and Verse* by Hilaire Belloc, (New York: McBride 1924.) p. 118.

Chapter 5: The Protestant Fear

1. Estimates herein contained are based on the report of the *Yearbook of American Churches for 1960*. Ed. by Benson Y. Landis (New York: National Council of the Churches of Christ in U.S.A., 1959.)

Chapter 6: The Protestant Principle

1. *Oliver Cromwell's Letters and Speeches*, ed. T. Carlyle. Letter 136. August 3, 1650. (New York: Scribner, 1897.) p. 187.